501
Cross Stitch
Designs
by
Sam Hawkins

for American School of Needlework, Inc.

Meredith® Press, New York

All of us at Meredith® Press are dedicated to offering you, our customer, the best crafts products possible. Please address your comments and suggestions to Customer Service Department, Meredith® Press, 150 East 52nd Street, New York, NY 10022.

Meredith® Press is an imprint of Meredith® Books:
President, Book Group: Joseph J. Ward
Vice-President, Editorial Director: Elizabeth P. Rice

For Meredith® Press:
Executive Editor: Maryanne Bannon
Associate Editor: Guido Anderau
Production Manager: Bill Rose

For American School of Needlework:
President: Jean Leinhauser
Executive Vice-President: Rita Weiss
Vice-President/Managing Editor: Bobbie Matela
Art Director: Carol Wilson Mansfield
Creative Director: Jane Cannon Meyers
Cross Stitch Editor: Ann Harnden
Associate Editors: Linda Causee and Meredith Montross

Book Design:
Joyce Lerner, Graphic Solutions, Inc-Chicago

ISBN: 0-696-04668-7 (hardcover)
ISBN: 0-696-20382-0 (softcover)
Library of Congress Card Catalog Number: 93-077495

Printed in the United States of America

10 9 8 7 6 5 4

Contents

A Word from Meredith® Press

Dear Cross Stitcher,

For the true cross stitcher, there is no such thing as having too many designs or motifs from which to pick and choose and inspire personal expressions of creativity. To satisfy the steady demand for new designs, thousands are published every year. One of the very best and most popular designers is Sam Hawkins. A big book compiling lots and lots of Sam's designs for easy reference seemed like a great idea. And so Meredith® Press is very pleased to offer this collection of Sam's designs by special arrangement with American School of Needlework.®

Happy Stitching!

Maryanne Bannon
Executive Editor
Meredith® Press

Counted Cross Stitch

Introduction

You'll find it being done on airplanes, in doctors' offices, and even in the supermarket check-out line.

You'll see it being done by children, senior citizens, and all ages in between.

It's addictive.

It is, in fact, counted cross stitch, today's most popular needlework skill.

The first embroidery stitch most of us learn is cross stitch, which as children we probably worked clumsily on stamped towels bearing statements such as "Monday is Wash Day, Tuesday is Ironing Day...." Or perhaps you decorated pillow cases with old fashioned ladies in full skirts with umbrellas.

Although we still use the same basic stitch, today cross stitch has become a highly sophisticated, absolutely charming skill.

Now, instead of working over stamped Xs, we work from charts onto perfectly blank evenweave fabric. The stitcher has the thrill of watching a colorful design take shape quickly and easily. No more the clumsy stitches of our childhoods—each counted cross stitch is perfectly even and perfectly spaced.

Cross stitch is addictive.

It's easy, quick and fun to do, and the materials are inexpensive. Cross stitchers collect charted designs and pattern books to such a degree that literally thousands of new designs are published each year.

One of the most popular cross stitch designers is Sam Hawkins, whose talents are showcased in this book of 501 small designs.

These designs—each a mini work of art—cover many subject areas, from kitchens to pets to sports. Here you'll find something to stitch for just about every friend and relative.

We've shown all the motifs stitched; a few of them we then made up into finished projects. For you, the fun is figuring out what motif to use for whatever project you want. You can use the motifs individually, or in combinations. We're sure you'll have fun combining your creativity with Sam's to create cherished pieces of counted cross stitch.

Jean Leinhauser

Jean Leinhauser, President
American School of Needlework®

Materials

Materials for counted cross stitch are few and inexpensive: a piece of evenweave fabric, a tapestry needle, some 6-strand cotton floss, and a charted design. An embroidery hoop is optional. All of these are readily available at most needlework shops.

Evenweave fabrics, designed especially for embroidery, are woven with the same number of vertical and horizontal threads per inch. Cross stitches are made over the intersections of the horizontal and vertical threads, and because the number of threads in each direction is equal, each stitch will be the same size and perfectly square.

Aida Cloth, a basketweave fabric in which horizontal and vertical threads are grouped, making the intersections for stitches very easy to see. Aida is woven with the intersections spaced in four different sizes: 11-count (11 stitches to the inch); 14-count (14 stitches to the inch); 16-count (16 stitches to the inch) and 18-count (18 stitches to the inch).

There is also 14-count Vinyl-weave™ Aida, which looks like Aida fabric but can be wiped clean and doesn't fray.

The number of stitches per inch of any evenweave fabric determines the size of a design after it is worked. The photos in **Fig 1** *show the same heart design worked on all four sizes of Aida. The more stitches to the inch, the smaller the design will be. Thus a design stitched on 18-count fabric will be considerably smaller than one stitched on 11-count fabric.*

Fig 1   11-count Aida

continued

xxxxxxxxxxxxxxxxxxxxxxx 3 xxxxxxxxxxxxxxxxxxxxx

Fig 1
continued

14-count Aida

16-count Aida

18-count Aida

Linen, a fabric that has become favored among cross stitchers, is woven with single vertical and horizontal threads; the most popular thread counts are 18 to 36 per inch. **Fig 2** shows the heart design worked on 28-count linen. Since cross stitches are made over two threads of linen, the finished size will be the same as the design worked on 14-count Aida.

Fig 2 28-count linen

Perforated Paper and Perforated Plastic—both evenly perforated at 14 stitches to the inch—are wonderful surfaces for cross stitch. They are easy to finish, as you just cut out the finished design and there is no raveling. Perforated Paper is more delicate, and tears easily; Perforated Plastic looks almost identical and is sturdy.

Waste Canvas (sometimes called tear-away canvas or blue-line canvas) is a disposable counted cross stitch surface. Its magic is that it lets you stitch on non-evenweave fabrics, such as T-shirts, sweatshirts, towels or sheets. It is an inexpensive, double-thread canvas (from 8 1/2 to 16 pairs of threads per inch) that provides a temporary, countable stitching background. The canvas—which has blue lines woven every 5th pair of threads as an aid in counting—is basted in desired position on the garment or fabric. Then the design is stitched just as for regular fabric counted cross stitch. After the design is finished, dampen the canvas surface and gently pull out the canvas threads.

Pre-made Projects

Do you want to make a cross-stitched fingertip towel, pillow or perhaps a baby bib, but you don't like to sew? Then you will love the many pre-made accessories available with the evenweave fabric made part of the construction. You'll find so many lovely pre-sewn items; in addition to those we've mentioned, there are placemats, kitchen accessories, afghans, bookmarks, and many baby accessories.

Needles

Use a blunt-pointed tapestry needle which slips between the threads, not through them. **Fig 3** will tell you which size needle is appropriate for each kind of fabric.

Floss

Any six-strand cotton embroidery floss can be used for cross stitch. The six-strand floss can be divided to work with one, two or three strands as required by the fabric. **Fig 3** tells how many floss strands to use with the various fabrics.

Fabric	Stitches per inch	Strands of Floss	Tapestry Needle Size
Aida	11	3	24
Aida	14	2	24 or 26
Aida	16	2	24 or 26
Aida	18	1 or 2	26
Perforated Paper/Plastic	14	3	24

Fig 3

For our charts the brands of embroidery floss colors are specified by number in the Color Keys. Each brand has its own color range, so these suggestions are not perfect color matches, but are appropriate substitutions. Cut floss into comfortable working lengths—we suggest about 18". Generic color names are given for each floss color in a design; for example, if there is only one green, it will be so named, but if there are three greens, they will be labeled lt (light), med (medium), and dk (dark).

Scissors

A pair of small, sharp-pointed scissors is necessary, especially for snipping misplaced stitches. You may want to hang your scissors on a chain or ribbon around your neck—you'll need them often.

Charts

Counted cross stitch designs are worked from charts. Each square on a chart represents one cross stitch. The symbol in each square represents the floss color to be used. Straight lines over or between symbols indicate backstitches. Each chart is accompanied by a Color Key, which gives the numbers of the suggested colors. If a color name appears without a preceding symbol and equal sign, the color is only used for one of the decorative stitches. Backstitches are indicated by straight lines and should be worked the length and direction shown. French Knots are designated by a dot or starburst symbol. Each chart also gives you the number of stitches in width, then height of the design area.

Charts can be foolers: the size of the charted design is not necessarily the size that your finished work will be. The worked size is determined by the number of threads per inch of the fabric you select. For example, if you work a motif that is 22 stitches wide and 11 stitches high on 11-count Aida, the worked design will be 2" wide and 1" high. Worked on 18-count Aida, the same design will be 1 1/4" wide and about 1/2" high.

We have included the chart for the heart design shown in **Figs 1** and **2**. If you are new to cross stitch, use it to learn this new skill.

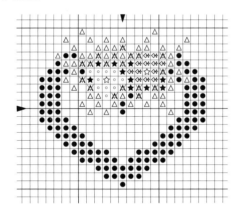

Here's My Heart

Design area: 21 wide x 20 high

		Anchor	Coats	DMC
∘	= med pink	894	26	3126
✪	= dk pink	335	42	3153
☆	= med yellow	725	306	2307
◇	= lt green	704	256	6238
★	= dk green	3345	268	6258
△	= lt blue	519	167	7167
✗	= med blue	799	130	7021

Getting Started

Unless otherwise directed, work your design centered on the fabric. Follow arrows to find center of charted design; count threads or fold fabric to find its center. Count up and over to the left on chart and fabric to begin cross stitching.

To begin, bring threaded needle to front of fabric. Hold an inch of the end against back, then anchor it with your first few stitches. To end threads and begin new ones next to existing stitches, weave through the backs of several stitches. Trim thread ends close to fabric. Because knots in embroidery cause lumps that show under the fabric when it's framed or sewn into finished projects, never begin or end with a knot.

The Stitches

Note: *Unless otherwise noted in the Color Key, use two strands of floss for all cross stitches and decorative stitches; use one or two strands, as desired, for backstitching.*

Cross Stitch

A single cross stitch is formed in two motions. Following the numbering in **Fig 4**, bring threaded needle up at 1, down at 2, up at 3, down at 4, completing the stitch. When working on Aida cloth, as in **Fig 1** on page 4, your stitch will cover one "block" of fabric.

When working on linen, as in **Fig 2** on page 4, your stitch will cover pairs of threads. The stitch crosses diagonally over two threads of the linen each way, as shown in **Fig 5**. Each square on the chart equals two vertical threads and two horizontal threads.

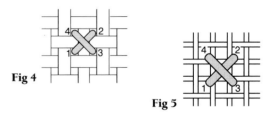

Fig 4

Fig 5

Work horizontal rows of stitches, **Fig 6**, whenever possible. Bring thread up at 1 and down at 2; repeat to end of row, forming first half of each stitch. Complete the stitches (3-4, 3-4) on the return journey right to left. Work second and subsequent rows below first row.

When a vertical row of stitches is appropriate, complete each stitch then proceed to the next, **Fig 7**. No matter how you work the stitches, make sure that all crosses slant in the same direction.

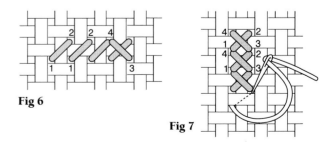

Fig 6

Fig 7

continued

Backstitch

Backstitches are usually worked after cross stitches have been completed. They may slope in any direction and are occasionally worked over more than one fabric block or thread. **Fig 8** shows the progression of several stitches; bring thread up at odd numbers, down at even numbers.

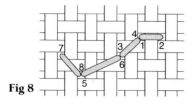

Fig 8

French Knot

Bring thread up where indicated on chart. Wrap floss once around needle, **Fig 9**, and reinsert needle close to where thread first came up. Hold wrapping thread tightly, close to surface of fabric. Pull needle through, letting thread go just as knot is formed. For a larger knot, use more strands of floss, but wrap only once.

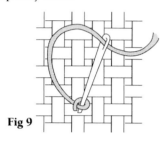

Fig 9

Lazy Daisy Stitch

This stitch creates pointed oval shapes that resemble flower petals. Bring thread up at center hole (1), **Fig 10**. Loop floss, insert needle in same hole, and bring it out two squares from center (2) or as indicated on chart, with loop beneath point of needle. Pull needle through, adjusting size and shape of loop. Stitch down over loop, one thread farther from center, to secure it. Repeat for each oval shape. Anchor ending thread especially well on the wrong side.

Eyelet

This is a technique rather than an individual stitch, used to create a radiating star shape, **Fig 11**. Make a series of straight stitches, always bringing thread up at outer edge of shape and stitching down at center. Work around the shape, clockwise or counterclockwise, making stitches the length and direction shown on chart.

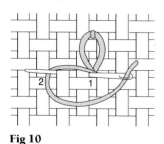

Fig 10

Fig 11

Straight Stitch

A straight stitch, **Fig 12**, is made like a long backstitch. Come up at one end of the stitch and down at the other.

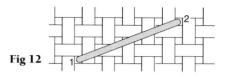

Fig 12

Running Stitch

This stitch resembles basting. Bring thread up at odd numbers and down at even numbers, **Fig 13**. Count squares to place stitches as indicated on the chart.

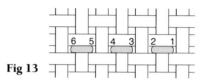

Fig 13

Planning a Project

Some of our designs are shown as suggested finished projects, but you can use the designs for other projects. Whichever project you work, select your chart and type of fabric. Next determine the finished dimensions of the stitched area. Divide the number of stitches in width by the number of stitches per inch of fabric. This tells you how many inches wide the fabric must be. Repeat for the height of the design.

Add enough additional fabric for unworked area around the design plus an additional 2" on each side for use in finishing and mounting.

Cut your fabric exactly true, right along the holes of the fabric. Some ravelling will occur as you handle the fabric; however, an overcast basting stitch, machine zigzag stitch, or masking tape around the raw edges will minimize ravelling.

It is best to start stitching at the top of the design (or the top of a color area) and work downward, whenever possible. This way your needle comes up in an empty hole and goes down in a used hole. This makes your work look neater and is easier than bringing the needle up through an already occupied hole.

Finishing

When you have finished stitching, dampen embroidery (or wash in lukewarm mild soap suds if soiled and rinse well); roll it briefly in a clean towel to remove excess moisture. Place embroidery face down on a dry, clean terry towel and iron carefully until dry and smooth. Make sure all thread ends are well anchored and clipped closely. Then proceed with desired finishing.

50 Floral Designs

The natural beauty of flowers has been translated into charted designs that are a joy to stitch. Think of the many relaxing hours you can spend watching these pretty little florals appear as you stitch away.

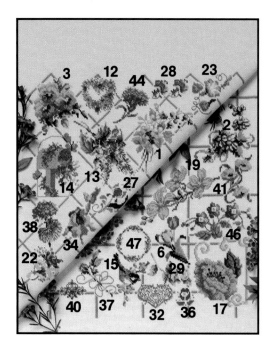

#1

Design size: 53 wide x 61 high

		DMC	Anchor	Coats
~	= very lt yellow	745	300	2350
◇	= lt yellow	743	297	2298
❈	= med yellow	742	303	2303
▨	= dk yellow	783	307	5307
□	= orange	3340	329	2324
△	= lt green	3348	265	6266
✛	= med green	3347	266	6256
◆	= dk green	3346	257	6258
■	= very dk green	895	246	6021
☆	= lt blue	3325	159	7976
▲	= med blue	312	147	7979
✕	= rust	920	339	3340
		= Backstitch:		

flowers—dk yellow (1 strand)
stems—dk green (1 strand)

#2

Design size: 51 wide x 48 high

			DMC	Anchor	Coats
▫	=	white	blanc	2	1001
O	=	lt pink	3733	75	3282
◉	=	med pink	3731	76	3176
~	=	lt yellow	745	300	2350
◇	=	med yellow	742	303	2303
⚹	=	dk yellow	783	307	5307
△	=	lt green	3348	265	6266
+	=	med green	704	256	6238
★	=	dk green	319	246	6246
◈	=	lt blue-gray	931	921	7052
▨	=	dk blue-gray	3750	816	7980
│	=	Backstitch: dk green (1 strand)			

#3

Design size: 46 wide x 49 high

			DMC	Anchor	Coats
▫	=	white	blanc	2	1001
□	=	yellow	726	295	2295
☆	=	orange	742	303	2303
◇	=	lt blue	341	117	7005
◈	=	med blue	340	118	7110
★	=	yellow-green	3346	257	6258
×	=	lt green	369	213	6015
+	=	med green	320	216	6017
◆	=	dk green	895	246	6021
~	=	very lt purple	211	108	4303
△	=	lt purple	554	96	4104
⚹	=	med purple	553	98	4097
■	=	dk purple	550	102	4101

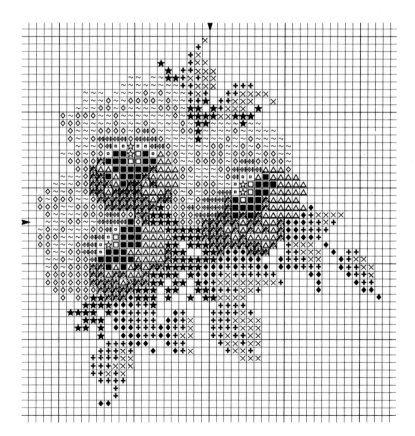

XXXXXXXXXXXXXXXXXXXXXXXXXXX 11 XXXXXXXXXXXXXXXXXXXXXXXX

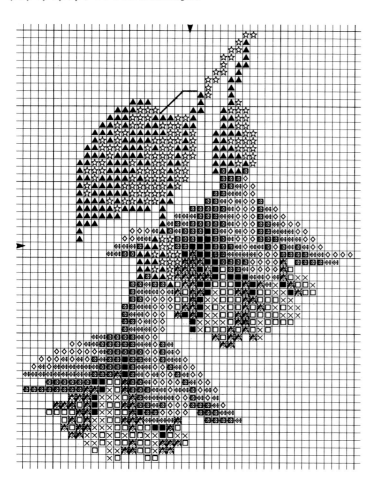

#4

Design size: 44 wide x 57 high

			DMC	Anchor	Coats
◇	=	lt pink	3716	25	3150
❖	=	med pink	3731	76	3176
▨	=	dk pink	815	43	3073
☆	=	lt green	368	240	6016
▲	=	med green	367	217	6018
×	=	lt purple	211	108	4303
□	=	med purple	554	96	4104
✼	=	dk purple	552	101	4092
■	=	very dk purple	550	102	4101
│	=	Backstitch: med green (1 strand)			

#5

Design size: 39 wide x 32 high

			DMC	Anchor	Coats
▫	=	white	blanc	2	1001
◇	=	lt rose	776	24	3125
❖	=	med rose	3731	76	3176
▨	=	dk rose	3350	42	3004
◎	=	orange	3341	328	2323
□	=	yellow	743	297	2298
▲	=	green	702	239	6226
△	=	lt blue	3325	160	7976
✼	=	med blue	322	978	7978
■	=	dk blue	312	147	7979
☆	=	purple	554	96	4104
★	=	gray-black	3799	236	8999
│	=	Backstitch:			

hearts & bird breasts—dk rose (1 strand)
bird outlines & beaks—med blue (1 strand)

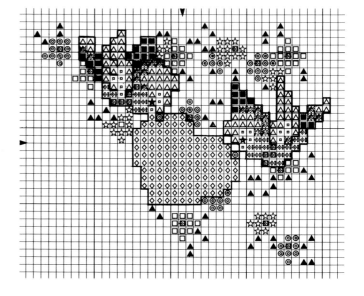

#6

Design size: 31 wide x 40 high

			DMC	Anchor	Coats
◇	=	very lt pink	963	49	3173
◈	=	lt pink	3716	25	3150
▣	=	med pink	3731	76	3176
■	=	dk pink	815	43	3073
○	=	lt red	894	26	3126
⊕	=	med red	891	35	3012
●	=	dk red	304	47	3410
×	=	lt yellow-green	3348	265	6266
☆	=	med yellow-green	704	256	6238
+	=	med green	702	239	6226
▲	=	dk green	895	246	6021

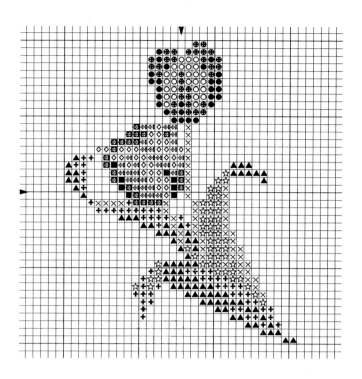

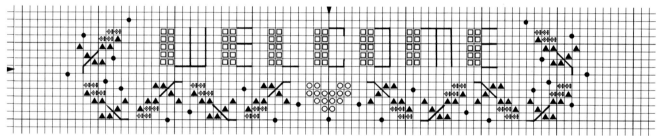

#7

Design size: 68 wide x 13 high

			DMC	Anchor	Coats
○	=	pink	894	26	3126
◈	=	red	304	47	3410
▲	=	green	701	227	6227
□	=	med turquoise	807	168	7168
		dk turquoise	3765	170	7162
•	=	French Knots: dk turquoise			
|	=	Backstitch: med turquoise			

#8

Design size: 47 wide x 13 high

			DMC	Anchor	Coats
▫	=	lt pink	3716	25	3150
◈	=	med pink	893	27	3127
○	=	yellow	744	301	2296
◉	=	gold	783	307	5307
▲	=	green	703	238	6238
◇	=	lt turquoise	3761	158	7159
⋊	=	med turquoise	996	433	7010
		purple	552	101	4092
●	=	rust	301	351	2326
|	=	Backstitch: purple			

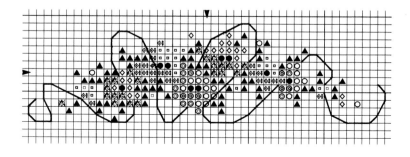

✕✕✕✕✕✕✕✕✕✕✕✕✕✕✕✕✕✕✕ 13 ✕✕✕✕✕✕✕✕✕✕✕✕✕✕✕✕✕✕✕

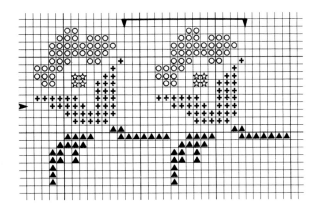

#9

Design size: 16-wide-repeat x 21 high

			DMC	Anchor	Coats
☆	=	yellow	744	301	2296
○	=	lt pink	3733	75	3282
+	=	med pink	3350	42	3004
▲	=	green	913	209	6020

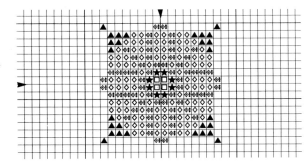

#10

Design size: 16 wide x 16 high

			DMC	Anchor	Coats
◇	=	lt pink	3716	25	3150
◈	=	dk pink	3350	42	3004
□	=	yellow	725	306	2307
▲	=	green	704	256	6238
★	=	brown	434	309	5365

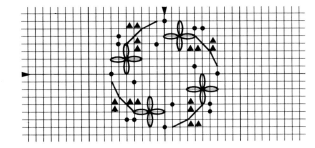

#11

Design size: 14 wide x 14 high

			DMC	Anchor	Coats
		pink	893	27	3127
▲	=	green	702	239	6226
		purple	552	101	4092
✧	=	Lazy Daisies: pink			
•	=	French Knots: purple			
|	=	Backstitch: green			

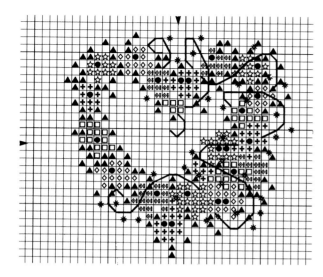

#12

Design size: 30 wide x 30 high

			DMC	Anchor	Coats
⬦	=	pink	893	27	3127
☆	=	orange	3341	328	2323
□	=	yellow	725	306	2307
▲	=	med green	703	238	6238
		dk green	700	229	6227
+	=	blue	3760	169	7169
◇	=	lavender	554	96	4104
		purple	552	101	4092
●	=	brown	433	371	5471
✳	=	French Knots: purple			
		=	Backstitch: dk green (1 strand)		

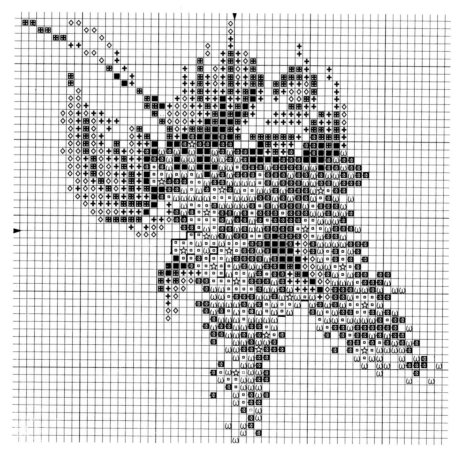

#13

Design size: 56 wide x 56 high

			DMC	Anchor	Coats
▫	=	white	blanc	2	1001
☆	=	yellow	742	303	2303
◇	=	lt green	3348	265	6266
+	=	med green	989	242	6017
⊞	=	dk green	3346	257	6258

			DMC	Anchor	Coats
■	=	very dk green	895	246	6021
ω	=	lt purple	554	96	4104
⊠	=	dk purple	552	101	4092
		=	Backstitch: dk purple (1 strand)		

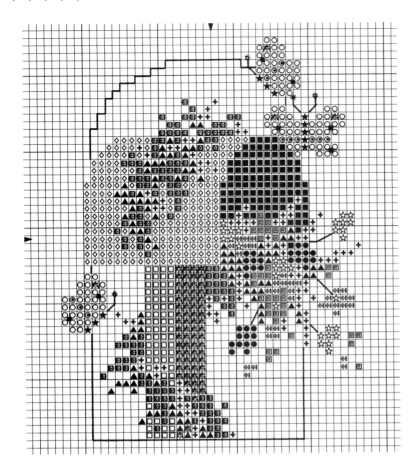

#14

Design size: 40 wide x 53 high

		DMC	Anchor	Coats
✲	= pink	893	27	3127
●	= red	304	47	3410
○	= lt orange	3340	329	2329
⊙	= dk orange	350	11	3111
☆	= yellow	743	297	2298
+	= lt green	704	256	6238
▲	= dk green	701	227	6227
⊡	= turquoise	996	433	7010
⊞	= purple	553	98	4097
□	= lt rust	402	347	3337
✕	= dk rust	301	351	2326
◇	= lt gray	928	900	8397
■	= dk gray	414	400	8399
★	= gray-black	3799	236	8999
✳	= French Knots: gray-black			
•	= French Knots: dk rust			
|	= Backstitch:			
	stems—dk green			
	frame outline—dk green (1 strand)			
	antennae—gray-black			

#15

Design size: 31 wide x 45 high

		DMC	Anchor	Coats
▫	= white	blanc	2	1001
○	= lt pink	3716	25	3150
◉	= med pink	3731	76	3176
	gold	783	307	5307
▲	= green	913	209	6020
◆	= brown	433	371	5471
✕	= lt gray	318	399	8511
□	= med gray	414	400	8399
✕	= dk gray	3799	236	8999
•	= French Knots: gold			
|	= Backstitch:			
	eye & tail feathers—white			
	stems—green			
	beak—dk gray (1 strand)			

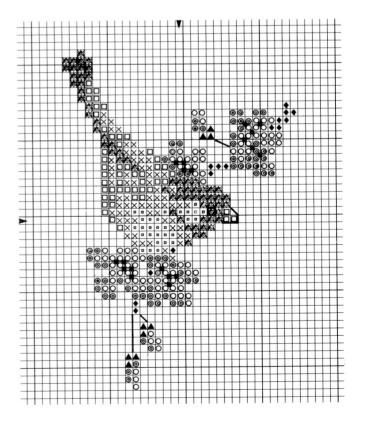

#16

Design size: 27 wide x 52 high

		DMC	Anchor	Coats
⬧ =	lt pink	894	26	3126
	med pink	893	27	3127
▲ =	red	498	20	3072
▫ =	yellow	743	297	2298
	med green	3347	266	6256
	dk green	3346	257	6258
+ =	lt blue	807	168	7168
★ =	dk blue	3765	169	7162

⬧ = Lazy Daisies: med green

• = French Knots:
    in Lazy Daisy border—med pink
    dots on "i"s—dk green
    isolated border dots—dk blue

| = Backstitch:
    lettering—dk green (1 strand)
    outline frame—dk blue

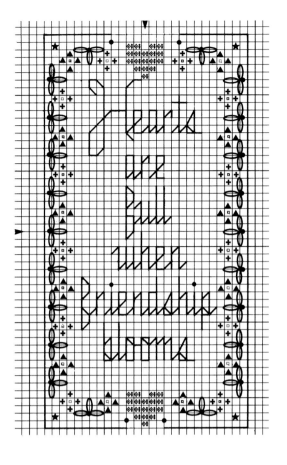

#17

Design size: 49 wide x 59 high

		DMC	Anchor	Coats
▫ =	very lt peach	353	8	3006
✕ =	lt peach	352	10	3008
⬧ =	med peach	350	11	3111
▨ =	dk peach	347	13	3013
□ =	lt yellow	726	295	2295
⋇ =	med yellow	783	307	5307
▲ =	dk yellow	782	308	5308
△ =	lt green	3364	843	6010
+ =	med green	3363	861	6269
★ =	dk green	319	246	6246
■ =	gray-black	3799	236	8999

| = Backstitch: gray-black

#18

Design size: 69 wide x 47 high

			DMC	Anchor	Coats
▫	=	white	blanc	2	1001
□	=	yellow	743	297	2298
△	=	lt green	368	240	6016
+	=	med green	367	216	6018
★	=	dk green	895	246	6021
◇	=	lt purple	211	108	4303
◉	=	med purple	553	98	4097
●	=	dk purple	550	102	4101
		lt rust	3778	884	2338
		dk rust	355	351	3340
✲	=	French Knots:			
		border—lt rust			
		lettering—dk rust			
|	=	Backstitch:			
		border—lt rust			
		lettering—dk rust (1 strand)			

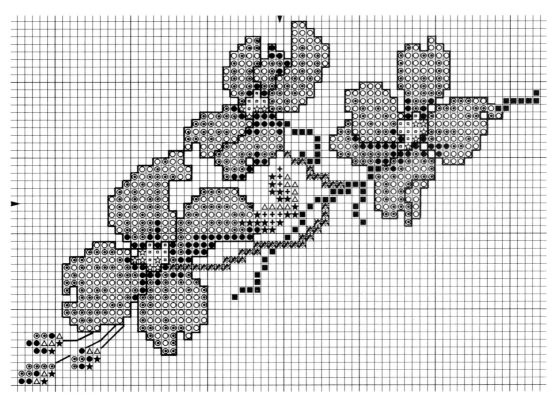

#19

Design size: 69 wide x 48 high

			DMC	Anchor	Coats
○	=	lt pink	945	778	3335
◎	=	med pink	3733	75	3282
●	=	dk pink	3731	76	3176
▫	=	yellow	743	297	2298
☆	=	gold	783	307	5307
△	=	lt green	3348	265	6266
+	=	med green	3347	266	6256
★	=	dk green	319	246	6246
✕	=	med brown	435	369	5371
■	=	dk brown	433	371	5471
│	=	Backstitch (all 1 strand):			

flower centers—med brown
flower petals—dk pink
stems—dk brown

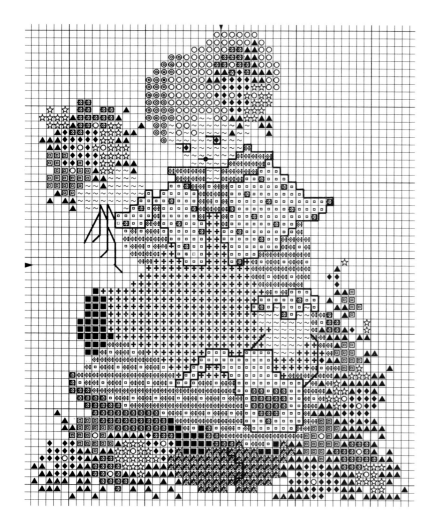

#20

Design size: 50 wide x 62 high

			DMC	Anchor	Coats
▫	=	white	blanc	2	1001
⊕	=	lt pink	3716	25	3150
⊠	=	dk pink	3731	76	3176
		red	815	43	3073
~	=	peach	353	8	3006
☆	=	orange	3341	328	2323
O	=	med yellow	744	301	2296
◉	=	dk yellow	743	297	2298
▲	=	green	319	246	6246
◆	=	lt turquoise	3761	158	7159
		dk turquoise	807	168	7168
+	=	lt blue-gray	931	921	7051
■	=	dk blue-gray	3750	816	7980
▣	=	purple	553	98	4097
⋈	=	med brown	434	309	5365
		dk brown	433	371	5471
		gray-black	3799	236	8999

• = French Knot: red
| = Backstitch:
    mouth—red
    stems—green
    around eyes—dk turquoise (1 strand)
    dress—lt blue-gray (1 strand)
    shoe—dk brown
    watering can outline—gray-black (1 strand)
    eyelashes & watering can handle—gray-black

#21

Design size: 33 wide x 34 high

			DMC	Anchor	Coats
∧	=	yellow	744	301	2296
◇	=	lt turquoise	3761	158	7159
⊕	=	med turquoise	3760	169	7169
★	=	dk turquoise	312	147	7979
△	=	lt green	3364	843	6010
⋈	=	dk green	319	246	6246

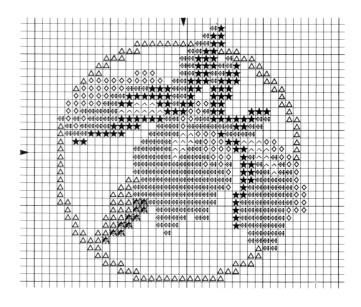

#22

Design size: 30 wide x 29 high

			DMC	Anchor	Coats
~	=	lt pink	3716	25	3150
⊗	=	med pink	3731	76	3176
⊡	=	dk pink	815	43	3073
●	=	very dk pink	3685	70	3089
×	=	lt yellow	745	300	2350
☆	=	med yellow	743	297	2298
		dk yellow	742	303	2303
◇	=	lt green	989	242	6017
+	=	med green	3346	257	6258
▲	=	dk green	319	246	6246
○	=	lt blue	807	168	7168
		dk blue	3765	170	7162
✿	=	French Knots: dk blue			
❘	=	Backstitch:			
		ribbon—dk yellow (1 strand)			
		stems—dk green			

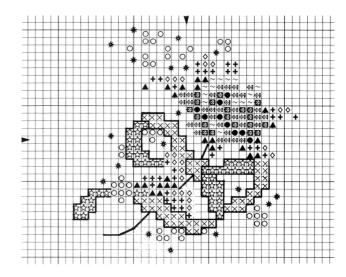

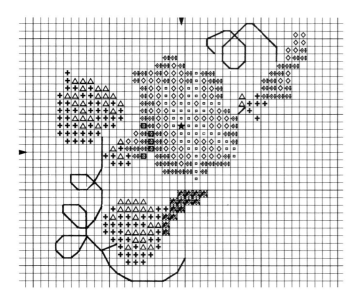

#23

Design size: 33 wide x 34 high

			DMC	Anchor	Coats
▫	=	white	blanc	2	1001
★	=	yellow	743	297	2298
△	=	lt green	368	240	6016
+	=	med green	320	216	6017
⋊	=	dk green	319	246	6246
◇	=	lt blue	3325	159	7976
⊗	=	med blue	334	977	7977
⊡	=	dk blue	3750	816	7980
❘	=	Backstitch: dk green (1 strand)			

#24

Design size: 19 wide x 19 high

			DMC	Anchor	Coats
⊗	=	pink	3731	76	3176
☆	=	yellow	725	306	2307
+	=	lt green	320	216	6017
▲	=	med green	319	246	6246
		blue	3760	169	7169
•	=	French Knots: blue			

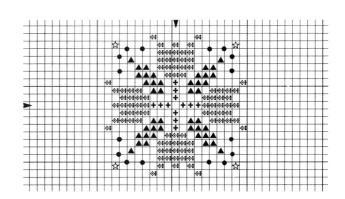

XXXXXXXXXXXXXXXXXXXXXXXXXX 21 XXXXXXXXXXXXXXXXXXXXXXXXXX

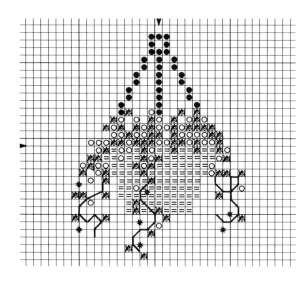

#25

Design size: 23 wide x 30 high

		DMC	Anchor	Coats
✗	= lt green	704	256	6238
	dk green	3346	257	6267
O	= turquoise	807	168	7168
=	= brown	3778	883	2338
●	= gray-black	3799	236	8999
✳	= French Knots: turquoise			
|	= Backstitch: dk green (1 strand)			

#26

Design size: 44 wide x 42 high

		DMC	Anchor	Coats
✤	= lt pink	894	26	3126
	med pink	891	35	3012
△	= lt green	704	256	6238
+	= med green	989	242	6017
★	= dk green	319	246	6246
O	= lt purple	554	96	4104
◎	= med purple	552	101	4092
~	= lt brown	437	362	5373
◇	= med brown	435	369	5365
|	= Backstitch:			
	hearts—med pink (1 strand)			
	leaf motifs on shutters—med green (1 strand)			

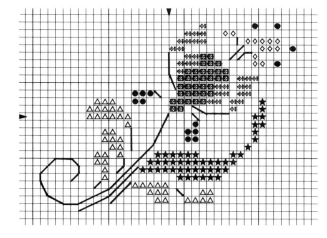

#27

Design size: 34 wide x 25 high

		DMC	Anchor	Coats
◇	= lt pink	894	26	3126
✤	= med pink	893	27	3127
▣	= med red	304	47	3410
●	= dk red	815	43	3073
△	= lt green	3347	266	6256
★	= dk green	895	246	6021
|	= Backstitch: (all 1 strand):			
	stamen end of flower—lt pink			
	sides of flower—med pink			
	dk red detached petals—dk red			
	small leaves—lt green			
	main stem & dk green leaf—dk green			

#28

Design size: 15 wide x 15 high

			DMC	Anchor	Coats
+	=	lt green	320	216	6017
▲	=	dk green	319	246	6246
∧	=	very lt purple	211	108	4303
◇	=	lt purple	554	96	4104
⌗	=	med purple	553	98	4097
⊞	=	dk purple	552	101	4092
■	=	very dk purple	550	102	4101
		=	Backstitch: dk green (1 strand)			

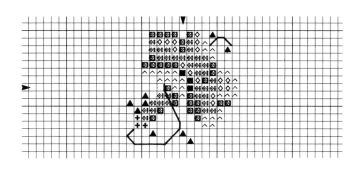

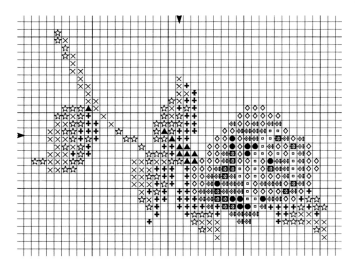

#29

Design size: 39 wide x 28 high

			DMC	Anchor	Coats
▫	=	white	blanc	2	1001
◇	=	very lt pink	963	49	3173
⌗	=	lt pink	3716	25	3150
⊞	=	med pink	3731	76	3176
●	=	dk pink	815	43	3073
×	=	very lt green	369	213	6015
☆	=	lt green	704	256	6238
+	=	med green	367	216	6018
▲	=	dk green	895	246	6021

#30

Design size: 33 wide x 35 high

			DMC	Anchor	Coats
		yellow	742	303	2303
★	=	lt green	704	256	6238
		dk green	702	239	6226
		blue	996	433	7010
•	=	French Knots: yellow			
		=	Backstitch:			
		bluebells—blue			
		stems—dk green			

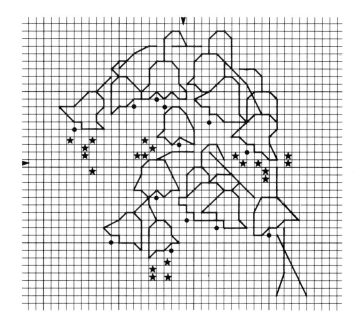

XXXXXXXXXXXXXXXXXXXXXXXXXXXXXXXX 23 XXXXXXXXXXXXXXXXXXXXXXXXXXXXXXXX

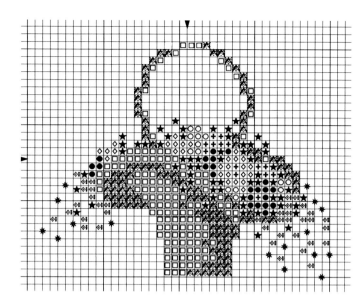

#31

Design size: 38 wide x 31 high

			DMC	Anchor	Coats
O	=	pink	894	26	3126
●	=	red	498	20	3072
+	=	yellow	743	297	2298
□	=	gold	437	362	5942
★	=	green	700	229	6227
◇	=	blue	996	433	7001
⊕	=	lt purple	554	96	4104
		med purple	552	101	4092
⋊	=	rust	921	349	2326
✳	=	French Knots: med purple			

#32

Design size: 30 wide x 19 high

			DMC	Anchor	Coats
O	=	lt pink	3733	75	3282
⊕	=	dk pink	3731	76	3176
▫	=	yellow	743	297	2298
▲	=	green	470	267	6261
		blue	3760	169	7169
		rust	301	351	2326
•	=	French Knots: blue			
|	=	Backstitch:			
		stems—green			
		heart outline—rust			

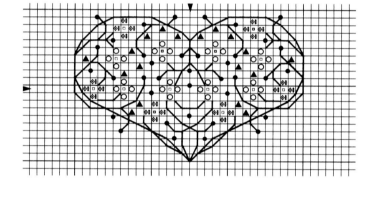

#33

Design size: 38 wide x 40 high

			DMC	Anchor	Coats
⊕	=	med orange	3341	328	2323
▨	=	dk orange	350	11	3111
□	=	yellow	743	297	2298
◇	=	lt green	989	242	6017
▲	=	dk green	319	246	6246
O	=	lt blue	3325	159	7976
●	=	med blue	334	977	7977
		rust	355	351	3340
|	=	Backstitch: rust			

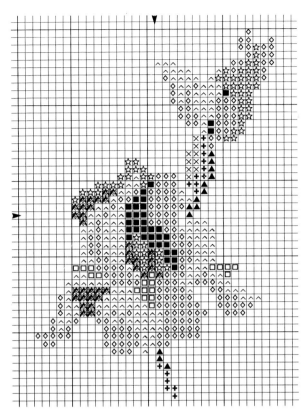

#34

Design size: 32 wide x 49 high

			DMC	Anchor	Coats
□	=	yellow	725	306	2307
×	=	lt green	3348	265	6266
+	=	med green	3347	266	6256
▲	=	dk green	3346	257	6258
∧	=	very lt turquoise	3761	158	7159
◇	=	lt turquoise	807	168	7168
☆	=	med turquoise	3760	169	7169
⋈	=	dk turquoise	3765	170	7162
■	=	purple	792	940	7022

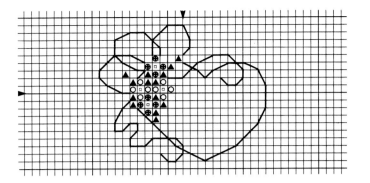

#35

Design size: 22 wide x 18 high

			DMC	Anchor	Coats
		pink	893	27	3127
▫	=	yellow	743	297	2298
▲	=	lt green	703	238	6238
		dk green	701	227	6227
O	=	lt turquoise	3761	158	7159
⊕	=	dk turquoise	996	433	7010
|	=	Backstitch:			
		heart—pink			
		ribbon—dk green (1 strand)			

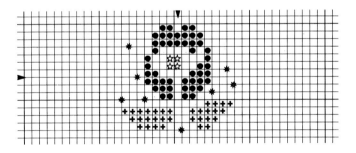

#36

Design size: 15 wide x 14 high

			DMC	Anchor	Coats
		lt red	891	35	3012
●	=	dk red	304	47	3410
☆	=	yellow	742	303	2303
+	=	green	701	227	6227
✳	=	French Knots: lt red			

#37

Design size: 34 wide x 39 high

		DMC	Anchor	Coats
◇ =	lt pink	776	24	3125
✿ =	med pink	3731	76	3176
▣ =	dk pink	815	43	3073
● =	very dk pink	3685	70	3089
△ =	lt green	3348	265	6266
+ =	med green	989	242	6017
★ =	dk green	319	246	6246
☐ =	turquoise	958	187	6187
│ =	Backstitch:			
	stem—dk green			
	ribbon—turquoise			

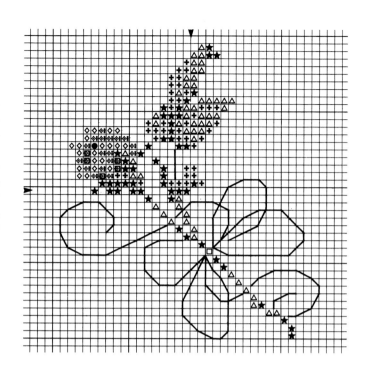

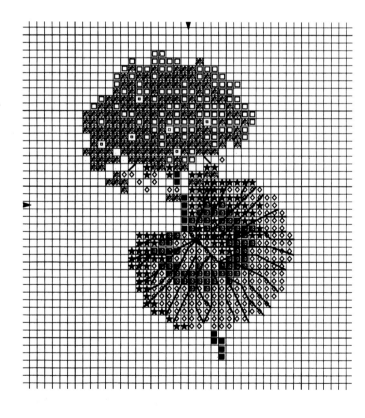

#38

Design size: 28 wide x 41 high

		DMC	Anchor	Coats
☐ =	med pink	894	26	3126
▧ =	dk pink	3712	10	3071
✖ =	red	304	47	3410
▫ =	yellow	742	303	2303
◇ =	lt green	369	213	6015
★ =	med green	320	216	6017
■ =	dk green	895	246	6021
│ =	Backstitch: dk green (1 strand)			

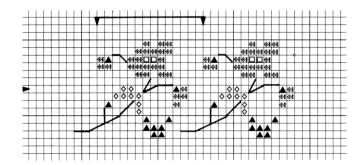

#39

Design size: 14-wide-repeat x 13 high

		DMC	Anchor	Coats
□	= yellow	744	301	2296
◇	= lt green	3363	861	6269
▲	= dk green	319	246	6246
✥	= purple	554	96	4104
│	= Backstitch: dk green			

#40

Design size: 24 wide x 16 high

		DMC	Anchor	Coats
∞	= green			
	Lazy Daisy	700	229	6227
✣	= purple			
	Lazy Daisy	552	101	4092
│	= Backstitch: green			

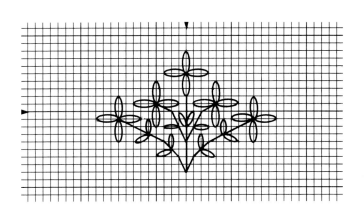

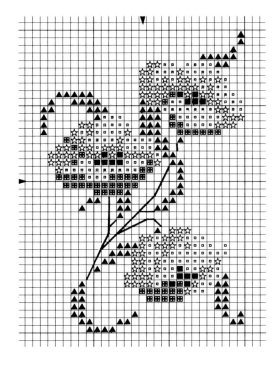

#41

Design size: 27 wide x 40 high

		DMC	Anchor	Coats
▫	= lt orange	945	778	3335
☆	= med orange	3341	328	2323
⊞	= dk orange	350	11	3111
▲	= green	3346	257	6258
■	= gray-black	3799	236	8999
│	= Backstitch: green			

#42

Design size: 44 wide x 44 high

		DMC	Anchor	Coats
	pink	3712	9	3071
◈ =	peach	352	10	3008
□ =	lt yellow	745	300	2292
☆ =	med yellow	743	297	2298
● =	gold	436	363	5943
▲ =	med green	367	217	6018
	dk green	319	246	6246
+ =	lt rust	3778	883	2338
	dk rust	355	351	3340
• =	French Knots:			
	dots on "i"s—dk rust			
	remaining knots—pink			
❘ =	Backstitch:			
	tendrils—dk green (1 strand)			
	lettering—dk rust (1 strand)			

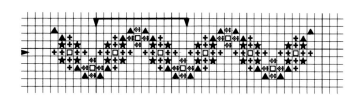

#44

Design size: 31 wide x 30 high

		DMC	Anchor	Coats
△ =	lt red	894	26	3126
✖ =	med red	891	35	3012
■ =	dk red	815	43	3073
◇ =	lt green	704	256	6238
+ =	med green	702	239	6226
★ =	dk green	700	229	6227

#43

Design size: 12-wide-repeat x 7 high

		DMC	Anchor	Coats
◈ =	pink	894	26	3126
□ =	yellow	743	297	2298
▲ =	turquoise	958	187	6187
+ =	lt purple	553	98	4097
★ =	dk purple	550	102	4101

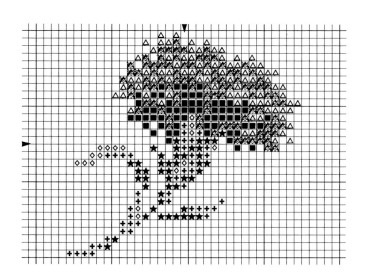

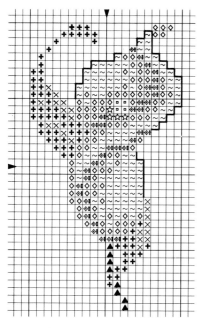

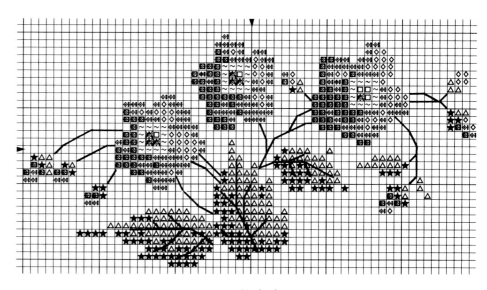

#45

Design size: 20 wide x 38 high

		DMC	Anchor	Coats
~	= white	blanc	2	1001
▫	= lt yellow	745	300	2350
☆	= med yellow	743	297	2298
◇	= lt blue	3761	158	7159
	med blue	3760	169	7169
◈	= dk blue	3765	170	7162
✕	= lt green	369	213	6015
+	= med green	3363	861	6269
▲	= dk green	319	246	6246
❘	= Backstitch: med blue (1 strand)			

#46

Design size: 60 wide x 31 high

		DMC	Anchor	Coats
~	= white	blanc	2	1001
◇	= lt pink	3716	25	3150
◈	= med pink	3731	76	3176
▨	= dk pink	815	43	3073
□	= med yellow	743	297	2298
✕	= dk yellow	783	307	5307
△	= lt green	704	256	6238
★	= med green	702	239	6226
	dk green	700	229	6227
	very dk green	895	246	6021
❘	= Backstitch:			
	stems—dk green			
	leaf veins—very dk green (1 strand)			

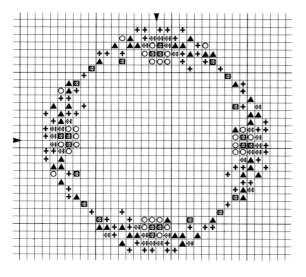

#47

Design size: 30 wide x 30 high

		DMC	Anchor	Coats
○	= lt red	776	24	3125
◈	= med red	893	27	3127
▨	= dk red	498	20	3072
+	= lt green	704	256	6238
▲	= dk green	701	227	6227

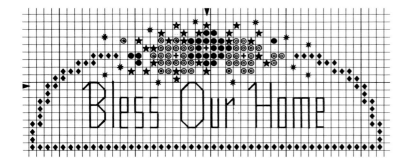

#48

Design size: 47 wide x 17 high

			DMC	Anchor	Coats
☉	=	lt pink	3716	25	3150
●	=	dk pink	893	27	3127
+	=	yellow	743	297	2298
★	=	green	704	256	6238
		purple	552	101	4092
◆	=	rust	3778	884	2338
✳	=	French Knots: dk pink			
│	=	Backstitch: purple			

#49

Design size: 65 wide x 37 high

			DMC	Anchor	Coats
✿	=	lt rose	3716	25	3150
▧	=	dk rose	3350	42	3004
□	=	yellow	744	301	2296
⊙	=	gold	742	303	2303
△	=	lt green	704	256	6238
		med green	3346	257	6267
★	=	dk green	895	246	6021
◆	=	blue	3761	158	7159
✖	=	purple	553	98	4097
~	=	lt tan	738	372	5372
◇	=	med tan	436	363	5943
■	=	brown	433	371	5471
│	=	Backstitch:			
		stems—med green			
		banner—brown (1 strand)			

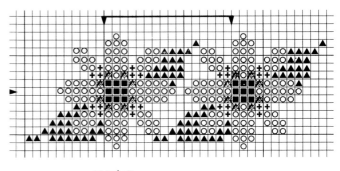

#50

Design size: 16-wide-repeat x 15 high

			DMC	Anchor	Coats
O	=	lt yellow	744	301	2296
+	=	med yellow	725	306	2307
✖	=	dk yellow	783	307	5307
▲	=	green	3347	266	6256
■	=	brown	355	351	3340

50 Kitchen Designs

Find the perfect design to decorate the center of the home—the kitchen—with cross stitch creations: fruits and vegetables, farm animals, cakes and pies.

my kitchen doesn't always look like this— sometimes it's even WORSE!

COOK'S EQUATIONS
3 TSP = 1 TBL
4 TBL = ¼ CUP
2 CUPS = 1 PINT
2 PINTS = 1 QUART

the ♥ of our home is the kitchen

God bless my kitchen and improve my cooking

Remember the miller when you eat your bread

I ♥ COFFEE

mom's kitchen

over easy

head COOK

IN THIS KITCHEN I REIGN SUPREME— IF YOU DON'T LIKE IT STARVE!

Hot bread makes the

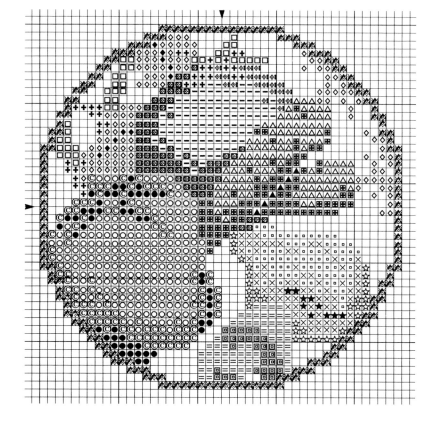

#1

Design size: 46 wide x 46 high

		DMC	Anchor	Coats
− =	lt red	351	11	3011
✵ =	med red	349	13	2335
▩ =	dk red	321	9046	3500
△ =	lt orange	740	316	2099
⊞ =	med orange	946	332	2330
▫ =	lt gold	676	891	2874
✕ =	med gold	783	307	5309
☆ =	dk gold	782	308	5308
★ =	very dk gold	780	310	5365
◇ =	lt yellow-green	704	256	6238
◆ =	dk yellow-green	905	258	6239
□ =	lt blue-green	954	203	6225
+ =	med blue-green	910	230	6031
○ =	lt green	913	209	6226
© =	med green	911	204	6227
● =	dk green	909	229	6228
▲ =	rust	919	341	2326
= =	lt tan	3774	880	3335
▣ =	med tan	407	914	3883
✖ =	brown	632	936	5936

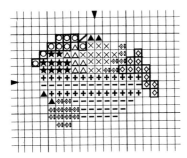

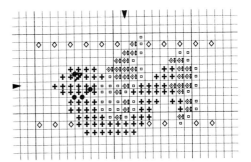

#2

Design size: 16 wide x 12 high

			DMC	Anchor	Coats
★	=	red	321	9046	3500
×	=	orange	740	316	2099
⊛	=	med yellow	726	295	2295
△	=	dk yellow	783	307	5309
◇	=	lt green	704	256	6238
		med green	905	258	6239
▲	=	dk green	986	246	6246
+	=	blue	792	940	7022
○	=	lt purple	554	96	4104
		med purple	552	101	4092
−	=	tan	676	891	2874

❘ = Backstitch:
  green grapes—med green (1 strand)
  purple grapes—med purple (1 strand)
  stem—dk green

#3

Design size: 23 wide x 13 high

			DMC	Anchor	Coats
		white	blanc	2	1001
◇	=	pink	3705	35	3012
□	=	lt blue	809	130	7021
⊛	=	med blue	798	137	7080
+	=	dk blue	796	133	7100
		gray-black	3799	236	8999
•	=	French Knots:			

  eye—white
  neck detail—pink

❘ = Backstitch: gray-black (1 strand)

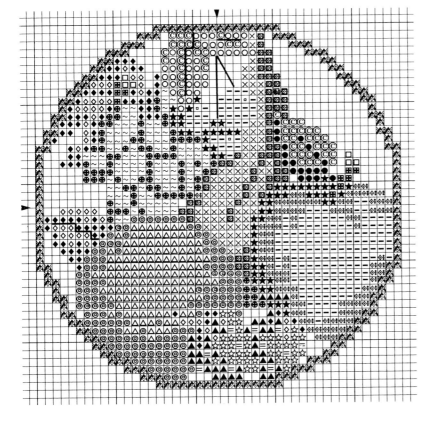

#4

Design size: 46 wide x 46 high

			DMC	Anchor	Coats
□	=	lt pink	963	49	3173
☆	=	med pink	3705	35	3012
▲	=	dk pink	349	13	2335
−	=	lt red	666	46	3046
⊛	=	med red	321	9046	3500
★	=	dk red	816	44	3000
△	=	lt orange	741	304	2314
◎	=	med orange	740	316	2099
=	=	yellow	726	295	2295
×	=	lt gold	676	891	2874
▣	=	dk gold	680	901	2876
◇	=	lt yellow-green	704	256	6238
◆	=	dk yellow-green	905	258	6239
○	=	lt green	913	209	6226
©	=	med green	911	204	6227
●	=	dk green	909	229	6228
~	=	lt purple	554	96	4104
⊕	=	med purple	552	101	4092
□	=	lt brown	407	914	3883
✄	=	med brown	632	936	5936
⊞	=	dk brown	300	352	5471

❘ = Backstitch: dk green

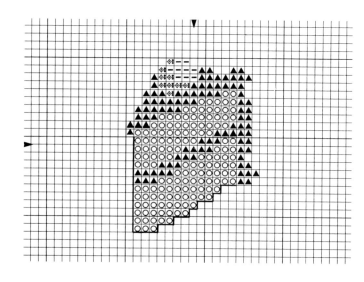

#5

Design size: 17 wide x 22 high

			DMC	Anchor	Coats
−	=	lt red	3705	35	3012
✛	=	dk red	321	9046	3500
O	=	yellow	727	293	2289
		lt gold	676	891	2874
		med gold	680	901	2876
▲	=	brown	300	352	5471
		= Backstitch (1 strand):			

cake side—lt gold
cake bottom—med gold

#6

Design size: 24 wide x 16 high

			DMC	Anchor	Coats
X	=	lt rose	3708	26	3126
▲	=	dk rose	309	42	3154
−	=	yellow	726	295	2295
◇	=	lt green	704	256	6238
◆	=	dk green	701	227	6227
✛	=	blue	793	121	7110
		= Backstitch:			

stems—dk green
leaves—dk green (1 strand)

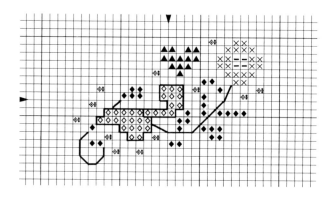

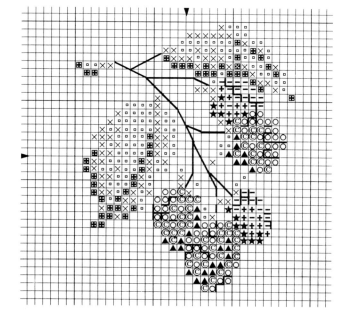

#7

Design size: 28 wide x 34 high

			DMC	Anchor	Coats
−	=	lt red	3708	26	3126
+	=	med red	321	9046	3500
★	=	dk red	816	44	3000
□	=	lt green	772	264	6253
X	=	med green	320	216	6017
⊞	=	dk green	986	246	6246
O	=	lt blue	794	120	7021
©	=	med blue	792	940	7022
▲	=	dk blue	791	941	7045
		= Backstitch:			

red berries—dk red (1 strand)
blue berries—dk blue (1 strand)
stems—dk green

#8

Design size: 27 wide x 23 high

			DMC	Anchor	Coats
□	=	white	blanc	2	1001
O	=	lt pink	760	9	3069
◆	=	med pink	3712	10	3071
⊗	=	blue	793	121	7110
		rust	221	896	3242
▲	=	gray-black	3799	236	8999
│	=	Backstitch:			

neckerchief—blue (1 strand)
eyelids & chin—rust (1 strand)
eyelashes—gray-black
remaining features—gray-black (1 strand)

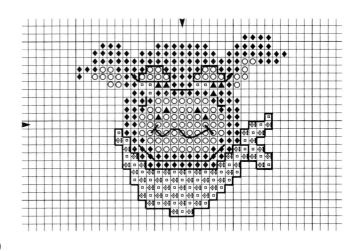

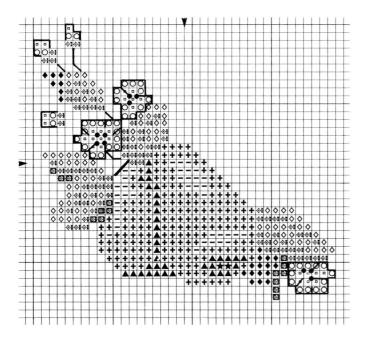

#9

Design size: 38 wide x 35 high

			DMC	Anchor	Coats
□	=	white	blanc	2	1001
–	=	lt yellow	727	293	2289
+	=	med yellow	725	306	2307
▲	=	dk yellow	782	308	5308
◇	=	lt green	772	264	6253
⊗	=	med green	704	256	6238
⊞	=	dk green	986	246	6246
◆	=	very dk green	319	878	6021
O	=	lt blue	800	128	7031
		dk blue	799	136	7030
★	=	brown	300	352	5471
•	=	French Knots: brown			
│	=	Backstitch:			

stems—dk green
blossoms—dk blue (1 strand)

#10

Design size: 37 wide x 22 high

			DMC	Anchor	Coats
□	=	white	blanc	2	1001
×	=	lt pink	3708	26	3126
◆	=	med pink	304	47	3410
–	=	lt green	369	213	6015
▲	=	dk green	909	229	6228
●	=	black	310	403	8403
│	=	Backstitch: lt green (1 strand)			

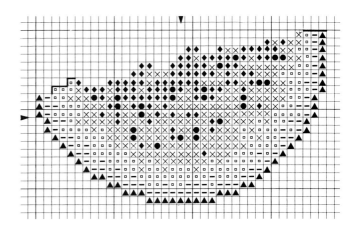

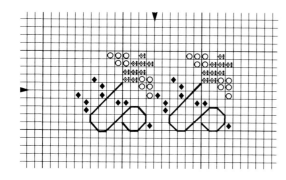

#11

Design size: 20 wide x 10 high

		DMC	Anchor	Coats
✦	= orange	740	316	2099
O	= yellow	726	295	2295
◆	= green	905	258	6239
|	= Backstitch: green			

#12

Design size: 34 wide x 16 high

		DMC	Anchor	Coats
▫	= white	blanc	2	1001
©	= yellow	742	303	2303
◆	= blue	799	136	7030
	gray	318	399	8511
|	= Backstitch: lettering—blue egg—gray (1 strand)			

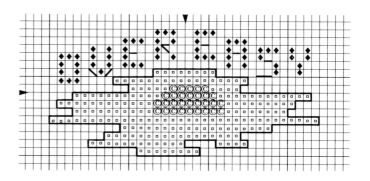

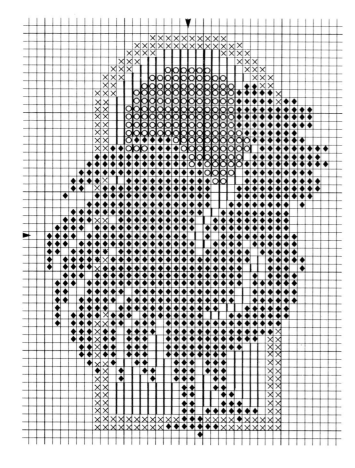

#13

Design size: 36 wide x 51 high

		DMC	Anchor	Coats
X	= pink	3708	26	3126
O	= yellow	726	295	2295
◆	= brown	632	936	5936
|	= Backstitch: pink (1 strand)			

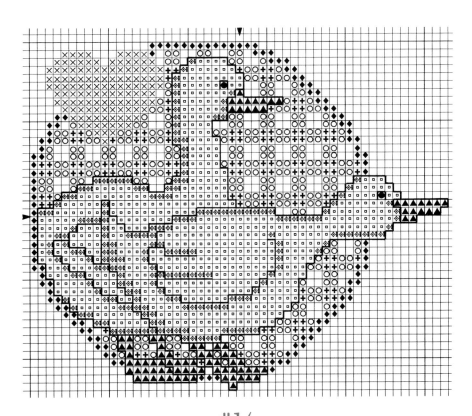

#14

Design size: 53 wide x 44 high

		DMC	Anchor	Coats
□ =	white	blanc	2	1001
✕ =	pink	3708	26	3126
○ =	lt red	760	9	3069
+ =	dk red	349	13	3046
▲ =	orange	740	316	2099
✧ =	lt blue	3752	343	7876
	dk blue	931	921	7052
◆ =	brown	300	352	5471
● =	gray-black	3799	236	8999
│ =	Backstitch (1 strand):			
	geese—dk blue			
	eyes, beaks, feet—gray-black			

#15

Design size: 30 wide x 28 high

		DMC	Anchor	Coats
✕ =	lt pink	3708	26	3126
▲ =	dk pink	3705	35	3012
◇ =	green	772	264	6253
	brown	632	936	5936
• =	French Knots: brown			
│ =	Backstitch: brown (1 strand)			

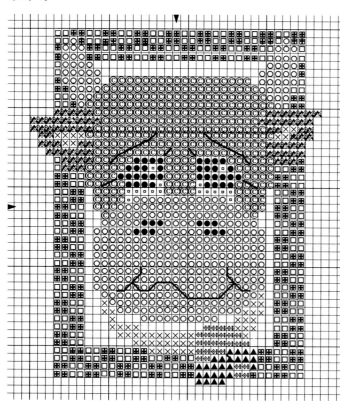

#16

Design size: 37 wide x 45 high

			DMC	Anchor	Coats
▫	=	white	blanc	2	1001
✕	=	pink	760	9	3069
✿	=	lt gold	676	891	2874
▲	=	dk gold	680	901	2876
☐	=	lt blue-gray	3752	343	7876
⊞	=	dk blue-gray	931	921	7052
○	=	very lt brown	437	362	5942
©	=	lt brown	435	369	5371
✖	=	med brown	301	351	2326
●	=	dk brown	938	381	5477
		=	Backstitch: dk brown		

#17

Design size: 41 wide x 46 high

			DMC	Anchor	Coats
▫	=	white	blanc	2	1001
○	=	lt red	666	46	3046
⊕	=	med red	304	47	3410
●	=	dk red	816	44	3000
✿	=	yellow-green	772	264	6253
−	=	lt green	369	213	6015
+	=	med green	320	216	6017
◆	=	dk green	319	246	6246
☐	=	gray	318	399	8511
▲	=	brown	938	381	5477

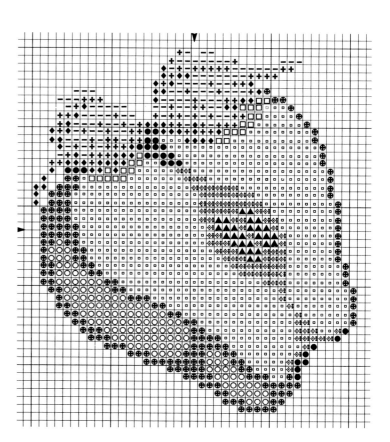

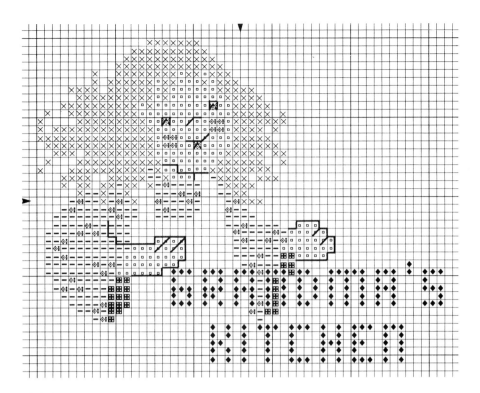

#18

Design size: 52 wide x 41 high

			DMC	Anchor	Coats
⊗	=	lt pink	3712	9	3071
◆	=	dk pink	816	44	3000
▫	=	peach	353	8	3006
×	=	orange	351	11	3011
—	=	lt green	369	213	6015
⊞	=	dk green	320	216	6017
		lt brown	407	914	3883
		med brown	632	936	5936
⋈	=	dk brown	300	352	5471
|	=	Backstitch:			

hands & sleeve—lt brown (1 strand)
eyes & chin—med brown (1 strand)
nose & mouth—dk brown

#19

Design size: 77 wide x 14 high

			DMC	Anchor	Coats
O	=	orange	3341	328	2323
×	=	lt brown	407	914	3883
◆	=	dk brown	632	936	5936
•	=	French Knots:			

border—lt brown
butterfly—dk brown

| \| | = | Backstitch: |

border—lt brown
lettering & butterfly—dk brown (1 strand)

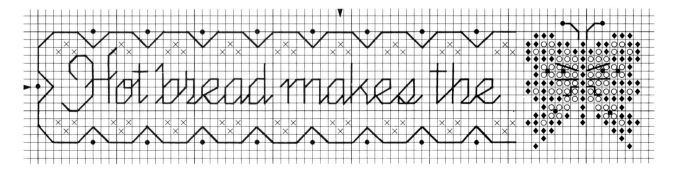

XXXXXXXXXXXXXXXXXXXXXXXX 41 XXXXXXXXXXXXXXXXXXXXXXX

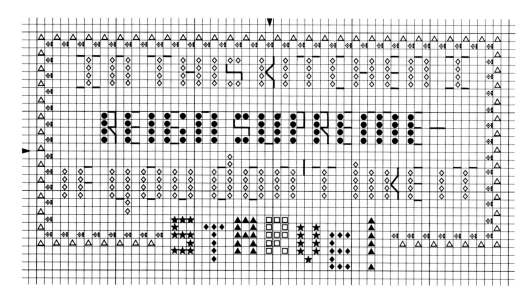

#20

Design size: 59 wide x 30 high

		DMC	Anchor	Coats
✧	= lt pink	3708	26	3126
★	= dk pink	309	42	3154
□	= orange	740	316	2099
◆	= green	701	227	6227
△	= lt blue	799	136	7030
▲	= dk blue	798	137	7080
◇	= lt brown	3772	679	5579
●	= dk brown	632	936	5936
		= Backstitch:			

    1st & 3rd line lettering—lt brown
    2nd line lettering—dk brown

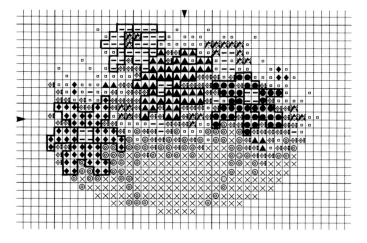

#21

Design size: 35 wide x 24 high

		DMC	Anchor	Coats
◆	= pink	3708	26	3126
⋈	= orange	741	304	2314
−	= yellow	726	295	2295
▲	= blue	809	130	7021
▫	= lt green	772	264	6253
✧	= dk green	319	246	6246
●	= purple	554	96	4104
×	= lt brown	3772	936	5579
◎	= dk brown	300	352	5471
		= Backstitch (optional):			

    flower outlines—to match each flower (1 strand)

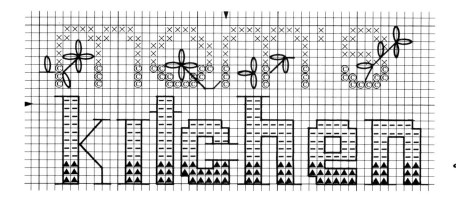

#22

Design size: 49 wide x 20 high

			DMC	Anchor	Coats
–	=	lt pink	3708	26	3126
▲	=	dk pink	309	42	3154
		green	911	204	6227
×	=	lt purple	554	96	4104
©	=	dk purple	552	101	4092
✿	=	Lazy Daisy			

flowers—dk pink
leaves—green

| = Backstitch (1 strand):
letters and letter outlines—dk pink
stems—green

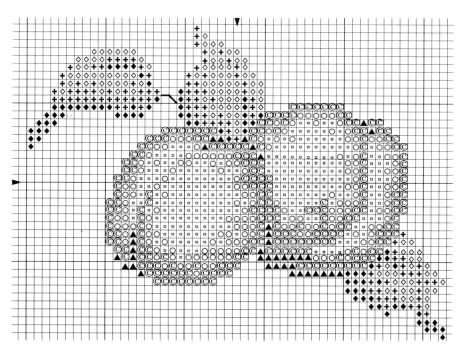

#23

Design size: 53 wide x 40 high

			DMC	Anchor	Coats
O	=	lt peach	3341	328	2323
©	=	med peach	352	8	3008
▲	=	dk peach	350	11	3111
▫	=	yellow	727	293	2289
◇	=	lt green	472	264	6253
+	=	med green	470	267	6268
◆	=	dk green	319	246	6246
	=	Backstitch: dk green			

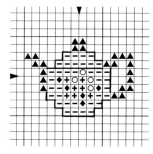

#24

Design size: 14 wide x 10 high

			DMC	Anchor	Coats
O	=	lt pink	3708	26	3126
+	=	dk pink	309	42	3154
◆	=	green	986	246	6246
–	=	lt brown	3774	880	3335
		med lt brown	3773	914	2337
▲	=	med brown	3772	679	5579
		dk brown	632	936	5936
	=	Backstitch (1 strand):			

teapot outline—med lt brown
lid line—dk brown

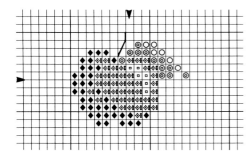

#25

Design size: 15 wide x 12 high

		DMC	Anchor	Coats
▫	= pink	3713	23	3173
✦	= lt red	321	9046	3500
◆	= dk red	498	20	3072
O	= lt green	704	256	6238
◉	= med green	905	258	6239
	dk green	986	246	6246
		= Backstitch: dk green		

#26

Design size: 18 wide x 26 high

		DMC	Anchor	Coats
O	= tan	739	387	5387
✦	= lt brown	435	369	5371
▲	= dk brown	300	352	5471
		= Backstitch: dk brown (1 strand)		

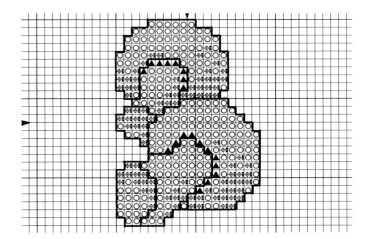

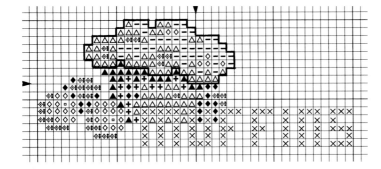

#27

Design size: 40 wide x 16 high

		DMC	Anchor	Coats
▫	= white	blanc	2	1001
✕	= pink	3705	35	3012
◇	= lt blue	3752	343	7876
✦	= med blue	793	121	7110
◆	= dk blue	796	133	7100
−	= very lt brown	950	4146	2336
△	= lt brown	3772	679	5579
+	= med brown	632	936	5936
▲	= dk brown	938	381	5477
		= Backstitch: med brown (1 strand)		

#28

Design size: 27 wide x 27 high

			DMC	Anchor	Coats
◇	=	lt pink	3708	26	3126
◈	=	med pink	309	42	3154
▲	=	dk pink	498	20	3072
–	=	med green	320	216	6017
		dk green	319	246	6246
✕	=	lt blue	809	130	7021
		med blue	798	137	7080
•	=	French Knots: med blue			
		=	Backstitch:			
		flowers—dk pink			
		tendrils—dk green			

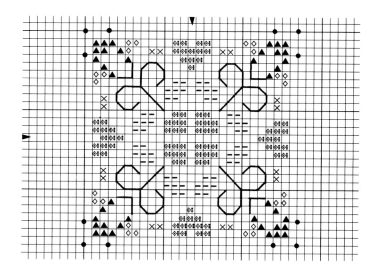

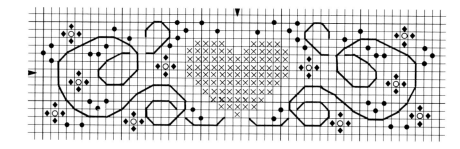

#29

Design size: 49 wide x 13 high

			DMC	Anchor	Coats
✕	=	pink	3705	35	3012
○	=	yellow	725	306	2307
		green	910	230	6031
◆	=	blue	799	136	7030
		purple	552	101	4092
•	=	French Knots: purple			
		=	Backstitch: green (1 strand)			

#30

Design size: 18 wide x 20 high

			DMC	Anchor	Coats
◈	=	pink	3708	26	3126
★	=	red	309	42	3154
○	=	yellow	725	306	2307
◆	=	green	991	189	6212
•	=	French Knots: red			
		=	Backstitch: green (1 strand)			

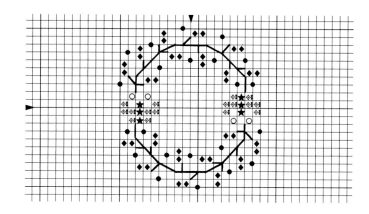

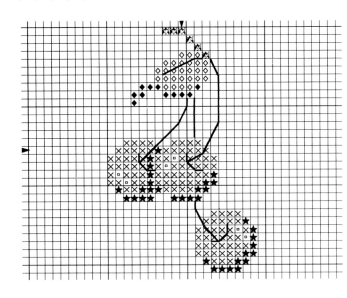

#31

Design size: 19 wide x 31 high

		DMC	Anchor	Coats
▫	= lt red	3708	26	3126
✕	= med red	321	9046	3500
★	= dk red	816	44	3000
◇	= lt green	954	203	6225
◆	= med green	911	204	6227
	dk green	991	189	6212
⋈	= brown	632	936	5936
│	= Backstitch: dk green			

#32

Design size: 35 wide x 37 high

		DMC	Anchor	Coats
▫	= white	blanc	2	1001
◇	= lt green	772	264	6253
▲	= med green	320	216	6017
	dk green	319	246	6246
○	= lt purple	211	108	4303
◉	= med purple	554	96	4104
●	= dk purple	552	101	4092
	very dk purple	550	102	4101
⋈	= brown	400	352	3340
│	= Backstitch (1 strand):			
	tendrils—dk green			
	grapes—very dk purple			

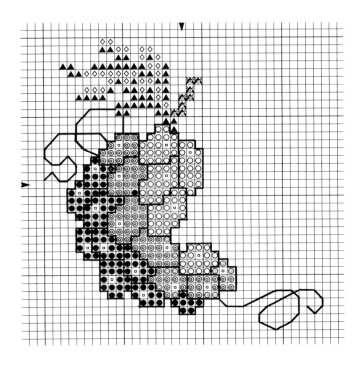

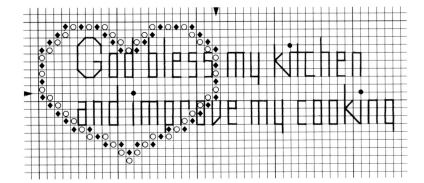

#33

Design size: 45 wide x 18 high

		DMC	Anchor	Coats
○	= lt pink	3712	9	3071
◆	= dk pink	498	20	3072
	turquoise	943	188	6187
•	= French Knots: turquoise			
│	= Backstitch: turquoise (1 strand)			

#34

Design size: 39 wide x 44 high

			DMC	Anchor	Coats
○	=	lt red	3705	35	3012
+	=	med red	321	9046	3500
▲	=	dk red	816	44	3000
◇	=	lt green	772	264	6253
◈	=	med green	320	216	6017
◆	=	dk green	319	246	6246
		=	Backstitch: med red			

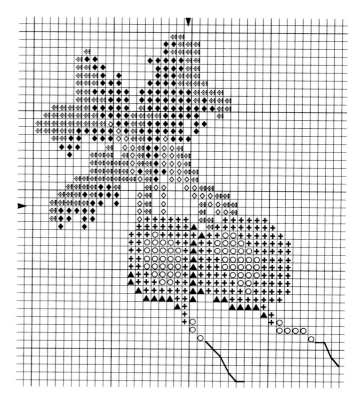

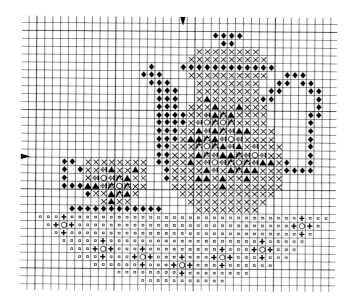

#35

Design size: 37 wide x 32 high

			DMC	Anchor	Coats
▫	=	cream	739	387	5387
+	=	pink	3708	26	3126
○	=	yellow	726	295	2295
▲	=	green	986	246	6246
×	=	lt blue	809	130	7021
◆	=	dk blue	798	137	7080
◈	=	lt purple	554	96	4104
✖	=	dk purple	552	101	4092

#36

Design size: 43 wide x 19 high

			DMC	Anchor	Coats
×	=	lt pink	3708	26	3126
◈	=	dk pink	3705	35	3012
◇	=	green	912	205	6031
©	=	blue	792	940	7022
	=	brown	632	936	5936
		=	Backstitch: brown (1 strand)			

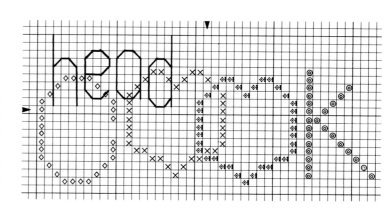

#37

Design size: 39 wide x 46 high

		DMC	Anchor	Coats
□	= white	blanc	2	1001
×	= very lt green	369	213	6015
O	= lt green	954	203	6225
+	= med green	703	238	6238
⊕	= dk green	911	204	6227
◆	= very dk green	991	189	6212
▲	= gray-black	3799	236	8999
•	= French Knot: gray-black			
│	= Backstitch: gray-black			

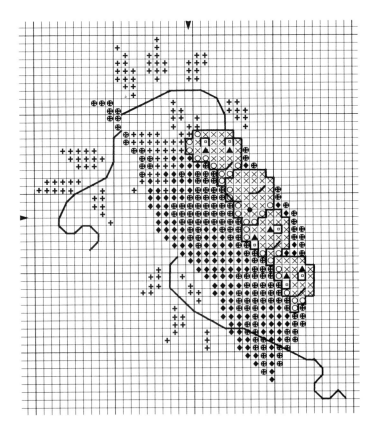

#38

Design size: 41 wide x 28 high

		DMC	Anchor	Coats
	blue	798	137	7080
O	= lt brown	407	914	3883
⊕	= med brown	632	936	5936
	dk brown	938	381	5477
•	= French Knot: blue			
│	= Backstitch (1 strand):			

lettering—blue
grains—lt brown
stem—dk brown

#39

Design size: 45 wide x 8 high

		DMC	Anchor	Coats
☆	= pink	3708	26	3126
✣	= med brown	3772	936	5579
▲	= dk brown	300	352	5471
│	= Backstitch: med brown, using 1 strand			

around cross stitched sections and
2 strands along extended lines

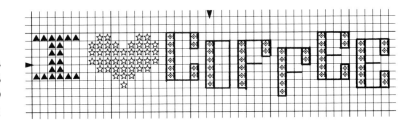

#40

Design size: 35 wide x 32 high

		DMC	Anchor	Coats
□	= white	blanc	2	1001
★	= lt pink	760	9	3069
☆	= dk pink	3712	10	3071
✕	= green	703	238	6238
✤	= blue	799	136	7030
▲	= brown	433	371	5471
✻	= gray-black	3799	236	8999
│	= Backstitch:			

   heart—dk pink

   lettering—to match each word, using
     1 strand around cross stitched sections
     and 2 strands along extended lines

   lambs—gray-black (1 strand)

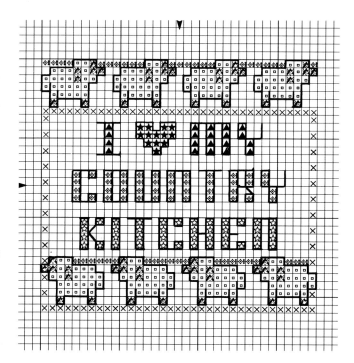

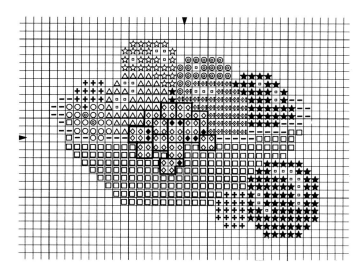

#41

Design size: 34 wide x 25 high

		DMC	Anchor	Coats
□	= white	blanc	2	1001
☆	= pink	3708	26	3126
★	= red	304	47	3410
✤	= orange	740	316	2099
△	= med yellow	726	295	2295
✚	= dk yellow	742	303	2303
○	= lt green	772	264	6253
◎	= med green	704	256	6238
─	= tan	437	362	5942
□	= brown	434	309	5365
◇	= lt purple	341	117	7005
◆	= med purple	3746	119	7110
│	= Backstitch: med purple (1 strand)			

#42

Design size: 45 wide x 20 high

		DMC	Anchor	Coats
☆	= red	321	9046	3500
✚	= yellow	726	295	2295
◆	= green	701	227	6227
□	= lt blue-gray	3752	343	7876
✤	= dk blue-gray	931	921	7052
│	= Backstitch: green			

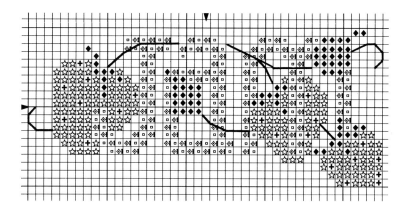

✕✕✕✕✕✕✕✕✕✕✕✕✕✕✕✕✕✕✕✕✕ **49** ✕✕✕✕✕✕✕✕✕✕✕✕✕✕✕✕✕✕✕✕✕

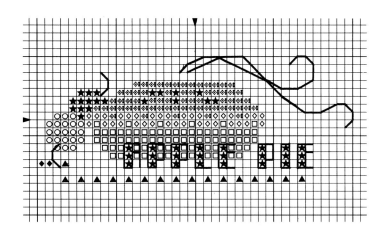

#43

Design size: 40 wide x 16 high

		DMC	Anchor	Coats
O	= lt red	3705	35	3012
★	= dk red	304	47	3410
◆	= green	986	246	6246
▲	= blue	798	137	7080
◇	= lt brown	437	362	5942
✧	= med brown	434	309	5365
□	= lt gray	318	399	8511
	dk gray	414	400	8399
│	= Backstitch:			

lettering—dk red (1 strand)
stems—green
steam—dk gray

#44

Design size: 33 wide x 27 high

		DMC	Anchor	Coats
O	= lt red	3705	35	3012
⊕	= dk red	498	20	3072
▫	= lt brown	437	362	5942
✧	= med brown	435	369	5371
▲	= dk brown	433	371	5471

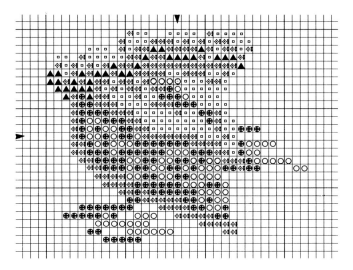

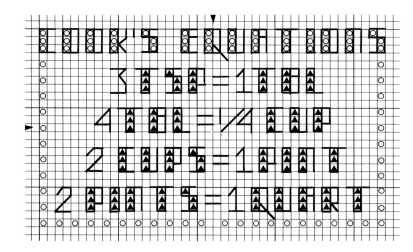

#45

Design size: 44 wide x 25 high

		DMC	Anchor	Coats
	red	321	9046	3500
O	= green	703	238	6238
▲	= blue	792	940	7022
│	= Backstitch (1 strand):			

numerals—red
green lettering—green
equal signs & blue lettering—blue

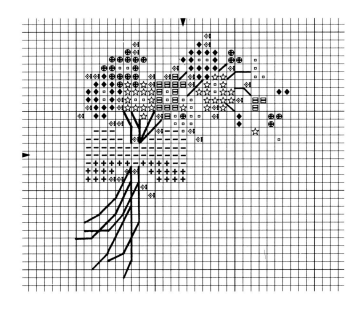

#46

Design size: 27 wide x 31 high

			DMC	Anchor	Coats
☆	=	pink	3708	26	3126
⊕	=	orange	351	11	3011
▫	=	yellow	726	295	2295
━	=	lt gold	676	891	2874
+	=	dk gold	783	307	5309
✥	=	green	986	246	6246
◆	=	blue	799	136	7030
⊟	=	purple	552	101	4092
❘	=	Backstitch: green (1 strand)			

#47

Design size: 25 wide x 25 high

			DMC	Anchor	Coats
▫	=	cream	746	386	2386
━	=	very lt pink	963	49	3173
O	=	lt pink	3708	26	3126
◉	=	med pink	309	42	3154
●	=	dk pink	816	44	3000
◆	=	lt green	772	264	6253
□	=	dk green	319	246	6246

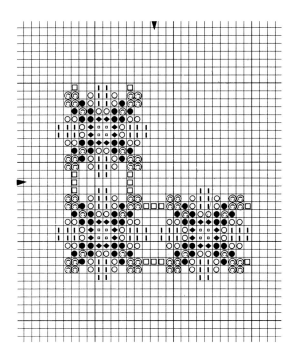

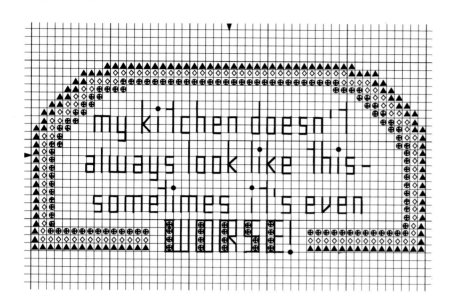

#48

Design size: 50 wide x 24 high

		DMC	Anchor	Coats
▲	= red	321	9046	3500
◇	= yellow	725	306	2307
⊕	= blue	798	137	7080
•	= French Knots:			
	dots on "i"s—red			
	exclamation point—blue			
│	= Backstitch (1 strand):			
	red lettering—red			
	blue lettering—blue			

#49

Design size: 17 wide x 17 high

		DMC	Anchor	Coats
◇	= lt pink	3708	26	3126
◆	= med pink	309	42	3154
	dk pink	816	44	3000
O	= green	772	264	6253
•	= French Knots: dk pink			
│	= Backstitch: dk pink			

Note: *Extended border stitches as desired.*

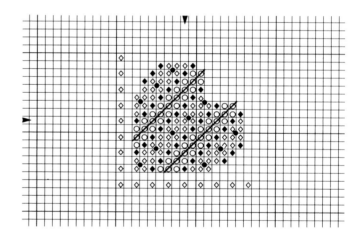

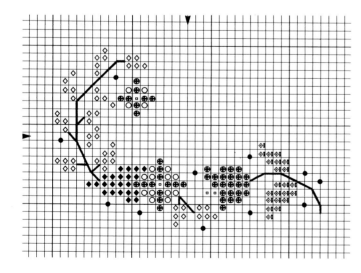

#50

Design size: 34 wide x 23 high

		DMC	Anchor	Coats
O	= lt pink	3708	26	3126
	med pink	3705	35	3012
⊕	= dk pink	309	42	3154
▫	= yellow	725	306	2307
◇	= lt green	703	238	6238
✪	= med green	701	227	6227
◆	= dk green	986	246	6246
•	= French Knots: med pink			
│	= Backstitch: dk green			

50
Baby
Designs

So many things that babies wear can be made extra special with the addition of a little stitchery —from delicate motifs with sweet feminine themes to humorous characters and feisty little boy designs.

#1

Design size: 54 wide x 41 high

		DMC	Anchor	Coats
□	= cream	746	386	1002
▫	= pink	3713	23	3068
✿	= med rose	956	40	3153
▩	= dk rose	321	47	3500
◇	= yellow	744	301	2296
☆	= med gold	742	303	2303
⊠	= dk gold	783	307	2308
○	= lt blue	3761	158	7159
+	= med blue	806	169	7169
◆	= dk blue	3765	170	7162
©	= rust	922	324	3337
■	= gray-black	3799	236	8514
•	= French Knots: med gold			
|	= Backstitch:			

    chin—med rose (1 strand)
    mouth—dk rose
    halo—dk gold
    eyes—gray-black (1 strand)

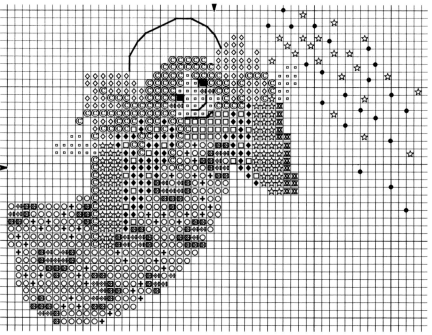

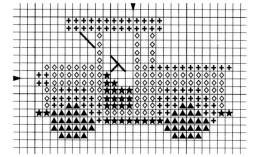

#2

Design size: 26 wide x 16 high

		DMC	Anchor	Coats
+	= yellow	743	297	2298
◇	= lt blue	826	161	7180
★	= dk blue	824	164	7182
▲	= gray-black	3799	236	8514
|	= Backstitch:			

    roof brace—lt blue
    steering wheel—gray-black

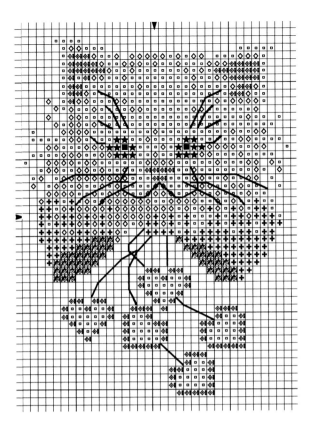

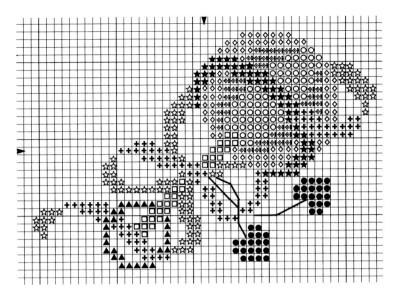

#3

Design size: 35 wide x 47 high

			DMC	Anchor	Coats
▫	=	cream	712	387	5387
✧	=	pink	3716	25	3150
◇	=	lt blue	3761	158	7159
★	=	dk blue	825	162	7181
+	=	lt purple	554	96	4104
⊠	=	dk purple	552	101	4092
■	=	gray-black	3799	236	8514
│	=	Backstitch:			
		ties—dk purple			
		mouth—gray-black			
		whiskers & eyebrows—gray-black (1 strand)			

#4

Design size: 45 wide x 31 high

			DMC	Anchor	Coats
✧	=	med pink	956	40	3153
●	=	dk pink	326	59	3019
+	=	lt yellow	744	301	2296
☆	=	dk yellow	743	297	2298
□	=	lt green	704	256	6238
★	=	dk green	702	239	6226
◇	=	lt blue	807	168	7168
▲	=	med blue	806	169	7169
○	=	purple	3609	85	4085
│	=	Backstitch: dk pink			

#5

Design size: 39 wide x 27 high

			DMC	Anchor	Coats
✧	=	med rose	956	40	3153
●	=	dk rose	326	59	3019
◇	=	yellow	743	297	2298
△	=	lt green	704	256	6238
★	=	dk green	701	227	6227
⊠	=	blue	806	169	7169
©	=	purple	553	98	4097
│	=	Backstitch: dk green (1 strand)			

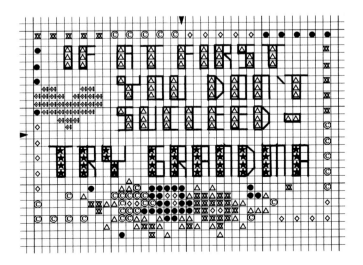

XXXXXXXXXXXXXXXXXXXXXX 57 XXXXXXXXXXXXXXXXXXXXXX

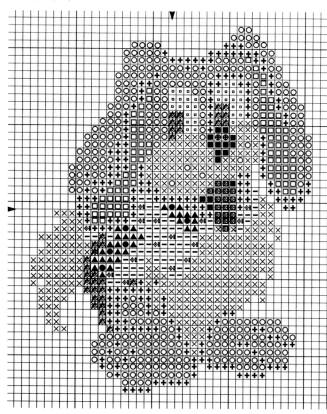

#6

Design size: 37 wide x 48 high

			DMC	Anchor	Coats
▫	=	white	blanc	2	1001
□	=	lt pink	963	49	3150
▨	=	dk pink	894	26	3126
✧	=	lt green	704	256	6238
●	=	dk green	702	239	6226
–	=	lt blue	3761	158	7159
▲	=	dk blue	807	168	7168
✕	=	tan	950	4146	2336
O	=	lt brown	407	883	3883
+	=	med brown	632	936	5356
▨	=	dk brown	938	381	5477
⊕	=	gray	414	400	8399
■	=	black	310	403	8403

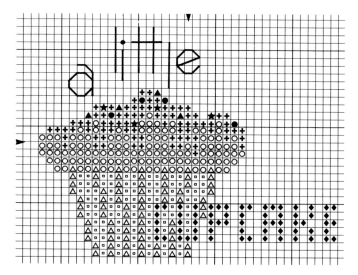

#8

Design size: 39 wide x 30 high

			DMC	Anchor	Coats
+	=	pink	957	50	3152
●	=	red	304	47	3410
▫	=	lt yellow	744	301	2296
△	=	med yellow	742	303	2303
▲	=	green	699	923	6228
★	=	blue	796	133	7100
◆	=	purple	552	101	4092
O	=	brown	632	936	5470
•	=	French Knot: green			
		=	Backstitch:			

    "a"—red

    "little"—green

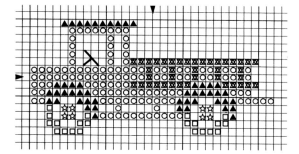

#7

Design size: 32 wide x 15 high

			DMC	Anchor	Coats
O	=	med red	321	47	3500
▲	=	dk red	498	20	3072
☆	=	yellow	743	297	2298
▨	=	gold	783	307	2308
□	=	gray-black	3799	236	8514
		=	Backstitch: gray-black			

#9

Design size: 57 wide x 59 high

		DMC	Anchor	Coats
–	= white	blanc	2	1001
◈	= lt pink	894	26	3126
●	= dk pink	892	28	3152
▫	= peach	754	778	3006
☆	= yellow	743	297	2298
O	= lt green	954	203	6020
◉	= med green	911	205	6227
+	= blue	825	162	7181
□	= lt tan	738	372	5372
✕	= med tan	436	363	5943
★	= brown	920	339	3340
|	= Backstitch:			
	eyes—brown			
	mouth—dk pink			

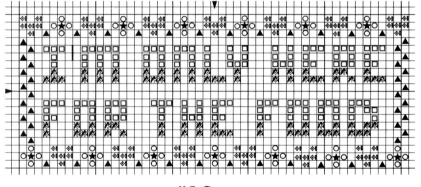

#10

Design size: 51 wide x 20 high

		DMC	Anchor	Coats
◈	= pink	956	40	3153
O	= yellow	743	297	2298
▲	= green	911	205	6227
□	= lt blue	3766	168	7168
✕	= med blue	806	169	7169
★	= rust	922	324	3337
|	= Backstitch: med blue			

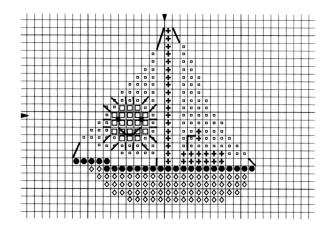

#11

Design size: 24 wide x 23 high

		DMC	Anchor	Coats
□	= cream	951	366	3335
●	= red	666	46	3046
□	= yellow	742	303	2303
◊	= blue	798	137	7080
+	= brown	632	936	5356
	gray-black	3799	236	8514
•	= French Knots: gray-black			
		= Backstitch: gray-black			

#12

Design size: 43 wide x 23 high

		DMC	Anchor	Coats
✦	= lt pink	957	50	3152
+	= med pink	956	40	3153
O	= lt yellow	744	301	2296
◉	= med yellow	725	306	2307
◊	= lt green	954	203	6020
☆	= med green	911	205	6227
△	= lt rust	922	324	3337
✗	= med rust	918	341	3340
■	= brown-black	3371	382	5382
		= Backstitch: brown-black (1 strand)			

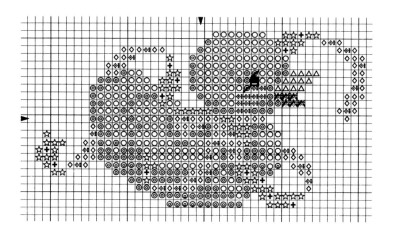

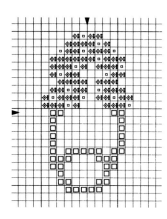

#13

Design size: 12 wide x 21 high

		DMC	Anchor	Coats
□	= white	blanc	2	1001
✦	= pink	956	40	3153
□	= yellow	725	306	2307

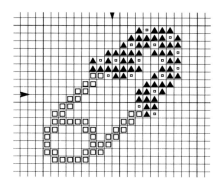

#14

Design size: 18 wide x 18 high

		DMC	Anchor	Coats
□	= white	blanc	2	1001
□	= yellow	725	306	2307
▲	= blue	798	137	7080

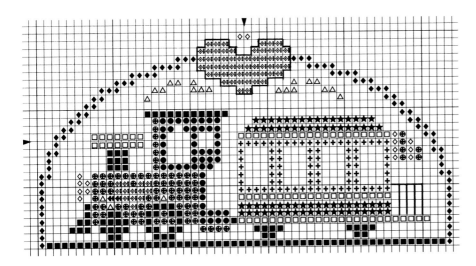

#15

Design size: 54 wide x 28 high

		DMC	Anchor	Coats
✧	= pink	963	49	3150
⊕	= med rose	956	40	3153
●	= dk rose	498	20	3072
◇	= yellow	743	297	2298
△	= lt green	472	264	6253
+	= med green	703	238	6238
★	= dk green	3346	257	6258

		DMC	Anchor	Coats
□	= tan	436	363	5943
◆	= gray	414	400	8399
■	= gray-black	3799	236	8514
		= Backstitch:			
	heart—med rose (1 strand)			
	tailgate—gray-black			

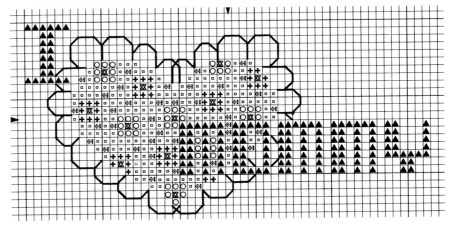

#16

Design size: 53 wide x 25 high

		DMC	Anchor	Coats
O	= pink	893	27	3127
▲	= green	911	205	6227
+	= blue	597	168	7168
▫	= lt tan	738	372	5372
✧	= med tan	435	369	5371
⊠	= dk tan	433	371	5471
		= Backstitch: dk tan			

#17 & 18

Design sizes: 17—28 wide x 35 high;
18—26 wide x 35 high

		DMC	Anchor	Coats
O	= white	blanc	2	1001
–	= cream	951	366	3335
✪	= lt pink	957	50	3152
⊠	= dk pink	956	40	3153
▫	= peach	754	778	3006
◇	= lt yellow	744	301	2296
☆	= dk yellow	783	307	2308
△	= lt turquoise	959	186	6186
◆	= dk turquoise	958	187	6187
+	= lt blue	3766	168	7168
★	= dk blue	806	169	7169
▲	= purple	3608	86	4086
©	= rust	922	324	3337
×	= lt brown	950	4146	2336
✺	= med brown	3772	679	5356
■	= dk brown	632	936	5470
	very dk brown	938	381	5477
•	= French Knots:			
	on blouse—dk pink			
	mouths—dk brown			
⎮	= Backstitch: very dk brown			

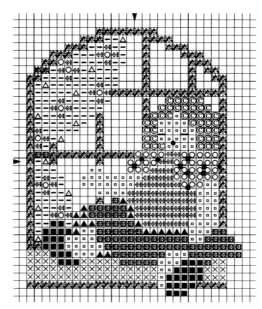

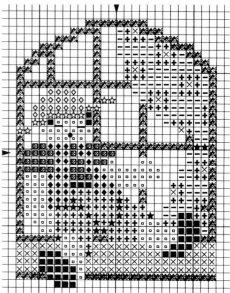

#19

Design size: 21 wide x 26 high

		DMC	Anchor	Coats
✪	= pink	956	40	3153
+	= red	326	59	3019
★	= blue	798	137	7080
■	= gray-black	3799	236	8514
⎮	= Backstitch: gray-black			

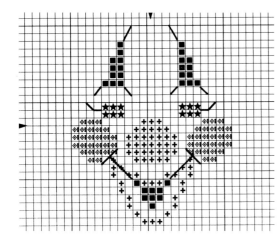

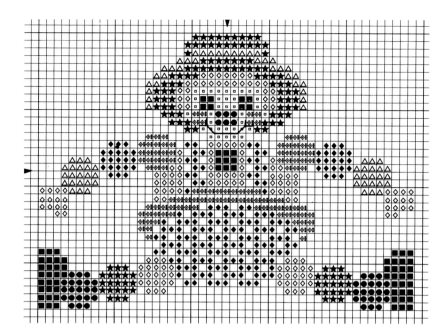

#20

Design size: 49 wide x 36 high

			DMC	Anchor	Coats
▫	=	lt pink	963	49	3150
◈	=	dk pink	956	40	3153
●	=	red	321	47	3500
◇	=	yellow	742	303	2303
△	=	lt green	912	204	6226
★	=	dk green	699	923	6228
◆	=	blue	798	137	7080
■	=	black	310	403	8403
|	=	Backstitch: red			

#21

Design size: 52 wide x 45 high

			DMC	Anchor	Coats
◇	=	lt yellow	744	301	2296
☆	=	dk yellow	726	295	2294
		green	911	205	6227
◉	=	rust	435	369	5365
▫	=	tan	738	372	5372
○	=	lt brown	407	883	3883
⊕	=	med brown	632	936	5356
▲	=	dk brown	938	381	5477
■	=	brown-black	3371	382	5382
•	=	French Knots: green			
|	=	Backstitch:			
		mouth—dk brown			
		eyes—brown-black (1 strand)			

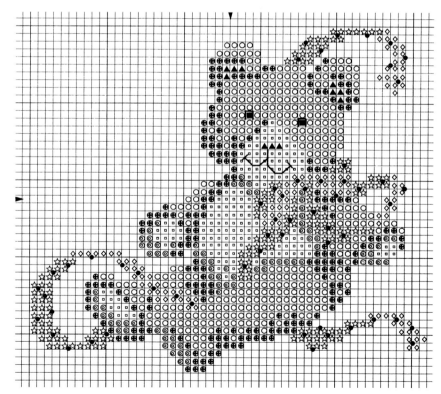

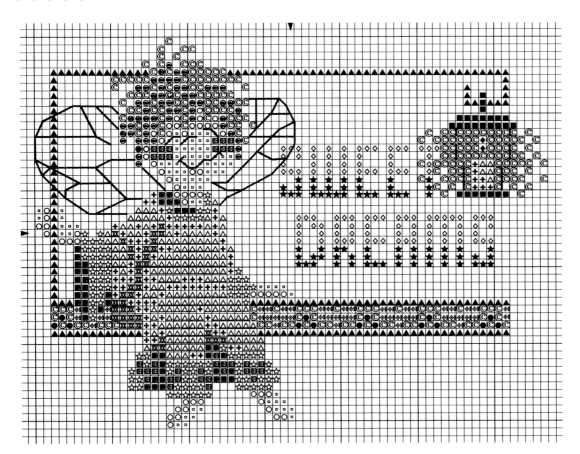

#22

Design size: 67 wide x 51 high

		DMC	Anchor	Coats
✤	= lt pink	957	50	3152
▩	= med pink	956	40	3153
▫	= lt peach	353	8	3008
O	= med peach	352	10	3011
◆	= orange	970	316	2327
©	= lt yellow	744	301	2296
☆	= dk yellow	725	306	2307
◉	= med gold	783	307	5363
⊞	= dk gold	782	308	2308
△	= lt green	954	203	6020
+	= med green	701	227	6227
⊠	= dk green	699	923	6228
●	= blue	825	162	7181
◇	= lt rust	922	324	3337
★	= med rust	920	339	3340
▲	= gray	317	400	8512
■	= gray-black	3799	236	8514
│	= Backstitch:			

wings—blue
eyes & mouth—gray-black
lantern—gray-black (1 strand)

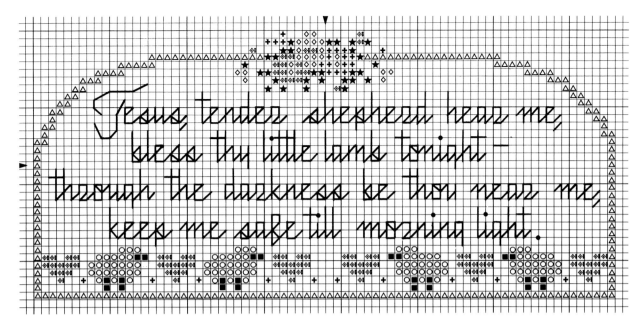

#24

Design size: 76 wide x 35 high

		DMC	Anchor	Coats
✥ =	pink	894	26	3126
◇ =	yellow	743	297	2298
△ =	lt green	912	204	6226
	med green	910	230	6227
★ =	dk green	699	923	6228

		DMC	Anchor	Coats
+ =	blue	807	168	7168
O =	tan	951	366	3335
■ =	gray-black	3799	236	8514
• =	French Knots: med green			
| =	Backstitch: med green (1 strand)			

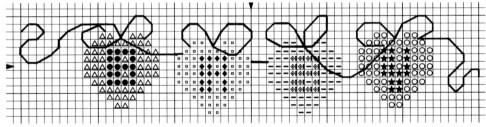

▲ #25

Design size: 60 wide x 13 high

		DMC	Anchor	Coats
– =	lt pink	963	49	3150
✥ =	dk pink	956	40	3153
▫ =	lt yellow	744	301	2296
◆ =	dk yellow	783	307	2308
O =	lt green	954	203	6020
★ =	dk green	700	229	6227
△ =	lt blue	3761	158	7159
● =	dk blue	806	169	7169
	purple	552	101	4092
| =	Backstitch: purple			

◄ #23

Design size: 27 wide x 35 high

		DMC	Anchor	Coats
✥ =	pink	956	40	3153
O =	yellow	743	297	2298
+ =	green	912	204	6226
★ =	blue	826	161	7180
◆ =	rust	922	324	3337
▫ =	tan	951	366	3335
	brown	801	357	5475
| =	Backstitch: brown			

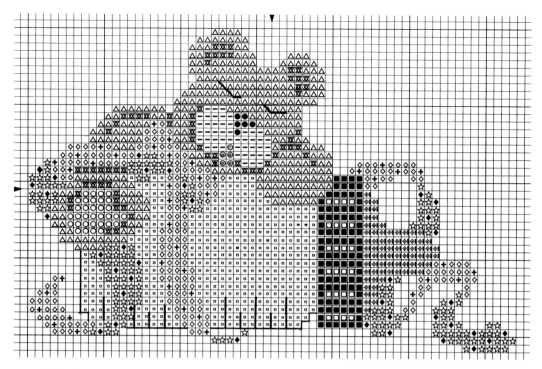

#26

Design size: 64 wide x 42 high

			DMC	Anchor	Coats
▫	=	cream	746	386	1002
O	=	lt pink	3716	25	3150
◉	=	med pink	3708	26	3126
◇	=	lt yellow	744	301	2296
☆	=	dk yellow	743	297	2298
+	=	lt green	704	256	6238
◆	=	med green	702	239	6226
−	=	tan	951	366	3335
◌⃰	=	rust	921	349	2326

			DMC	Anchor	Coats
△	=	lt brown	407	883	3883
⋈	=	med brown	918	341	3340
●	=	dk brown	938	381	5477
□	=	gray	318	399	8511
■	=	gray-black	3799	236	8514
		=	Backstitch:			

eyes—dk brown

milk bottle & markings—gray

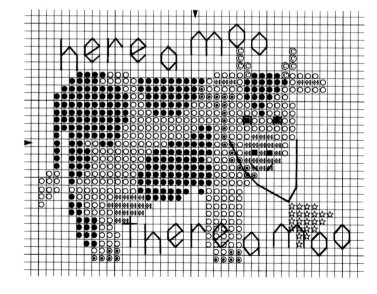

#27

Design size: 41 wide x 31 high

			DMC	Anchor	Coats
©	=	cream	951	366	3335
◌⃰	=	pink	893	27	3127
☆	=	yellow	725	306	2307
		purple	552	101	4092
O	=	lt brown	950	4146	3336
◉	=	med brown	3772	936	5356
●	=	dk brown	801	357	5475
■	=	gray-black	3799	236	8514
		=	Backstitch:			

lettering & bell rope—purple

eyes & mouth—gray-black (1 strand)

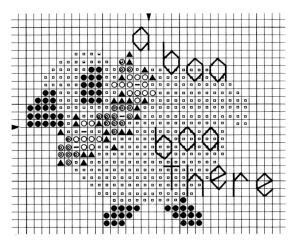

#28

Design size: 32 wide x 26 high

			DMC	Anchor	Coats
▫	=	cream	950	4146	2336
O	=	lt peach	3341	328	2329
◉	=	dk peach	921	349	2326
–	=	yellow	742	303	2303
▲	=	green	909	229	6228
●	=	brown	801	357	5475
│	=	Backstitch: brown			

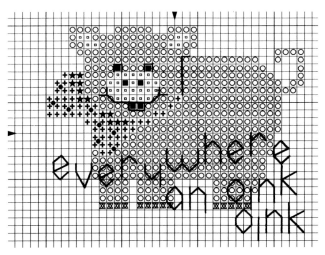

#29

Design size: 34 wide x 28 high

			DMC	Anchor	Coats
		white	blanc	2	1001
▫	=	lt pink	963	49	3150
O	=	med pink	894	26	3126
		dk pink	956	40	3153
+	=	lt turquoise	807	168	7168
★	=	dk turquoise	3765	169	7162
✖	=	brown	632	936	5356
■	=	black	310	403	8403
•	=	French Knots: white			
│	=	Backstitch:			
		neckline—dk pink			
		lettering—dk turquoise			
		eyes & mouth—black (1 strand)			

#30

Design size: 45 wide x 51 high

			DMC	Anchor	Coats
▫	=	cream	746	386	1002
◇	=	lt tan	437	362	5942
+	=	med tan	407	883	3883
✖	=	dk tan	632	936	5356
O	=	lt brown	950	4146	2336
⊕	=	med brown	920	339	3340
▲	=	dk brown	801	357	5475
■	=	black	310	403	8403
│	=	Backstitch: black (1 strand)			

XXXXXXXXXXXXXXXXXXXXXXXXXXXXXX 67 XXXXXXXXXXXXXXXXXXXXXXXXXXXXXX

#31

Design size: 36 wide x 28 high

			DMC	Anchor	Coats
□	=	cream	712	387	5387
✛	=	lt pink	893	27	3127
		dk pink	891	35	3012
O	=	yellow-orange	741	304	2314
▲	=	green	3346	257	6258
◇	=	blue	3761	158	7159
■	=	black	310	403	8403
|	=	Backstitch:			

lettering—dk pink
eye—black (1 strand)

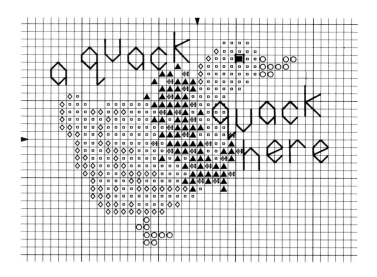

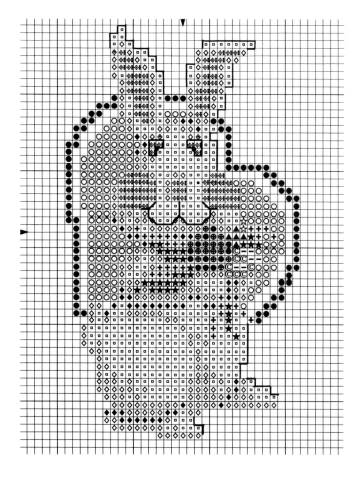

#32

Design size: 31 wide x 54 high

			DMC	Anchor	Coats
□	=	cream	746	386	1002
✛	=	very lt pink	963	49	3150
O	=	lt pink	894	26	3126
⊕	=	med pink	891	35	3012
●	=	dk pink	304	47	3410
−	=	lt yellow	744	301	2296
©	=	med yellow	742	303	2303
+	=	lt green	954	203	6020
★	=	dk green	910	230	6228
◇	=	lt blue	3766	168	7168
◆	=	dk blue	806	169	7169
☆	=	lt purple	554	96	4104
▲	=	dk purple	550	102	4101
		gray	414	400	8399
•	=	French Knots: gray			
|	=	Backstitch: gray			

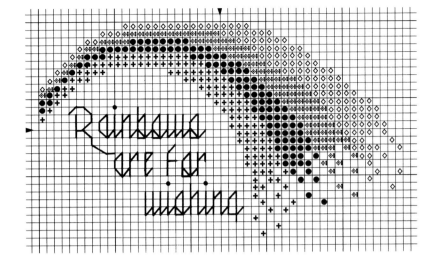

#33

Design size: 48 wide x 28 high

			DMC	Anchor	Coats
●	=	red	321	47	3500
◈	=	orange	970	316	2327
◇	=	yellow	743	297	2298
		green	700	229	6227
+	=	blue	797	132	7100
•	=	French Knots: green			
		=	Backstitch: green (1 strand)			

#34

Design size: 50 wide x 57 high

			DMC	Anchor	Coats
▫	=	white	blanc	2	1001
◉	=	lt red	892	28	3152
●	=	dk red	321	47	3500
○	=	lt yellow	743	297	2298
◎	=	dk yellow	741	304	2314
▲	=	green	910	230	6228
+	=	lt blue	799	131	7030
★	=	med blue	797	132	7100
◈	=	lt brown	437	362	5942
▨	=	dk brown	434	309	5365
■	=	gray-black	3799	236	8514
•	=	French Knots: green			
		=	Backstitch:			
			lettering—green			
			raindrops—med blue			
			eye—gray-black (1 strand)			

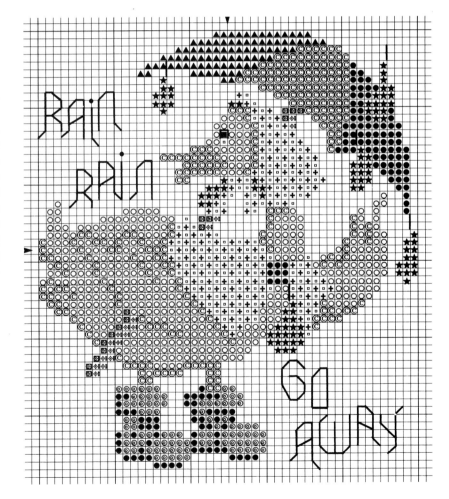

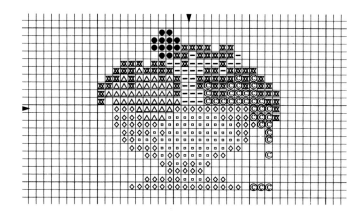

#35

Design size: 24 wide x 21 high

			DMC	Anchor	Coats
▫	=	white	blanc	2	1001
−	=	cream	746	386	1002
©	=	lt pink	956	40	3153
●	=	med pink	326	59	3019
◇	=	blue	827	159	7159
△	=	lt brown	407	883	3883
☒	=	med brown	801	357	5475

#36

Design size: 46 wide x 23 high

			DMC	Anchor	Coats
☐	=	white	blanc	2	1001
▫	=	cream	739	387	5387
✿	=	lt pink	3716	25	3150
−	=	med pink	957	50	3152
▨	=	dk pink	956	40	3153
▲	=	green	702	239	6226
☆	=	blue	827	159	7159
◇	=	tan	738	372	5372
◆	=	lt green	922	324	3337
❘	=	Backstitch:			

    "L"—tan

    heart—med pink

    stems—green

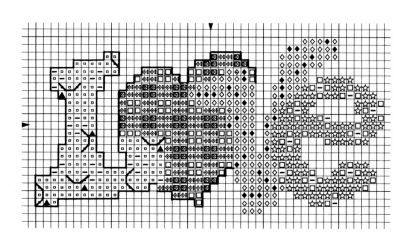

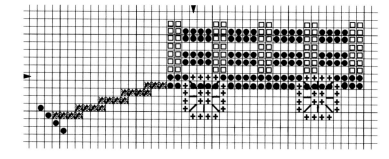

#37

Design size: 43 wide x 15 high

			DMC	Anchor	Coats
●	=	red	321	47	3500
☐	=	lt brown	437	362	5942
☒	=	dk brown	433	371	5471
+	=	gray-black	3799	236	8514
❘	=	Backstitch: gray-black			

#38

Design size: 45 wide x 61 high

			DMC	Anchor	Coats
□	=	white	blanc	2	1001
✕	=	lt pink	3713	23	3068
✧	=	med pink	957	50	3152
▩	=	dk pink	956	40	3153
●	=	very dk pink	326	59	3019
▫	=	lt peach	754	778	3006
		med peach	758	868	3336
○	=	yellow	743	297	2298
©	=	gold	783	307	2308
▲	=	green	700	229	6227
★	=	blue	826	161	7180
−	=	tan	951	366	3335
◇	=	med brown	632	936	5356
⚹	=	dk brown	918	341	3340
		gray	762	397	8510
■	=	gray-black	3799	236	8514

| = Backstitch:
    chin & arms—med peach
    stems—green
    tear—blue
    ruffle—gray
    eyes, eyebrows, mouth—gray-black

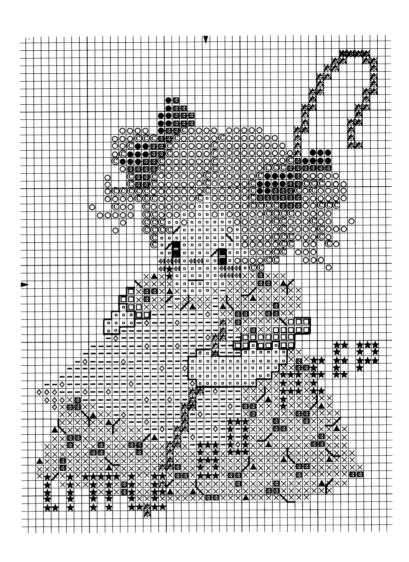

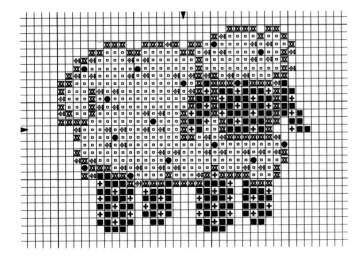

#39

Design size: 33 wide x 27 high

			DMC	Anchor	Coats
✧	=	lt pink	956	40	3153
●	=	med pink	326	59	3019
+	=	blue	807	168	7168
▫	=	lt tan	738	372	5372
✕	=	med tan	435	369	5371
■	=	brown	801	357	5475

#40

Design size: 40 wide x 21 high

		DMC	Anchor	Coats
✣ =	lt pink	894	26	3126
▲ =	med pink	326	59	3019
— =	lt yellow	725	306	2307
✗ =	med yellow	783	307	2308
○ =	lt green	954	203	6020
⊕ =	med green	911	205	6227
◇ =	lt blue	813	160	7161
★ =	med blue	825	162	7181
• =	French Knots: med green			
| =	Backstitch: med green			

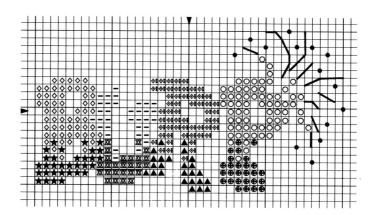

#41

Design size: 40 wide x 57 high

		DMC	Anchor	Coats
☆ =	med pink	957	50	3152
▲ =	dk pink	326	59	3019
■ =	red	666	46	3046
✣ =	orange	970	316	2327
◇ =	yellow	743	297	2298
★ =	green	910	230	6228
+ =	blue	825	162	7181
✗ =	purple	550	102	4101
△ =	lt blue	3761	158	7159
◆ =	med blue	806	169	7169
○ =	lt brown	950	4146	2336
⊙ =	med brown	3772	936	5356
● =	dk brown	938	381	5477
| =	Backstitch: dk brown (1 strand)			

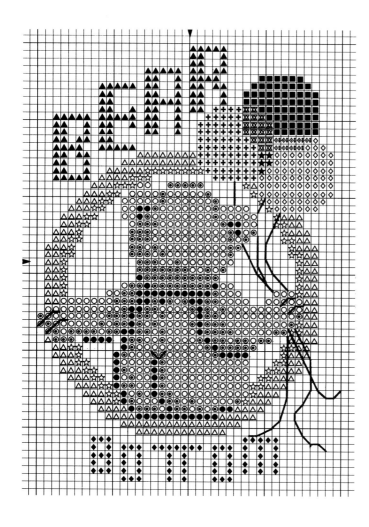

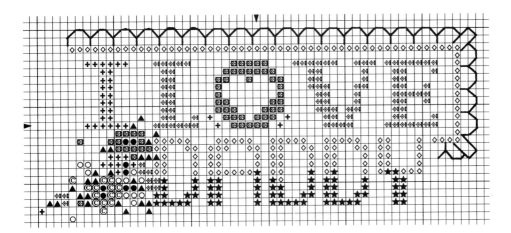

#42

Design size: 57 wide x 25 high

		DMC	Anchor	Coats
❖ =	lt pink	3708	26	3126
▩ =	dk pink	3706	28	3127
O =	yellow	743	297	2298
◇ =	lt green	954	203	6020
★ =	med green	912	204	6226
▲ =	very dk green	909	229	6228
© =	lt blue	3766	168	7168
+ =	dk blue	806	169	7169
● =	brown	407	883	3883
| =	Backstitch: very dk green			

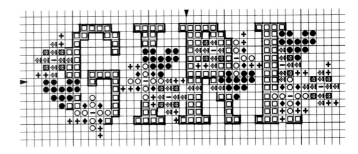

#43

Design size: 40 wide x 15 high

		DMC	Anchor	Coats
□ =	cream	951	366	3335
❖ =	lt rose	963	49	3150
▩ =	med rose	957	50	3152
● =	dk rose	956	40	3153
− =	yellow	726	295	2294
+ =	green	702	239	6226
O =	lt purple	3609	85	4085
◆ =	med purple	553	98	4097
| =	Backstitch: med rose			

#44

Design size: 27 wide x 34 high

		DMC	Anchor	Coats
❖ =	lt pink	956	40	3153
▩ =	dk pink	326	59	3019
◎ =	lt red	321	9046	3500
● =	dk red	304	47	3410
☆ =	orange	741	304	2314
▫ =	yellow	726	295	2294
+ =	gold	783	307	2308
− =	lt blue	826	161	7180
◆ =	dk blue	824	164	7182
◇ =	med green	912	204	6226
▲ =	dk green	699	923	6228
✖ =	rust	922	324	3337
	black	310	403	8403
| =	Backstitch: black			

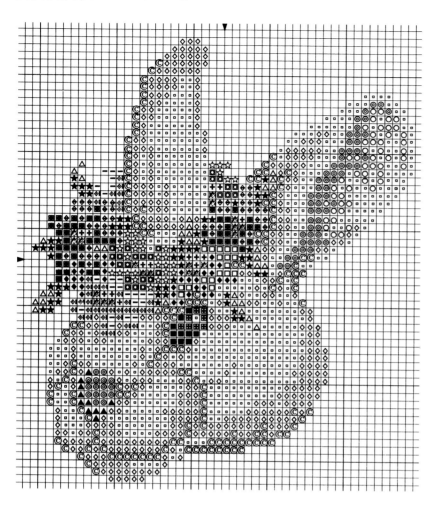

#45

Design size: 50 wide x 58 high

			DMC	Anchor	Coats
▫	=	cream	712	387	5387
◈	=	lt pink	957	50	3152
▣	=	dk pink	956	40	3153
○	=	peach	3341	328	2323
–	=	lt orange	741	304	2314
✧	=	med orange	970	316	2327
☆	=	lt yellow	744	301	2296
▨	=	med yellow	742	303	2303
△	=	lt green	703	238	6238
★	=	dk green	986	246	6211
◇	=	lt blue	3761	158	7159
©	=	med blue	825	162	7181
□	=	lt purple	554	96	4104
◆	=	med purple	553	98	4097
◉	=	lt rust	922	324	3337
▲	=	med rust	920	339	3340
+	=	lt brown	407	883	3883
✶	=	med brown	632	936	5356
⊞	=	med gray	317	400	8512
■	=	dk gray	3799	236	8514
		black	310	403	8403
∣	=	Backstitch: black (1 strand)			

#46

Design size: 42 wide x 38 high

			DMC	Anchor	Coats
▫	=	lt pink	3716	25	3150
✧	=	med pink	956	40	3153
●	=	dk pink	326	59	3019
◇	=	yellow	743	297	2298
☆	=	gold	741	304	2314
◆	=	med green	912	204	6226
✶	=	dk green	909	229	6228
○	=	lt blue	809	130	7021
▲	=	dk blue	798	137	7080
+	=	rust	922	324	3337
–	=	lt brown	436	363	5943
©	=	med brown	433	371	5471
■	=	black	310	403	8403
•	=	French Knots: dk blue			
∣	=	Backstitch:			
		swing—dk green			
		eye—black (1 strand)			

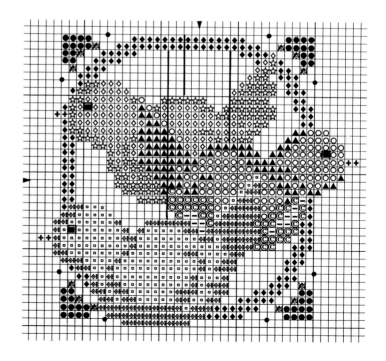

#47

Design size: 40 wide x 35 high

			DMC	Anchor	Coats
O	=	lt gold	744	301	2296
+	=	med gold	725	306	2307
⊠	=	green	3347	266	6256
▲	=	blue	825	162	7181
◇	=	lt purple	3608	86	4086
★	=	med purple	552	101	4092
•	=	French Knots: med purple			
		=	Backstitch: med purple			

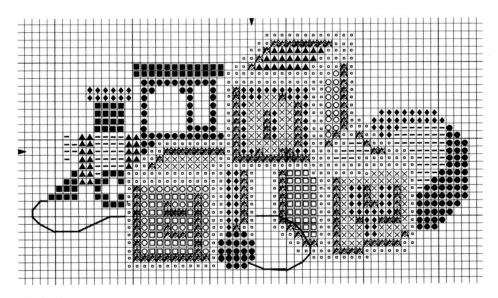

#48

Design size: 57 wide x 31 high

			DMC	Anchor	Coats
O	=	lt red	666	46	3046
●	=	dk red	304	47	3410
✕	=	orange	3341	328	2323
–	=	yellow	743	297	2298
◆	=	green	3347	266	6256
☐	=	lt blue	809	130	7021
▲	=	dk blue	798	137	7080
▫	=	lt brown	738	372	5372
⚒	=	dk brown	919	341	2326
■	=	black	310	403	8403
|	=	Backstitch: black			

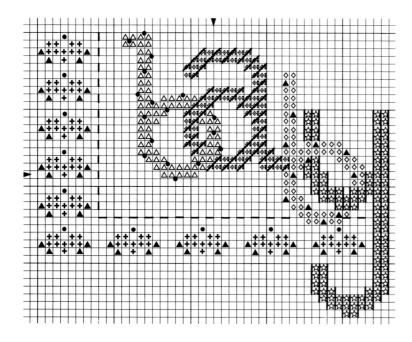

#49

Design size: 46 wide x 37 high

		DMC	Anchor	Coats
✿ =	lt pink	893	27	3127
+ =	dk pink	326	59	3019
◇ =	yellow	726	295	2294
△ =	lt green	954	203	6020
▲ =	med green	911	205	6227
☆ =	lt blue	809	130	7021
	dk blue	797	132	7100
--- =	Running Stitch: dk blue			
• =	French Knots:			
	on "B"—dk pink			
	above hearts—dk blue			
❘ =	Backstitch:			
	on "A"—dk pink			
	on "Y"—dk blue			

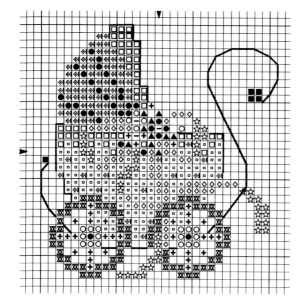

#50

Design size: 31 wide x 33 high

		DMC	Anchor	Coats
□ =	cream	746	386	1002
▫ =	lt pink	963	49	3150
✿ =	med pink	956	40	3153
● =	dk pink	326	59	3019
− =	orange	3340	329	2324
○ =	yellow	743	297	2298
◇ =	lt green	954	203	6020
☆ =	med green	911	205	6227
▲ =	dk green	909	229	6228
+ =	blue	798	137	7080
⊠ =	lt brown	407	883	3883
■ =	dk brown	632	936	5356
❘ =	Backstitch:			
	buggy—med pink (1 strand)			
	handle—dk brown			

Whatever your favorite sport may be, you will find a cross stitch design for it here: baseball, basketball, soccer, golf, sailing, fishing, boxing, jogging—even designs for football widows, spectator sportsmen and coaches.

GOLF

a beautiful walk
spoiled by
a small white ball

SOFTBALL

I'D RATHER BE
FISHING

Basketball

GRIDIRON

COACH

WORKOUT

DOUBLES

swimming

FOOTBALL
WIDOW

HOCKEY   JOGGER

SQUARE CIRCLE

fishing:
A JERK AT ONE
END OF A LINE
WAITING ON A
JERK FROM THE
OTHER END

Volleyball

BIRDIE?

WRESTLING
GET A GRIP ON IT

I'D RATHER HAVE
A BAD DAY ON THE GOLF
COURSE THAN A GOOD
DAY AT THE OFFICE!

LITTLE
LEAGUE   RACING

DEVOTED
SPECTATOR
SPORTSMAN

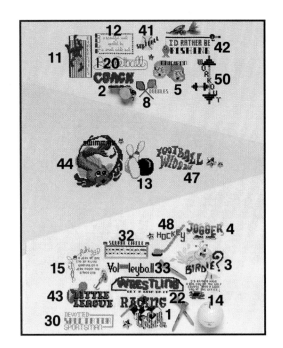

#1

Design size: 49 wide x 37 high

			DMC	Anchor	Coats
▫	=	white	blanc	2	1001
★	=	red	321	9046	3500
□	=	blue	798	137	7080
◇	=	brown	407	914	3883
●	=	gray-black	3799	236	8999
|	=	Backstitch: gray-black			

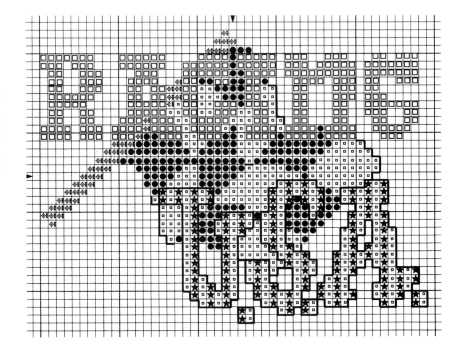

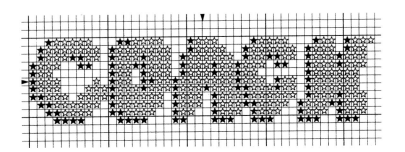

#2

Design size: 44 wide x 11 high

		DMC	Anchor	Coats
☆ =	med red	321	9046	3500
★ =	dk red	815	43	3073

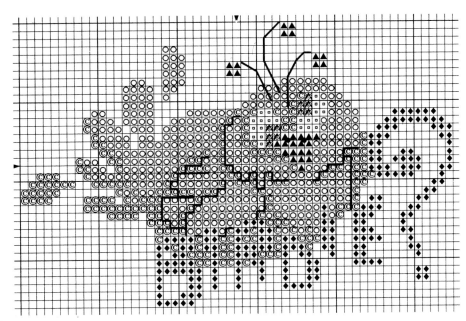

#3

Design size: 55 wide x 36 high

		DMC	Anchor	Coats
▫ =	white	blanc	2	1001
▲ =	orange	970	316	2327
O =	lt yellow	744	301	2296
© =	med yellow	725	306	2307
	dk yellow	783	307	5309

		DMC	Anchor	Coats
◆ =	green	561	212	6211
✖ =	blue	824	164	7182
• =	French Knots: blue			
⏐ =	Backstitch:			
	topknot—orange			
	feathers—dk yellow			

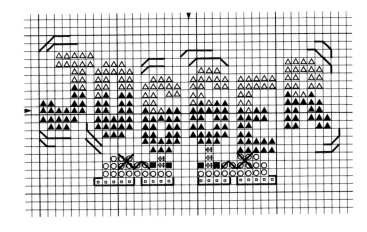

#4

Design size: 38 wide x 19 high

		DMC	Anchor	Coats
▫ =	white	blanc	2	1001
▲ =	red	321	9046	3500
△ =	orange	3340	329	2324
❖ =	peach	754	778	3146
O =	blue	826	161	7180
■ =	gray-black	3799	236	8999
⏐ =	Backstitch:			
	upper shaking marks—orange			
	lower shaking marks—red			
	laces & soles—gray-black			

#5

Design size: 36 wide x 23 high

			DMC	Anchor	Coats
~	=	peach	754	778	3146
©	=	orange	3340	329	2324
◇	=	lt green	564	203	6020
◆	=	dk green	561	212	6211
□	=	tan	437	362	5942
⊞	=	rust	400	352	3340
❖	=	brown	436	363	5943
▲	=	gray-black	3799	236	8999
┃	=	Backstitch: gray-black			

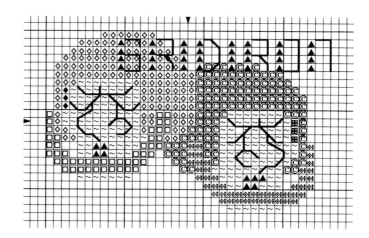

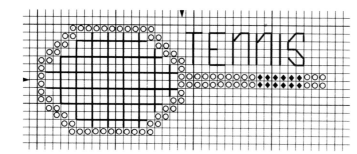

#6

Design size: 37 wide x 14 high

			DMC	Anchor	Coats
◆	=	blue	798	137	7080
○	=	brown	407	914	3883
		blue-black	3750	816	7980
┃	=	Backstitch: lettering—blue mesh—blue-black			

#7

Design size: 33 wide x 37 high

			DMC	Anchor	Coats
—	=	med red	3712	9	3071
+	=	dk red	815	43	3073
©	=	yellow	726	295	2295
△	=	lt purple	554	96	4104
▲	=	dk purple	552	101	4092
○	=	lt brown	407	914	3883
✖	=	dk brown	632	936	5936
◆	=	blue-black	3750	816	7980
•	=	French Knots: blue-black			
┃	=	Backstitch: lettering & lines—blue-black			

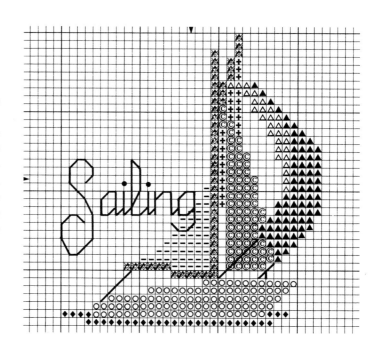

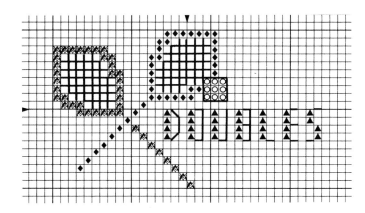

#8

Design size: 34 wide x 20 high

			DMC	Anchor	Coats
▲	=	orange	970	316	2327
O	=	tan	437	362	5942
◆	=	rust	400	352	3340
✻	=	brown	801	357	5475
│	=	Backstitch:			

lettering—orange
ball—tan
rust racket—rust
brown racket—brown

#9

Design size: 38 wide x 33 high

			DMC	Anchor	Coats
O	=	white	blanc	2	1001
✦	=	lt pink	754	778	3146
		red	815	43	3073
		blue	825	162	7181
©	=	tan	738	372	5372
		gray	414	400	8399
●	=	gray-black	3799	236	8999
│	=	Backstitch:			

stitch lines—red
lettering—blue
seam line—gray
eyebrows, eyes & nose—gray-black

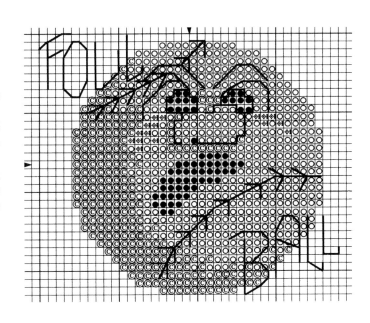

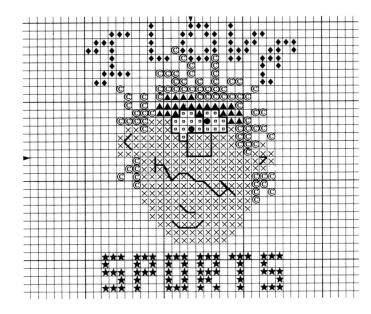

#10

Design size: 27 wide x 34 high

			DMC	Anchor	Coats
▫	=	white	blanc	2	1001
★	=	red	321	9046	3500
▲	=	orange	3340	329	2324
×	=	lt peach	754	778	3146
		dk peach	3712	9	3071
©	=	gold	725	306	2307
◆	=	turquoise	959	186	6185
		gray	414	400	8399
●	=	gray-black	3799	236	8999
│	=	Backstitch:			

ears, nose, chin—dk peach
mouth—gray
eyes—gray-black

#11

Design size: 28 wide x 44 high

		DMC	Anchor	Coats
□	= white	blanc	2	1001
⬥✢	= pink	3712	9	3071
♦	= green	700	229	6228
⊟	= turquoise	959	186	6185
○	= tan	437	362	5942
▲	= rust	400	352	3340
⊠	= med brown	433	371	5471
	dk brown	801	357	5475
•	= French Knots: dk brown			
|	= Backstitch:			

    border lines—green
    lettering—turquoise
    muzzle—med brown
    top of head & foot—dk brown

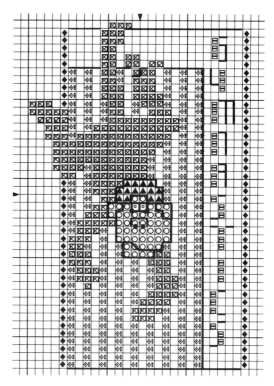

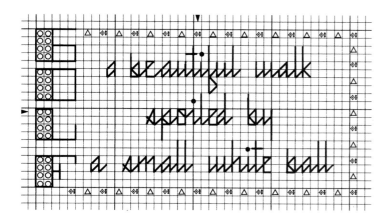

#12

Design size: 41 wide x 21 high

		DMC	Anchor	Coats
	orange	3340	329	2324
△	= lt blue-gray	931	921	7052
⬥✢	= dk blue-gray	930	922	7980
○	= rust	400	352	3340
•	= French Knots: orange			
|	= Backstitch:			

    "GOLF"—rust
    "a...ball"—orange

#13

Design size: 30 wide x 39 high

		DMC	Anchor	Coats
□	= cream	746	386	2386
☆	= med red	321	9046	3500
★	= dk red	815	43	3073
©	= lt brown	437	362	5942
	med brown	434	309	5365
□	= gray	318	399	8511
▲	= gray-black	3799	236	8999
|	= Backstitch: med brown			

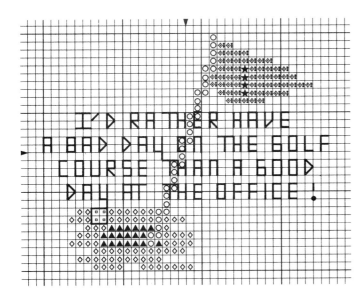

#14

Design size: 36 wide x 30 high

			DMC	Anchor	Coats
□	=	white	blanc	2	1001
★	=	red	304	47	3410
✦	=	yellow	726	295	2295
◇	=	green	562	210	6031
○	=	med brown	436	363	5943
		dk brown	433	371	5471
▲	=	brown-black	3371	382	5382
•	=	French Knot: dk brown			
		=	Backstitch:		
		lettering—dk brown			
		ball—brown-black			

#15

Design size: 34 wide x 40 high

			DMC	Anchor	Coats
○	=	white	blanc	2	1001
★	=	red	321	9046	3500
△	=	yellow	726	295	2295
		brown	632	936	5936
		blue-gray	931	921	7052
		gray-black	3799	236	8999
•	=	French Knots: blue-gray			
		=	Backstitch:		
		"A jerk...other end"—brown			
		"fishing" & fishing line—blue-gray			
		hook, bobber ends & outlines—gray-black			

#16

Design size: 32 wide x 24 high

			DMC	Anchor	Coats
		green	562	210	6031
×	=	blue	826	161	7180
		=	Backstitch: green		

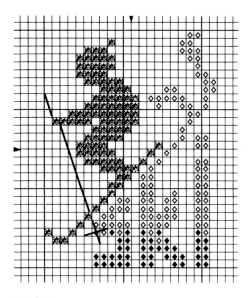

#17

Design size: 22 wide x 30 high

			DMC	Anchor	Coats
◇	=	lt blue	809	130	7021
◆	=	dk blue	798	137	7080
✖	=	brown	632	936	5936
|	=	Backstitch: brown			

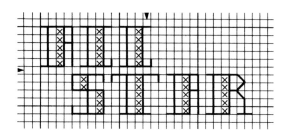

#19

Design size: 27 wide x 11 high

			DMC	Anchor	Coats
✕	=	blue	798	137	7080
|	=	Backstitch: blue			

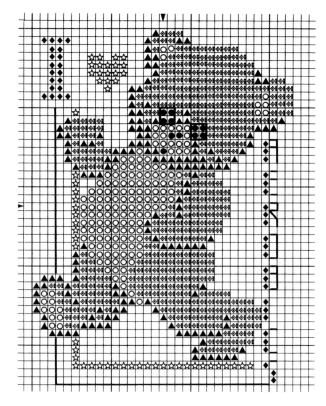

#18

Design size: 33 wide x 45 high

			DMC	Anchor	Coats
☆	=	pink	893	27	3127
◆	=	turquoise	959	186	6185
O	=	tan	3774	880	3335
✧	=	lt brown	407	914	3883
▲	=	med brown	632	936	5936
●	=	gray-black	3799	236	8999
|	=	Backstitch: letters & border line—turquoise eyes—gray-black			

#20

Design size: 58 wide x 14 high

			DMC	Anchor	Coats
◆	=	blue	797	132	7023
|	=	Backstitch: blue			

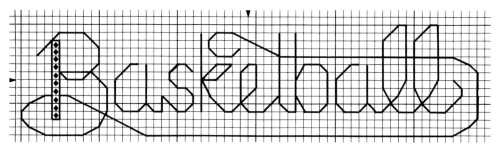

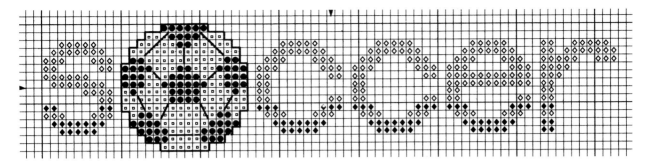

#21

Design size: 73 wide x 16 high

		DMC	Anchor	Coats
▫	= white	blanc	2	1001
◇	= lt green	563	208	6210
◆	= dk green	561	212	6211
●	= gray-black	3799	236	8999
│	= Backstitch: gray-black			

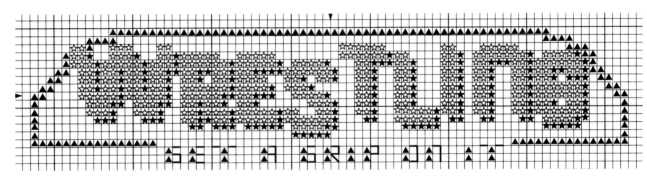

#22

Design size: 76 wide x 17 high

		DMC	Anchor	Coats
☆	= med red	321	9046	3500
★	= dk red	815	43	3073
▲	= gray-black	3799	236	8999
│	= Backstitch: gray-black			

#23

Design size: 57 wide x 19 high

		DMC	Anchor	Coats
★	= med red	321	9046	3500
	dk red	498	20	3072
✿	= orange	3340	329	2324
○	= gold	725	306	2307
│	= Backstitch: dk red			

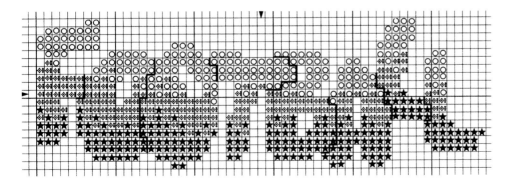

#24

Design size: 47 wide x 14 high

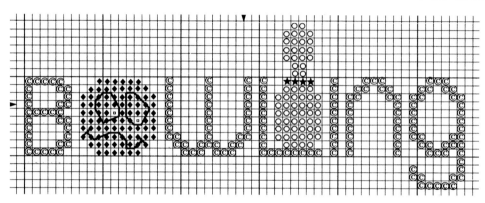

		DMC	Anchor	Coats
□	= white	blanc	2	1001
☐	= green	562	210	6031
	med blue	798	137	7080
▲	= dk blue	797	132	7023
⊕	= lt gray	318	399	8511
	dk gray	414	400	8399
✗	= brown	407	914	3883
		= Backstitch:		

"I'D...BE"—med blue

marks & outline on ball—dk gray

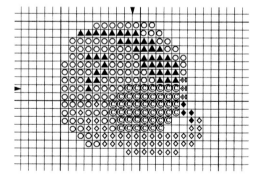

#25

Design size: 56 wide x 21 high

		DMC	Anchor	Coats			DMC	Anchor	Coats
□	= white	blanc	2	1001	©	= brown	632	936	5936
★	= red	304	47	3410	◆	= gray-black	3799	236	8999
O	= yellow	745	300	2350			= Backstitch: white			

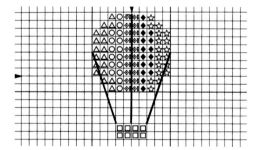

#26

Design size: 10 wide x 16 high

		DMC	Anchor	Coats
☆	= pink	893	27	3127
◆	= orange	970	316	2327
O	= yellow	726	295	2295
⊕	= green	703	238	6238
△	= blue	798	137	7080
□	= brown	433	371	5471
	brown-black	3371	382	5382
		= Backstitch: brown-black			

#27

Design size: 18 wide x 17 high

		DMC	Anchor	Coats
▲	= red	304	47	3410
O	= yellow	725	306	2307
⊕	= med gold	783	307	5309
©	= dk gold	782	308	5308
◇	= lt gray	318	399	8511
◆	= dk gray	414	400	8399

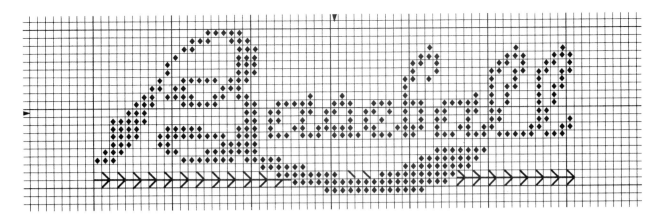

#28

Design size: 61 wide x 21 high

		DMC	Anchor	Coats
◆	= red	321	9046	3500
	gray-black	3799	236	8999
│	= Backstitch:			
	stitches—red			
	seamline—gray-black			

#29

Design size: 49 wide x 13 high

		DMC	Anchor	Coats
▫	= white	blanc	2	1001
✕	= lt blue	813	160	7161
✢	= med blue	826	161	7180
◆	= dk blue	824	164	7182
▲	= gray	414	400	8399
│	= Backstitch: gray			

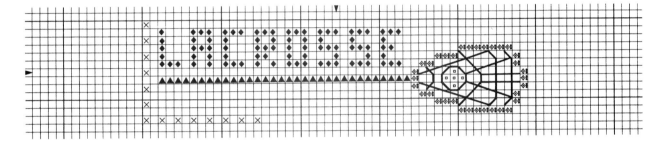

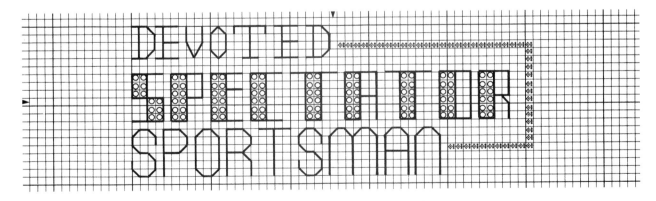

#30

Design size: 51 wide x 19 high

		DMC	Anchor	Coats
○	= orange	3340	329	2324
✢	= med blue	813	160	7161
	dk blue	825	162	7181

│ = Backstitch:
"SPECTATOR"—orange
"DEVOTED" & "SPORTSMAN"—dk blue

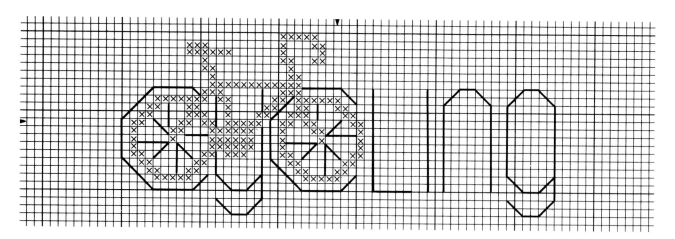

#31

Design size: 55 wide x 23 high

		DMC	Anchor	Coats
	red	498	20	3072
X =	gray-black	3799	236	8999
| =	Backstitch:			
	lettering—red			
	bicycle—gray-black			

#32

Design size: 48 wide x 19 high

		DMC	Anchor	Coats
★ =	red	304	47	3410
© =	yellow	726	295	2295
O =	gold	676	891	2874
♦ =	blue	798	137	7080
△ =	lt gray	318	399	8511
▲ =	dk gray	3799	236	8999
| =	Backstitch: blue			

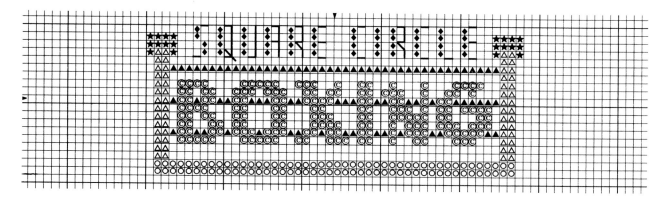

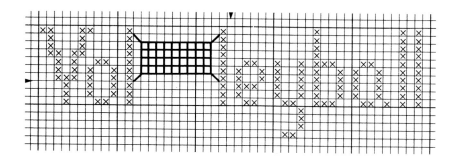

#33

Design size: 49 wide x 14 high

		DMC	Anchor	Coats
X =	gray-black	3799	236	8999
| =	Backstitch: gray-black			

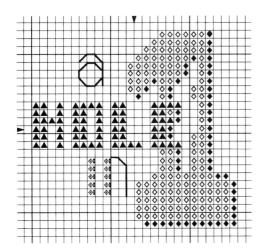

#34

Design size: 26 wide x 25 high

		DMC	Anchor	Coats
◇	= med red	321	9046	3500
◆	= dk red	815	43	3073
▲	= green	700	229	6228
❖	= blue	825	162	7181
	brown	801	357	5475
│	= Backstitch: brown			

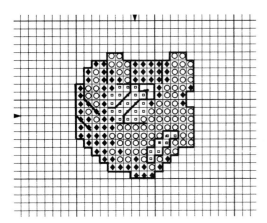

#36

Design size: 15 wide x 16 high

		DMC	Anchor	Coats
▫	= white	blanc	2	1001
	red	815	43	3073
O	= lt brown	437	362	5942
◆	= med brown	434	309	5365
	dk brown	801	357	5475
│	= Backstitch:			
	baseball—red			
	glove—dk brown			

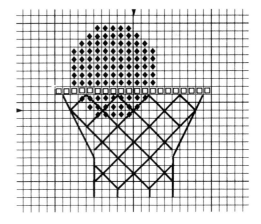

#35

Design size: 30 wide x 25 high

		DMC	Anchor	Coats
▫	= white	blanc	2	1001
★	= red	304	47	3410
O	= yellow	726	295	2295
	blue	826	161	7180
❖	= brown	632	936	5936
□	= gray	414	400	8399
●	= gray-black	3799	236	8999
•	= French Knot: brown			
│	= Backstitch:			
	fly feather—yellow			
	line—blue			
	lettering—brown			
	bobber—gray			

#37

Design size: 20 wide x 22 high

		DMC	Anchor	Coats
□	= gold	725	306	2307
◆	= brown	434	309	5365
	gray-black	3799	236	8999
│	= Backstitch: gray-black (2 strands)			

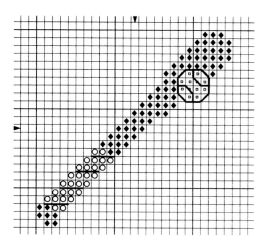

#38

Design size: 25 wide x 25 high

			DMC	Anchor	Coats
▫	=	white	blanc	2	1001
		red	498	20	3072
O	=	lt brown	437	362	5942
◆	=	med brown	435	369	5371
ǀ	=	Backstitch: red			

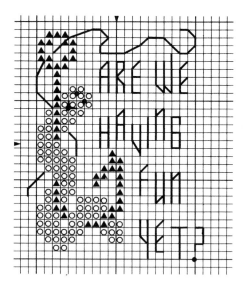

#39

Design size: 22 wide x 29 high

			DMC	Anchor	Coats
		red	304	47	3410
▲	=	gray	414	400	8399
O	=	brown	407	914	3883
		gray-black	3799	236	8999
•	=	French Knots:			
		mouth & question mark—red			
		eyes—gray-black			
ǀ	=	Backstitch:			
		lettering—red			
		fishing line—gray-black			

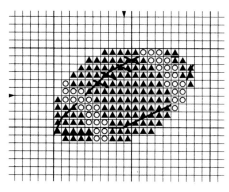

#40

Design size: 18 wide x 12 high

			DMC	Anchor	Coats
O	=	white	blanc	2	1001
▲	=	brown	400	352	3340
		gray-black	3799	236	8999
ǀ	=	Backstitch: gray-black			

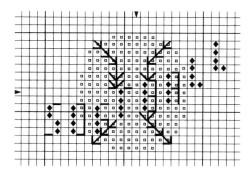

#41

Design size: 23 wide x 15 high

		DMC	Anchor	Coats
▫	= cream	951	366	3335
	red	815	43	3073
◆	= gray-black	3799	236	8999
|	= Backstitch:			
	stitching—red			
	seamline & lettering—gray-black			

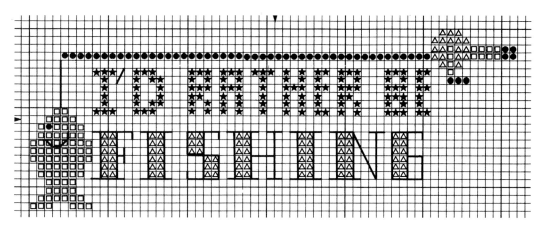

#42

Design size: 62 wide x 23 high

		DMC	Anchor	Coats
★	= red	498	20	3072
△	= blue-gray	930	922	7980
□	= gray	318	399	8511
●	= gray-black	3799	236	8999

|	= Backstitch:
	apostrophe—red
	lettering—blue-gray
	fishing line—gray
	fish mouth—gray-black

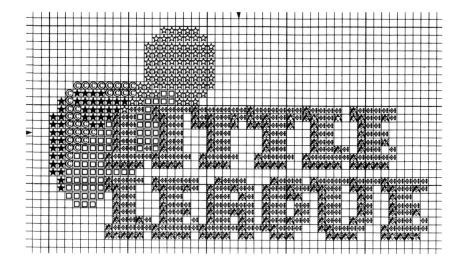

#43

Design size: 48 wide x 27 high

		DMC	Anchor	Coats
☆	= lt red	3712	9	3071
★	= dk red	304	47	3410
◎	= gold	725	306	2307
✣	= blue	826	161	7180
□	= blue-gray	931	921	7052
✘	= blue-black	3750	816	7980

XXXXXXXXXXXXXXXXXXXXXXXXXXXXXX 93 XXXXXXXXXXXXXXXXXXXXXXXXXXXX

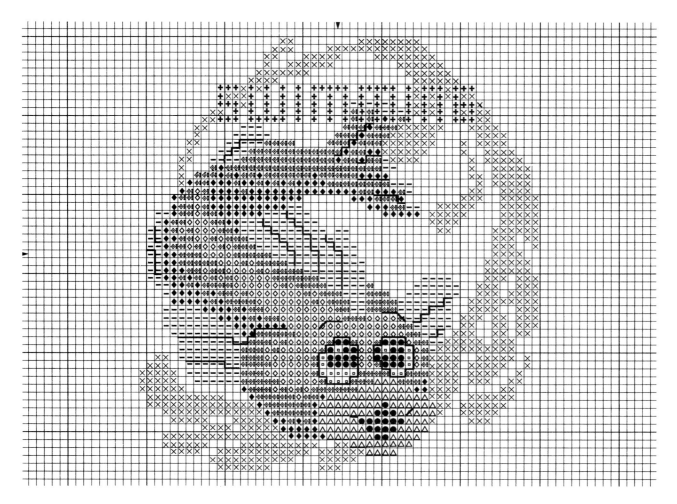

#44

Design size: 51 wide x 55 high

		DMC	Anchor	Coats
▫	= white	blanc	2	1001
△	= yellow-green	702	239	6226
▬	= lt green	564	203	6020
◇	= med green	563	208	6210
◈	= dk green	562	210	6031
◆	= very dk green	561	212	6211
✕	= lt blue	798	137	7080
✛	= dk blue	796	133	7100
●	= gray-black	3799	236	8999
		= Backstitch:		
		fins—dk green		
		tail—very dk green		
		eyebrows, eyes & mouth—gray-black		

#45

Design size: 13 wide x 11 high

		DMC	Anchor	Coats
◆	= red	321	9046	3500
✖	= gray-black	3799	236	8999

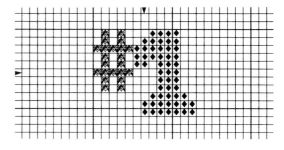

#46

Design size: 24 wide x 44 high

			DMC	Anchor	Coats
▫	=	white	blanc	2	1001
★	=	red	321	9046	3500
©	=	yellow	725	306	2307
♦	=	green	562	210	6031
✚	=	lt blue	799	131	7030
▲	=	dk blue	798	137	7080
✧	=	purple	552	101	4092
✕	=	med brown	407	914	3883
		dk brown	632	936	5936
☐	=	lt gray	318	399	8511
		dk gray	414	400	8399
●	=	gray-black	3799	236	8999
│	=	Backstitch:			

   towel—dk blue
   pocket—dk brown
   clubs—dk gray
   wheel—gray-black

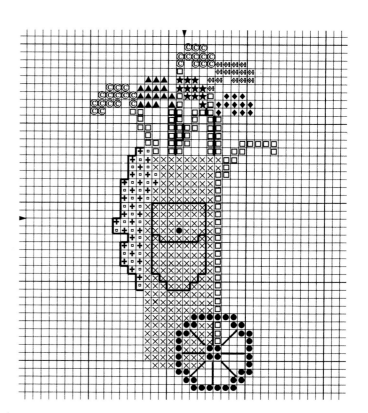

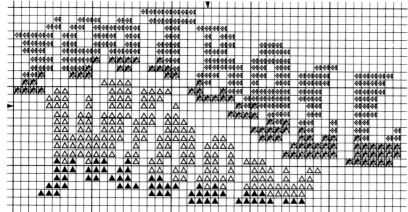

#47

Design size: 49 wide x 25 high

			DMC	Anchor	Coats
△	=	med pink	893	27	3127
▲	=	dk pink	498	20	3072
✧	=	med brown	301	351	2326
✖	=	dk brown	801	357	5475

#48

Design size: 34 wide x 34 high

			DMC	Anchor	Coats
✚	=	orange	970	316	2327
♦	=	green	701	227	6227
✧	=	brown	436	363	5943
©	=	gray	318	399	8511
●	=	gray-black	3799	236	8999

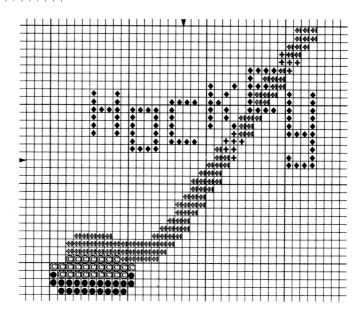

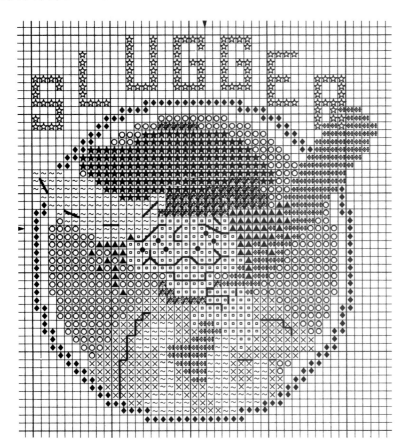

#49

Design size: 44 wide x 49 high

			DMC	Anchor	Coats
~	=	cream	746	386	2386
✕	=	lt red	3712	9	3071
★	=	med red	304	47	3410
▲	=	orange	970	316	2327
▫	=	peach	754	778	3146
O	=	yellow	744	301	2296
◆	=	green	701	227	6227
☆	=	blue	798	137	7080
✇	=	brown	434	309	5365
		gray-black	3799	236	8999
🔅	=	black	310	403	8403
•	=	French Knots: orange			
ǀ	=	Backstitch:			
		shirt—med red			
		face & fingers—gray-black			

#50

Design size: 31 wide x 50 high

			DMC	Anchor	Coats
		white	blanc	2	1001
◆	=	blue	825	162	7181
O	=	lt gray	415	398	8398
©	=	dk gray	414	400	8399
▲	=	gray-black	3799	236	8999
ǀ	=	Backstitch: white			

50
Pet Designs

From snakes to kittens, here are a wide variety of lovable creatures: dogs, horses, pigs, monkeys, turtles, birds—even a pet peeve.

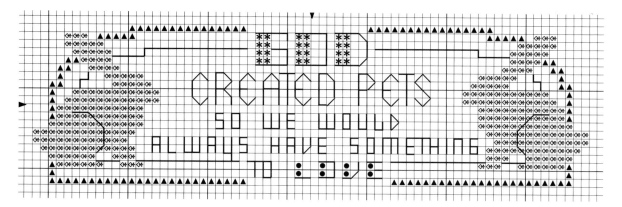

#1

Design size: 70 wide x 20 high

		Anchor	**Coats**	**DMC**
✣ =	lt pink	25	3125	3326
● =	dk pink	76	3087	3688
▲ =	green	265	6266	3348
	turquoise	169	7169	3765
✳ =	purple	110	4301	208
	brown	936	5936	632
| =	Backstitch:			

   "love"—dk pink
   inner border, "created pets"—turquoise
   "GOD"—purple
   bunny legs, "so...to"—brown

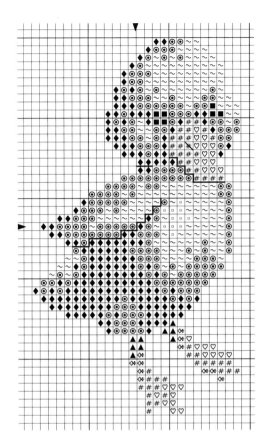

#2

Design size: 26 wide x 47 high

			Anchor	Coats	DMC
▫	=	white	1	1001	blanc
♡	=	lt orange	313	2302	742
#	=	med orange	1003	3336	922
~	=	lt yellow	305	2295	743
⊙	=	med yellow	306	2307	725
◆	=	dk yellow	308	5308	781
◈	=	med rust	1049	5356	301
▲	=	dk rust	352	5471	300
■	=	gray-black	1041	8501	844
│	=	Backstitch: gray-black			

#3

Design size: 34 wide x 42 high

			Anchor	Coats	DMC
▫	=	white	1	1001	blanc
◈	=	lt pink	24	3173	963
➤	=	med pink	76	3087	3688
○	=	lt gray	234	8510	762
⊠	=	med gray	235	8513	414
●	=	dk gray	400	8999	317
		very dk gray	401	8514	413
▲	=	blue-black	152	7160	939
│	=	Backstitch:			
		mouse outline—med gray			
		whiskers, tail—very dk gray			

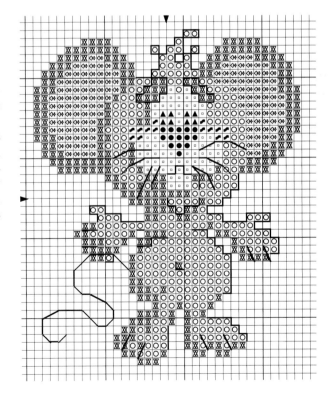

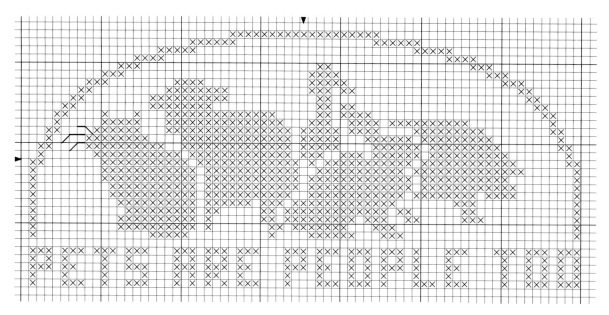

#4

Design size: 69 wide x 32 high

		Anchor	Coats	DMC
X	= blue-gray	921	7052	931
		= Backstitch: blue-gray			

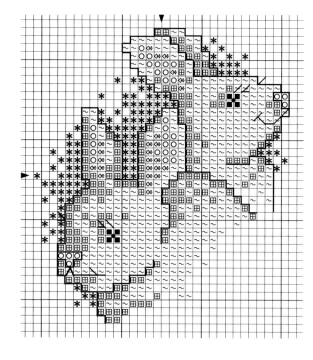

#5

Design size: 32 wide x 37 high

		Anchor	Coats	DMC
~	= white	1	1001	blanc
O	= lt pink	24	3173	963
✧	= med pink	26	3126	894
✱	= green	265	6266	3348
⊞	= lt blue-gray	1032	7876	3752
	dk blue-gray	921	7052	931
■	= blue-black	152	7160	939
•	= French Knots: white			
		= Backstitch:			

bunnies (except facial
features)—dk blue-gray
eyelashes, mouths—blue-black

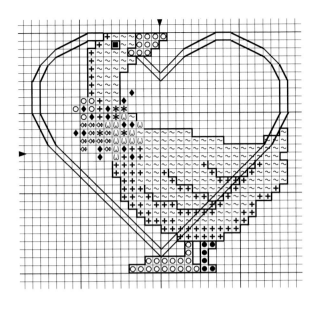

#6

Design size: 32 wide x 30 high

			Anchor	Coats	DMC
~	=	white	1	1001	blanc
✧	=	pink	26	3126	894
		red	59	3019	326
O	=	lt orange	323	2323	3341
●	=	dk orange	329	2327	3340
✳	=	yellow	288	2288	445
◆	=	green	258	6268	987
+	=	blue	1032	7876	3752
ω	=	purple	110	4301	208
		gray	235	8513	414
■	=	gray-black	1041	8501	844
		=	Backstitch:		

heart shapes—red
goose—gray
eye—gray-black

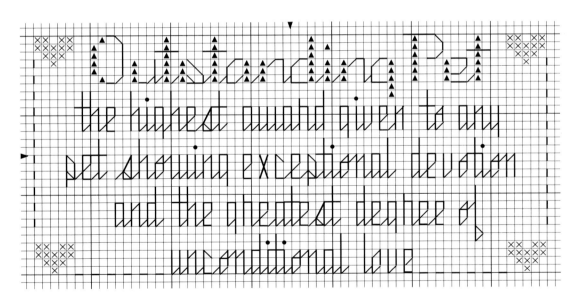

#7

Design size: 64 wide x 30 high

			Anchor	Coats	DMC
✕	=	pink	26	3126	894
		med red	1025	3013	347
		dk red	1005	3410	816
▲	=	gray	401	8514	413
•	=	French Knots: to match lettering			

- - - = Running Stitch: med red
| = Backstitch:
  "unconditional love"—med red
  "Outstanding Pet"—gray
  remaining lettering—dk red

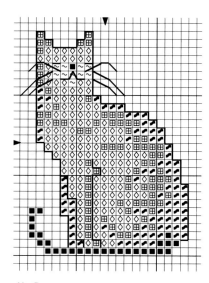

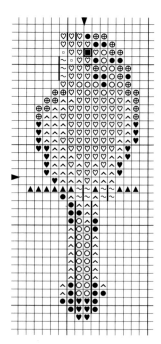

#8

Design size: 21 wide x 28 high

		Anchor	Coats	DMC
~	= white	1	1001	blanc
◇	= lt gray	234	8510	762
⊞	= med gray	399	8401	318
◣	= dk gray	400	8999	317
■	= gray-black	401	8514	413
│	= Backstitch:			
	whiskers, leg & body outline—dk gray			
	mouth—gray-black			
	eyes—gray-black (2 strands)			

#9

Design size: 14 wide x 36 high

		Anchor	Coats	DMC
▫	= white	1	1001	blanc
♥	= turquoise	187	6186	958
♡	= very lt blue-green	928	7053	3761
○	= lt blue-green	1038	7168	519
∧	= med blue-green	1039	7169	518
⊕	= dk blue-green	169	7162	3765
●	= blue	133	7100	820
~	= tan	362	5942	729
▲	= brown	358	5475	433
■	= gray	400	8999	414
│	= Backstitch:			
	tail—dk blue-green			
	head—blue			
	feet—brown			
	beak, eye—gray			

#10

Design size: 41 wide x 44 high

		Anchor	Coats	DMC
▫	= white	1	1001	blanc
✛	= pink	1022	3069	760
☆	= lt yellow	305	2295	743
★	= dk yellow	306	2307	725
◤	= gold	308	5308	781
◆	= green	266	6010	3347
✖	= med brown	370	5349	434
●	= dk brown	359	5472	801
✕	= med gray	398	8398	415
	dk gray	235	8513	414
■	= brown-black	382	5382	3371
│	= Backstitch:			
	ears—med gray			
	face—dk gray			

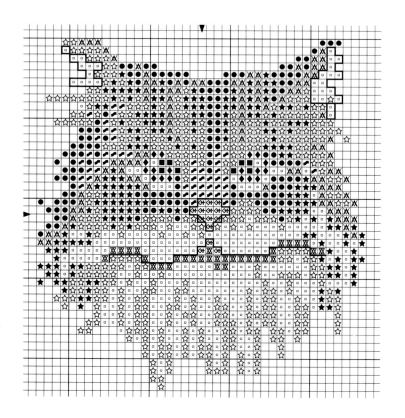

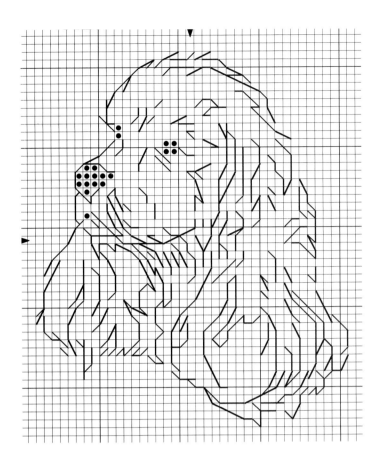

#11

Design size: 39 wide x 47 high

		Anchor	Coats	DMC
●	= brown	936	5936	632
|	= Backstitch: brown			

#12

Design size: 39 wide x 38 high

		Anchor	Coats	DMC
~	= white	1	1001	blanc
○	= lt orange	313	2302	742
●	= med orange	1003	3336	922
★	= yellow	305	2295	743
◇	= lt green	265	6266	3348
◆	= dk green	246	6246	986
♡	= lt blue	128	7031	800
♥	= dk blue	130	7021	809
■	= blue-gray	978	7978	312
|	= Backstitch:			

bow—med orange (2 strands)
goose—blue-gray

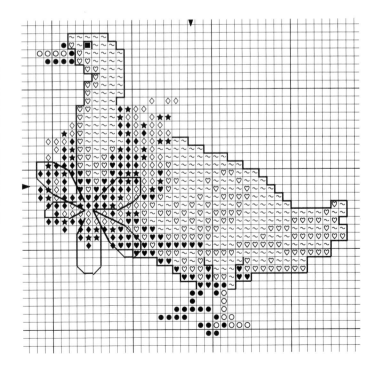

#13

Design size: 33 wide x 53 high

		Anchor	Coats	DMC
▫ =	white	1	1001	blanc
✳ =	peach	1012	2331	754
✕ =	rust	349	5309	434
∪ =	med brown	378	5578	841
◣ =	dk brown	358	5475	433
∧ =	lt gray	234	8510	762
☐ =	med gray	399	8511	318
⊠ =	dk gray	235	8513	414
◆ =	very dk gray	400	8999	317
■ =	black	403	8403	310
• =	French Knots: white			
| =	Backstitch:			
	below nose—dk brown			
	jaw, head outlines—very dk gray			
	eye creases—black			

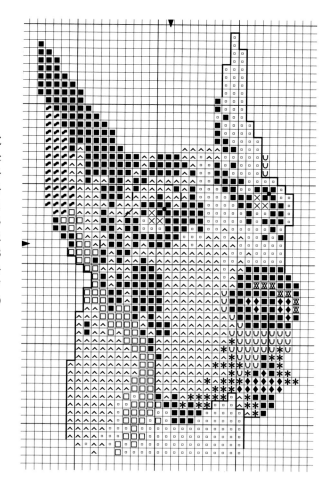

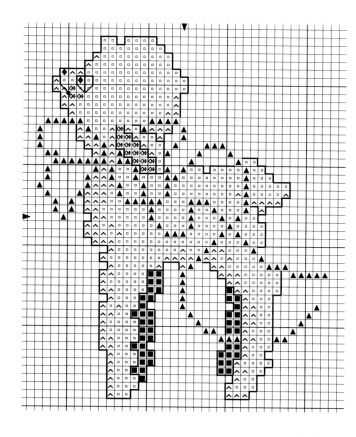

#14

Design size: 37 wide x 45 high

		Anchor	Coats	DMC
▫ =	white	1	1001	blanc
✧ =	pink	26	3126	894
▲ =	green	204	6210	563
∧ =	lt blue	1032	7876	3752
■ =	med blue	978	7978	312
	blue-gray	921	7052	931
◆ =	blue-black	152	7160	939
• =	French Knot: blue-black			
| =	Backstitch:			
	body outlines—blue-gray			
	mouth & eye—blue-black			

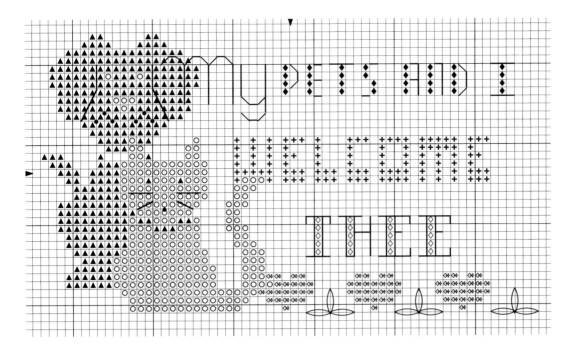

#15

Design size: 62 wide x 35 high

			Anchor	Coats	DMC
❖	=	lt pink	25	3125	3326
		dk pink	59	3019	326
○	=	yellow	891	5363	676
◇	=	lt green	265	6266	3348
◆	=	dk green	258	6268	987
+	=	blue	1039	7168	518
▲	=	brown	355	5349	975
•	=	French Knots:			

    puppy face—yellow
    kitty mouth—brown

◊ = Lazy Daisies: blue
\ = Straight Stitches: kitty whiskers—brown
| = Backstitch:
    "my"—dk pink
    puppy ears—yellow
    "pets and I," "thee"—dk green

#16

Design size: 19 wide x 50 high

			Anchor	Coats	DMC
▫	=	white	1	1001	blanc
⊕	=	med red	1025	3013	347
⦷	=	dk red	1028	3089	3685
★	=	yellow	305	2295	743
✳	=	gold	363	5943	436
△	=	lt blue	130	7021	809
❖	=	med blue	131	7080	798
▲	=	dk blue	132	7143	797
^	=	gray	399	8511	318
■	=	blue-black	152	7160	939
		=	Backstitch: blue-black			

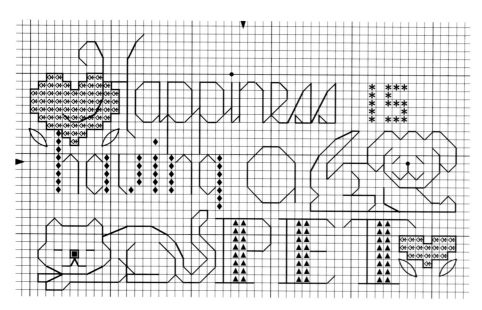

#17

Design size: 53 wide x 32 high

		Anchor	Coats	DMC
⬖ =	pink	24	3173	963
	rose	78	3089	601
◆ =	green	205	6031	912
✳ =	turquoise	187	6186	958
▲ =	purple	110	4301	208
■ =	brown	360	5476	898
• =	French Knots:			
	dot on "i"—rose			
	puppy nose—brown			

◗ = Lazy Daisies—turquoise

| = Backstitch:
    hearts, "Happiness," "a"—rose
    "having"—green
    "pet"—purple
    pets—brown

#18

Design size: 52 wide x 31 high

		Anchor	Coats	DMC
● =	rose	1022	3069	760
◆ =	green	266	6010	3347
✕ =	turquoise	187	6186	958
○ =	tan	368	5345	437
	rust	1014	2339	355
| =	Backstitch:			
	"I"—green			
	"horse"—rust			

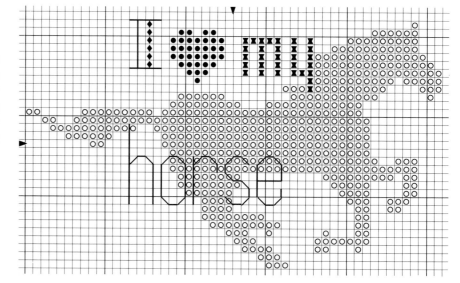

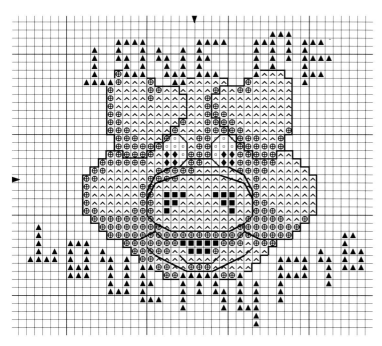

#19

Design size: 42 wide x 37 high

		Anchor	Coats	DMC
□	= white	1	1001	blanc
⌃	= lt pink	24	3173	963
⊕	= med pink	1022	3069	760
◆	= blue	132	7143	797
▲	= brown	371	5470	434
	gray	235	8513	414
■	= gray-black	1041	8501	844
|	= Backstitch: gray			

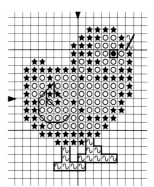

#20

Design size: 14 wide x 18 high

		Anchor	Coats	DMC
∿	= orange	328	2324	3341
○	= yellow	305	2295	743
★	= gold	306	2307	725
	gray	401	8514	413
●	= blue-black	152	7160	939
|	= Backstitch: gray			

#21

Design size: 40 wide x 45 high

		Anchor	Coats	DMC
□	= white	1	1001	blanc
✵	= pink	24	3173	963
◆	= turquoise	188	6187	943
○	= lt tan	366	3335	951
⊕	= med tan	368	5345	437
△	= lt brown	369	5347	435
✗	= med brown	371	5470	434
▲	= dk brown	360	5476	898
■	= brown-black	381	5381	938
•	= French Knots: brown-black			
|	= Backstitch: brown-black			

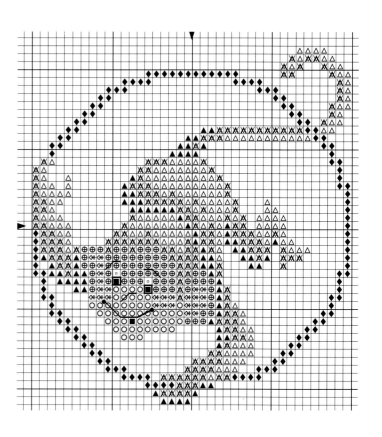

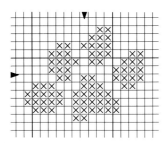

#22

Design size: 15 wide x 12 high

	Anchor	Coats	DMC
X = brown	352	5471	300

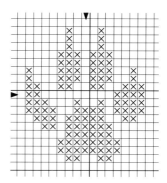

#23

Design size: 15 wide x 17 high

	Anchor	Coats	DMC
X = brown	358	5475	433

#24

Design size: 18 wide 16 high

	Anchor	Coats	DMC
∗ = orange	323	2323	3341
◆ = turquoise	188	6187	943
blue	131	7080	798
blue-black	152	7160	939

• = French Knots:
  bubbles—blue
  eyes—blue-black

| = Backstitch:
  fish outlines—orange
  bowl—blue
  fish fins—blue-black

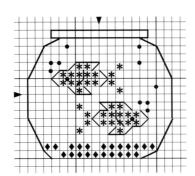

#25

Design size: 39 wide x 39 high

	Anchor	Coats	DMC
▫ = white	1	1001	blanc
∗ = peach	1012	2331	754
O = lt orange	313	2302	742
● = dk orange	1003	3336	922
∿ = yellow	295	2295	726
▲ = green	245	6211	986
◞ = blue	1039	7168	518
■ = gray-black	1041	8501	844
	= Backstitch: gray-black			

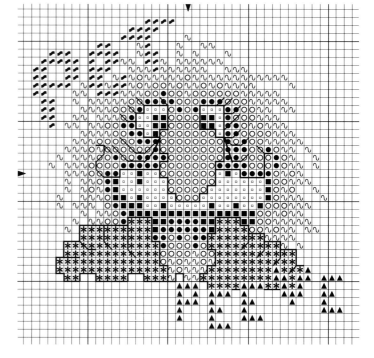

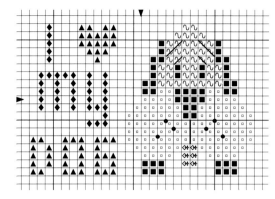

#26

Design size: 28 wide x 19 high

			Anchor	Coats	DMC
✧	=	pink	26	3126	894
▲	=	red	1025	3013	347
♦	=	blue	132	7143	797
▫	=	lt rust	347	5347	402
∿	=	dk rust	349	5309	3776
■	=	brown-black	382	5382	3371
•	=	French Knots: brown-black			
		=	Backstitch: brown-black		

#27

Design size: 33 wide x 35 high

			Anchor	Coats	DMC
▫	=	lt yellow-green	265	6266	3348
⊕	=	med yellow-green	239	6226	702
✕	=	med green	230	6031	699
♦	=	dk green	879	6880	500
✖	=	gray	235	8513	414
■	=	black	403	8403	310
•	=	French Knots: med green			
		=	Backstitch:		
			lettering—med green		
			fly—black		
			mouth—black (2 strands)		

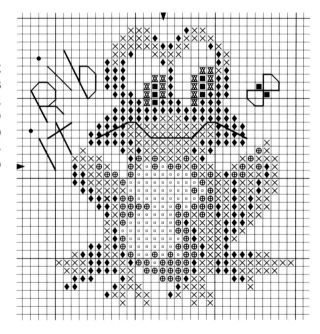

#28

Design size: 33 wide x 38 high

			Anchor	Coats	DMC
▫	=	white	1	1001	blanc
∧	=	lt pink	24	3173	963
#	=	med pink	26	3126	894
●	=	dk pink	76	3087	3688
○	=	lt gray	398	8398	415
⊙	=	med gray	399	8511	318
		dk gray	236	8514	3799
■	=	gray-black	1041	8501	844
╲	=	Straight Stitches: gray-black			
		=	Backstitch:		
			lettering—dk pink		
			motion marks—dk gray		
			mouth, whiskers—gray-black		

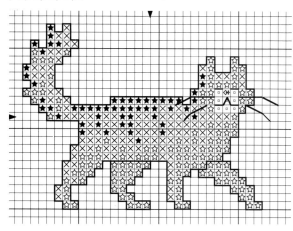

#29

Design size: 32 wide x 23 high

		Anchor	Coats	DMC
□	= white	1	1001	blanc
✿	= pink	1022	3069	760
☆	= lt gold	361	5375	738
✕	= med gold	363	5943	436
★	= dk gold	309	5309	781
	very dk gold	310	5365	780
	gray	401	8514	413
│	= Backstitch:			

   outline—very dk gold
   eyes, whiskers—gray

#30

Design size: 43 wide x 34 high

		Anchor	Coats	DMC
□	= white	1	1001	blanc
◇	= cream	366	3335	951
✿	= lt pink	24	3173	963
▲	= med pink	25	3125	3326
○	= lt brown	376	5576	950
+	= med brown	369	5347	435
	med dk brown	355	5349	975
■	= dk brown	357	5475	433
●	= brown-black	382	5382	3371
│	= Backstitch:			

   muzzle—med dk brown
   eyes—brown-black

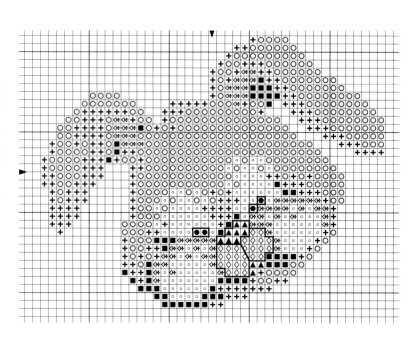

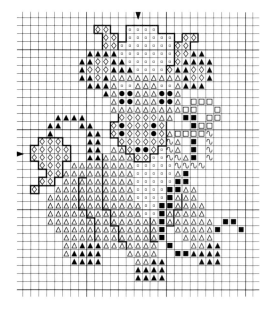

#31

Design size: 27 wide x 32 high

		Anchor	Coats	DMC
□	= white	1	1001	blanc
◇	= cream	386	2386	745
□	= lt green	259	6250	772
∿	= med green	265	6266	3348
■	= dk green	258	6268	987
△	= lt brown	347	5347	402
	med brown	349	5309	434
▲	= dk brown	351	3340	400
●	= brown-black	382	5382	3371
│	= Backstitch:			

   tail, horns, top of head, muzzle—med brown
   body—dk brown

#32

Design size: 30 wide x 29 high

			Anchor	Coats	DMC
□	=	white	1	1001	blanc
✧	=	pink	25	3125	3326
◇	=	lt green	259	6250	772
◆	=	dk green	258	6268	987
		purple	110	4301	208
○	=	lt gray	398	8398	415
		med gray	235	8513	414
●	=	gray-black	1041	8501	844
		=	Backstitch:		

ribbon—purple

lamb (except eyelashes & mouth)—med gray

eyelashes & mouth—gray-black

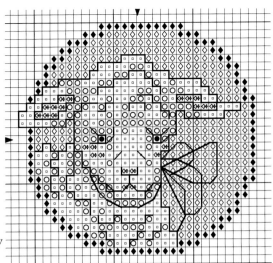

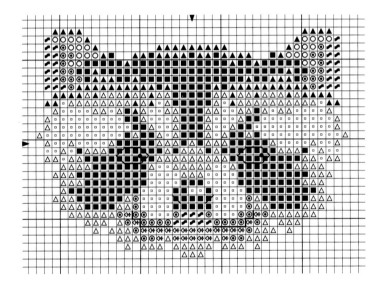

#33

Design size: 39 wide x 29 high

			Anchor	Coats	DMC
□	=	white	1	1001	blanc
△	=	lt brown	376	5576	950
✧	=	med brown	379	5379	840
▲	=	dk brown	936	5936	632
○	=	lt gray	234	8510	762
◉	=	med gray	399	8511	318
✎	=	dk gray	400	8999	414
■	=	black	403	8403	310
•	=	French Knots: white			
		=	Backstitch:		

eyes, nose—white

muzzle—dk gray

#34

Design size: 33 wide x 27 high

			Anchor	Coats	DMC
□	=	white	1	1001	blanc
○	=	lt pink	23	3068	3713
✧	=	med pink	26	3126	894
●	=	dk pink	59	3019	326
◇	=	lt gray	399	8511	318
∿	=	med gray	235	8513	414
		dk gray	400	8999	317
✖	=	gray-black	1041	8501	844
		=	Backstitch:		

"cat"—dk pink

eyebrows—dk gray

whiskers, mouth—gray-black

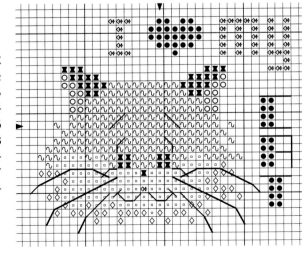

#35

Design size: 30 wide x 32 high

			Anchor	Coats	DMC
□	=	white	1	1001	blanc
✧	=	pink	25	3125	3326
○	=	tan	361	5375	738
⊕	=	lt brown	347	5347	402
✳	=	med brown	349	5309	3776
◣	=	dk brown	352	5471	300
✕	=	very dk brown	360	5476	898
◆	=	black	403	8403	310
•	=	French Knot: lt brown			
│	=	Backstitch: very dk brown			

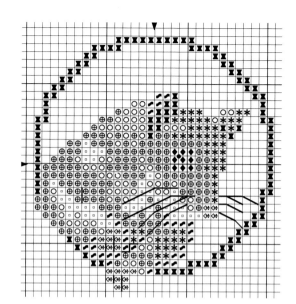

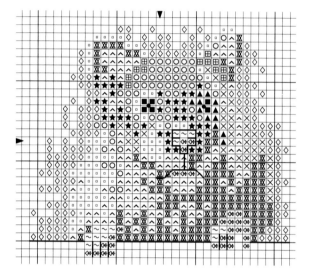

#36

Design size: 33 wide x 29 high

			Anchor	Coats	DMC
□	=	white	1	1001	blanc
~	=	lt pink	24	3173	963
✧	=	med pink	26	3126	894
◇	=	blue	129	7020	809
○	=	lt tan	361	5375	738
★	=	med tan	362	5942	729
⊞	=	lt brown	368	5345	437
✕	=	med brown	369	5347	435
▲	=	dk brown	355	5349	975
∧	=	lt gray	397	8232	762
✕	=	med gray	399	8511	318
		dk gray	400	8999	414
■	=	black	403	8403	310
•	=	French Knots: white			
│	=	Backstitch:			
		baseline—dk brown			
		nose, mouth, paws—dk gray			

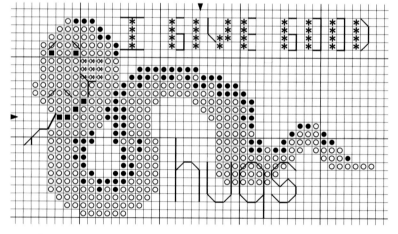

#37

Design size: 44 wide x 25 high

			Anchor	Coats	DMC
✧	=	pink	1024	3071	3328
○	=	lt green	265	6266	3348
●	=	dk green	258	6268	987
✳	=	med turquoise	1039	7168	518
		dk turquoise	169	7169	3765
■	=	gray-black	1041	8501	844
│	=	Backstitch:			
		"I...Good"—med turquoise			
		"hugs"—dk turquoise			
		facial features, tongue—gray-black			

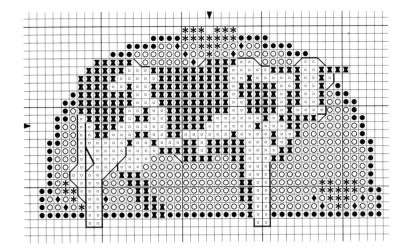

#38

Design size: 43 wide x 25 high

			Anchor	Coats	DMC
▫	=	white	1	1001	blanc
✱	=	pink	26	3126	894
◆	=	green	258	6268	987
○	=	lt blue	1032	7876	3752
●	=	med blue	921	7052	931
✕	=	gray-black	1041	8501	844
│	=	Backstitch: gray-black			

#39

Design size: 46 wide x 33 high

			Anchor	Coats	DMC
		red	1005	3410	816
✱	=	green	205	6031	912
⌃	=	med blue	1038	7169	519
		dk blue	1039	7168	518
●	=	brown	936	5936	632
│	=	Backstitch:			
		hearts—red			
		lettering—dk blue			

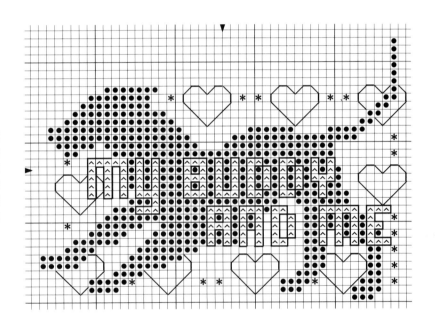

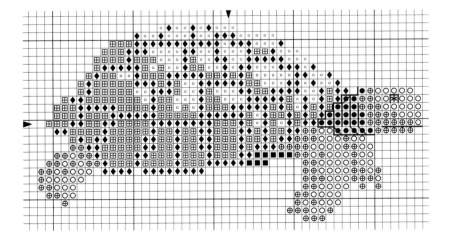

#40

Design size: 48 wide x 25 high

			Anchor	Coats	DMC
○	=	gold	891	5363	676
▫	=	lt green	259	6250	772
⊞	=	med green	266	6010	3347
◆	=	dk green	844	6844	733
■	=	very dk green	269	6269	936
⊕	=	med brown	1046	5371	435
●	=	dk brown	357	5475	801
✱	=	brown-black	382	5382	3371
│	=	Backstitch: brown-black			

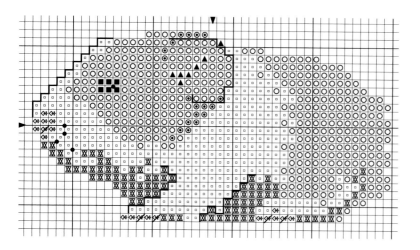

#41

Design size: 45 wide x 24 high

			Anchor	Coats	DMC
□	=	white	1	1001	blanc
✣	=	pink	1022	3069	760
○	=	lt brown	369	5347	435
⊙	=	med brown	358	5475	433
▲	=	dk brown	360	5476	898
■	=	brown-black	382	5382	3371
⊠	=	med gray	399	8511	318
		dk gray	235	8513	414
•	=	French Knots:			
		eye—white			
		muzzle—pink			
│	=	Backstitch:			
		top of head—lt brown			
		ear—med brown			
		nose, feet, leg—dk gray			

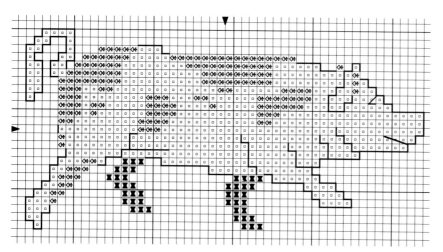

#42

Design size: 50 wide x 25 high

			Anchor	Coats	DMC
□	=	peach	1012	2331	754
✣	=	med brown	349	5309	434
⊠	=	dk brown	352	5471	300
│	=	Backstitch: dk brown			

#43

Design size: 16 wide x 16 high

		Anchor	Coats	DMC
red		1025	3013	347
brown		936	5936	632
│ =	Backstitch:			
	lettering—red			
	kitty—brown			

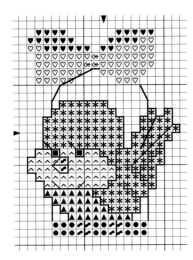

#44

Design size: 19 wide x 26 high

		Anchor	Coats	DMC
∧	= lt yellow	300	2350	745
✳	= med yellow	295	2295	726
▲	= dk yellow	298	2298	725
◢	= orange	323	2323	3341
♡	= lt blue	1032	7876	3752
✛	= med blue	921	7052	931
♥	= dk blue	978	7978	312
●	= brown	355	5349	975
	gray	400	8999	414
■	= blue-black	152	7160	939
|	= Backstitch:			
	feet—brown			
	bird—gray			
	swing—gray (2 strands)			
	eyelashes—blue-black			

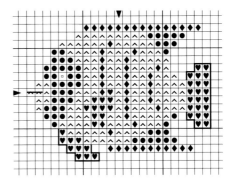

#45

Design size: 23 wide x 17 high

		Anchor	Coats	DMC
▫	= white	1	1001	blanc
♥	= yellow	295	2295	726
∧	= orange	323	2323	3341
◆	= blue	132	7143	797
●	= brown	355	5349	975
\	= Straight Stitch: brown			
|	= Backstitch: orange			

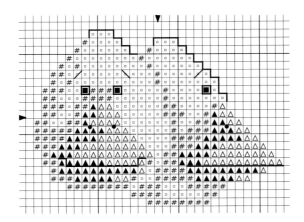

#46

Design size: 31 wide x 22 high

		Anchor	Coats	DMC
▫	= white	1	1001	blanc
△	= yellow	303	2303	742
▲	= orange	329	2327	3340
#	= med gray	398	8398	415
	dk gray	235	8513	414
■	= gray-black	1041	8501	844
•	= French Knots: gray-black			
|	= Backstitch:			
	head, mouth—dk gray			
	eyes, brows—gray-black			

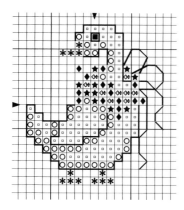

#47

Design size: 17 wide x 20 high

			Anchor	Coats	DMC
□	=	white	1	1001	blanc
✧	=	pink	76	3087	3688
✱	=	orange	328	2324	3341
★	=	yellow	305	2295	743
		lt green	239	6226	702
◆	=	dk green	258	6268	987
O	=	lt blue-gray	1032	7876	3752
		dk blue-gray	921	7052	931
■	=	blue-black	152	7160	939
│	=	Backstitch:			
		bow—lt green			
		duck—dk blue-gray			

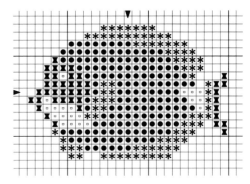

#48

Design size: 25 wide x 17 high

			Anchor	Coats	DMC
□	=	white	1	1001	blanc
✱	=	yellow	295	2295	726
●	=	blue	132	7143	797
X	=	black	403	8403	310

#49

Design size: 26 wide x 19 high

			Anchor	Coats	DMC
□	=	white	1	1001	blanc
✔	=	yellow	297	2294	444
ω	=	orange	328	2324	3341
■	=	black	403	8403	310
│	=	Backstitch: black			

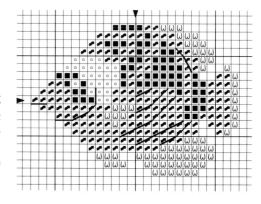

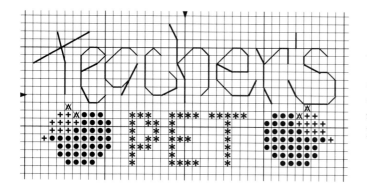

#50

Design size: 38 wide x 18 high

			Anchor	Coats	DMC
●	=	red	1025	3013	347
+	=	green	258	6268	987
✱	=	blue	1039	7168	518
⋈	=	brown	357	5475	801
		brown-black	382	5382	3371
│	=	Backstitch: brown-black			

50 House Designs

From a cozy cottage to a royal castle, you'll love creating the homes in this chapter. As you build each little house stitch by stitch, you'll be amazed at the amount of detail in each little charted design.

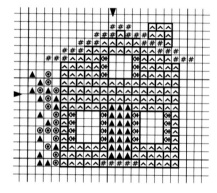

#1

Design size: 21 wide x 18 high

		Anchor	Coats	DMC
◈ =	lt pink	25	3125	3326
▲ =	dk pink	38	3176	961
◉ =	green	266	6010	3347
∧ =	rust	1013	2338	3778
# =	med gray	235	8513	414
	dk gray	400	8999	317
| =	Backstitch: dk gray			

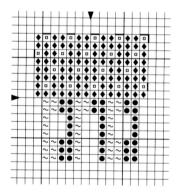

#2

Design size: 14 wide x 16 high

		Anchor	Coats	DMC
▫ =	white	2	1001	blanc
● =	red	1025	3013	347
~ =	tan	368	5345	437
◆ =	blue	1035	7052	930
| =	Backstitch: blue			

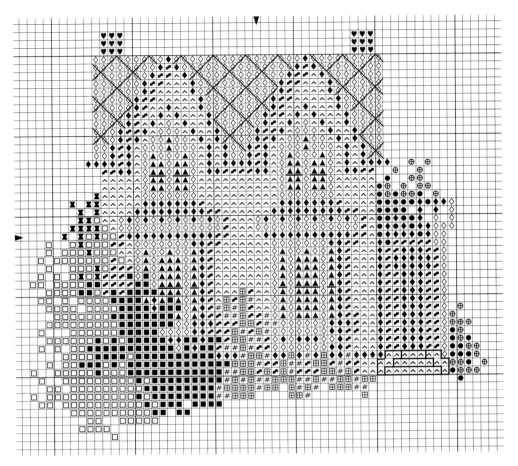

#3

Design size: 57 wide x 51 high

		Anchor	Coats	DMC
⊕	= med pink	25	3125	3326
●	= dk pink	42	3154	326
♥	= red	43	3044	814
#	= yellow	305	2295	743
□	= lt green	265	6266	3348
⊞	= med green	257	6258	988
■	= dk green	246	6246	986
✘	= very dk green	1044	6021	895

		Anchor	Coats	DMC
◇	= lt blue-gray	976	7876	3752
◆	= dk blue-gray	1034	7051	931
∧	= lt gray	398	8398	415
◣	= dk gray	400	8999	414
▲	= gray-black	1041	8501	844
		= Backstitch:		
	windows—lt gray			
	roof, stoop—dk gray			

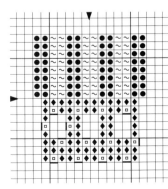

#4

Design size: 14 wide x 16 high

		Anchor	Coats	DMC
▫	= white	2	1001	blanc
●	= red	1025	3013	347
~	= tan	368	5345	437
◆	= blue	1035	7052	930
		= Backstitch: blue		

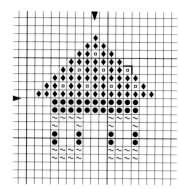

#5

Design size: 15 wide x 16 high

			Anchor	Coats	DMC
□	=	white	2	1001	blanc
●	=	red	1025	3013	347
~	=	tan	368	5345	437
◆	=	blue	1035	7052	930
		=	Backstitch: blue			

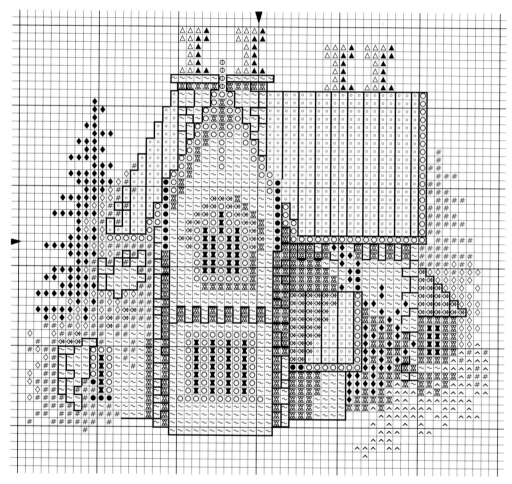

#6

Design size: 58 wide x 54 high

			Anchor	Coats	DMC				Anchor	Coats	DMC
∧	=	yellow-green	253	6253	472	△	=	lt brown	1008	2337	3773
◇	=	lt green	264	6250	772	▲	=	dk brown	936	5936	632
#	=	med green	266	6010	3347	~	=	lt gray	234	8510	762
◆	=	dk green	212	6211	561	⊠	=	med gray	399	8511	318
∘	=	lt blue	1032	7876	3752			dk gray	400	8999	317
⊕	=	med blue	1034	7051	931	◗	=	gray-black	1041	8501	844
○	=	lt rust	1013	2338	3778			=	Backstitch: dk gray			
●	=	med rust	1004	3337	920						

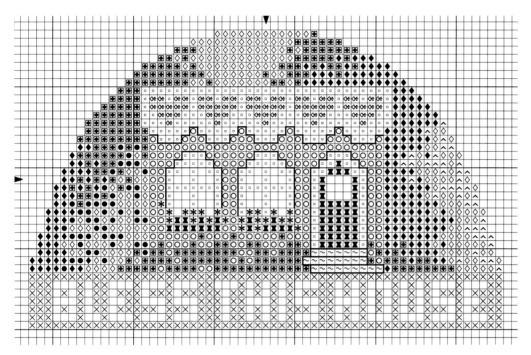

#7

Design size: 59 wide x 37 high

		Anchor	Coats	DMC
⋄ =	pink	38	3176	961
● =	red	42	3154	326
∧ =	yellow	305	2295	743
✕ =	med yellow-green	256	6267	704
⊞ =	dk yellow-green	257	6258	988
◇ =	lt green	240	6020	966
◆ =	dk green	212	6211	561
○ =	blue	128	7031	800
✳ =	purple	111	4300	553
▫ =	lt brown	376	5576	950
	med brown	349	5309	3776
✗ =	dk brown	351	3340	400
∼ =	lt gray	398	8398	415
	dk gray	400	8999	414
❙ =	Backstitch:			

roof, windows, door—med brown
steps—dk gray

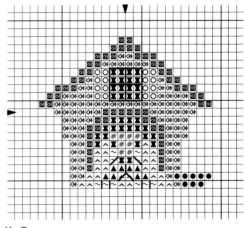

#8

Design size: 22 wide x 19 high

		Anchor	Coats	DMC
∼ =	white	2	1001	blanc
○ =	pink	25	3125	3326
● =	red	1025	3013	347
⋄ =	lt blue-gray	1033	7050	932
▨ =	dk blue-gray	1035	7052	930
∧ =	lt brown	376	5576	950
# =	med brown	1007	5579	3772
▲ =	dk brown	936	5936	632
✗ =	black	403	8403	310
❙ =	Backstitch:			

window—lt brown
dog face—black

#9

Design size: 29 wide x 26 high

		Anchor	Coats	DMC
✤ =	med pink	31	3127	3708
● =	dk pink	42	3154	326
✕ =	gold	891	5363	676
◆ =	green	245	6211	986
△ =	lt blue	1038	7169	519
▲ =	dk blue	169	7162	517
◟ =	Lazy Daisies: green			
• =	French Knots: dk blue			
❙ =	Backstitch:			
	roof pattern—dk pink			
	lettering, leaves, stems—green			

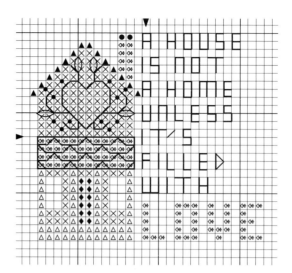

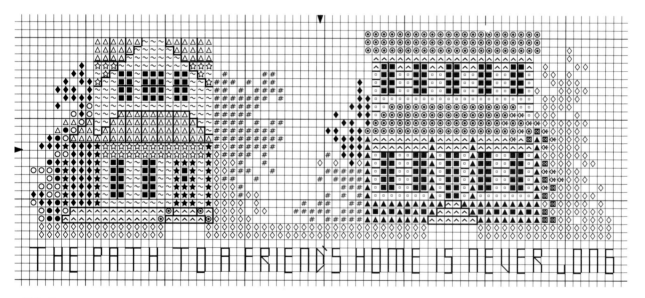

#10

Design size: 73 wide x 30 high

		Anchor	Coats	DMC			Anchor	Coats	DMC
▫ =	white	2	1001	blanc	☆ =	lt brown	368	5345	437
~ =	cream	275	2386	3770	★ =	dk brown	351	3340	400
✤ =	lt pink	25	3125	3326	⌃ =	lt gray	398	8398	415
▨ =	dk pink	38	3176	961	◉ =	med gray	235	8513	414
◇ =	lt green	259	6250	772		dk gray	236	8514	3799
# =	med green	243	6239	703	■ =	black	403	8403	310
◆ =	dk green	268	6269	469	❙ =	Backstitch:			
△ =	lt blue-gray	1033	7050	932		windows—cream			
▲ =	dk blue-gray	1035	7052	930		lettering—dk blue-gray			
○ =	lt purple	96	4104	3608		roof, siding, steps—dk gray			
● =	dk purple	100	4107	327					

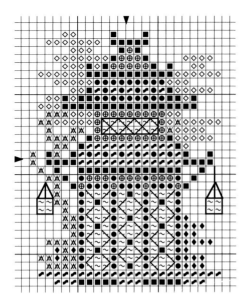

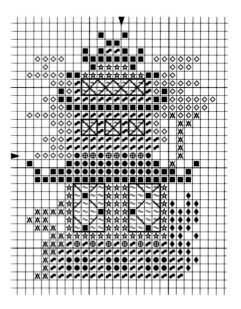

#11

Design size: 24 wide x 32 high

		Anchor	Coats	DMC
~	= cream	386	2386	745
⊕	= med red	1021	3068	761
●	= dk red	1025	3013	347
◇	= lt green	1042	6875	504
◆	= dk green	210	6031	562
⬎	= blue-gray	1034	7051	931
⋊	= brown	370	5356	434
■	= black	403	8403	310
|	= Backstitch: black			

#12

Design size: 24 wide x 31 high

		Anchor	Coats	DMC
~	= cream	386	2386	745
⊕	= med red	1021	3068	761
●	= dk red	1025	3013	347
◇	= lt green	1042	6875	504
◆	= dk green	210	6031	562
☆	= lt blue-gray	976	7876	3752
⬎	= dk blue-gray	1034	7051	931
⋊	= brown	370	5356	434
■	= black	403	8403	310
|	= Backstitch: black			

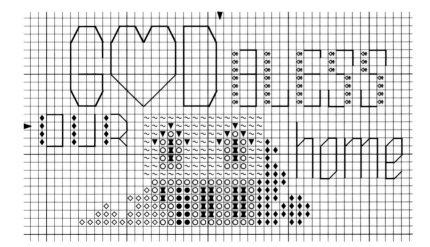

#13

Design size: 45 wide x 25 high

		Anchor	Coats	DMC
○	= lt pink	48	3067	818
	med pink	42	3154	326
●	= dk pink	43	3044	814
◇	= lt green	264	6253	472
◆	= dk green	266	6010	3347
✛	= blue	979	7979	312
	purple	99	4092	552
~	= lt blue-gray	976	7876	3752
▼	= dk blue-gray	1035	7052	930
⬕	= blue-black	152	7160	939
|	= Backstitch:			
	"G," "D"—med pink			
	"O"—dk pink			
	"our"—dk green			
	"bless"—blue			
	"home"—purple			

#14

Design size: 35 wide x 32 high

			Anchor	Coats	DMC
O	=	lt pink	48	3067	818
⊕	=	med pink	55	3001	604
●	=	red	1005	3410	816
▲	=	green	210	6031	562
~	=	lt blue-gray	848	6006	927
⊠	=	dk blue-gray	851	7227	924
⋈	=	brown	358	5475	433
		=	Backstitch:			
		windows—med pink			
		lettering—brown			

#15

Design size: 31 wide x 25 high

			Anchor	Coats	DMC
~	=	cream	386	2386	745
+	=	pink	38	3176	961
◇	=	lt green	264	6253	472
⊕	=	med green	267	6267	3346
◆	=	dk green	258	6268	987
⊕	=	lt blue	1032	7876	3752
★	=	med blue	1034	7051	931
#	=	brown	351	3340	400
■	=	gray-black	1041	8501	844
		=	Backstitch:			
		checkerboard border—med blue			
		roof—brown			

#16

Design size: 63 wide x 24 high

			Anchor	Coats	DMC
▫	=	pink	1023	3069	3712
O	=	lt green	264	6253	472
●	=	dk green	267	6267	3346
✧	=	lt blue-gray	1032	7876	3752
▲	=	dk blue-gray	1034	7051	931
∧	=	lt purple	108	4302	210
★	=	dk purple	110	4301	208
		brown	351	3340	400
•	=	French Knots: brown			
│	=	Backstitch:			
		border—dk blue-gray			
		lettering—brown			

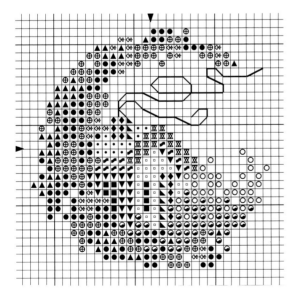

#17

Design size: 30 wide x 30 high

			Anchor	Coats	DMC
✧	=	lt pink	25	3125	3326
▲	=	dk pink	38	3176	961
•	=	lt gold	386	2386	745
▨	=	med gold	891	5363	676
◣	=	dk gold	309	5309	781
O	=	lt yellow-green	265	6266	3348
◖	=	med yellow-green	257	6258	988
⊕	=	lt blue-green	206	6209	955
●	=	dk blue-green	211	6213	562
▫	=	lt blue-gray	1032	7876	3752
		med blue-gray	1033	7050	932
▼	=	dk blue-gray	1034	7051	931
◤	=	lt rust	1013	2338	3778
◆	=	dk rust	1014	2339	355
■	=	gray-black	1041	8501	844
│	=	Backstitch: med blue-gray			

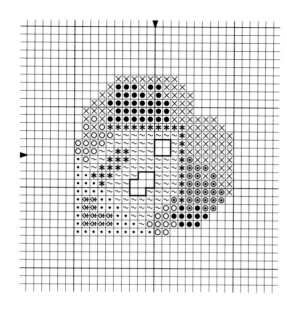

#18

Design size: 20 wide x 20 high

			Anchor	Coats	DMC
~	=	cream	386	2386	745
✿	=	pink	38	3176	961
✱	=	orange	323	2323	3341
•	=	very lt green	1043	6015	369
O	=	lt green	265	6266	3348
⊙	=	med green	267	6267	3346
●	=	dk green	212	6211	561
✕	=	blue	128	7031	800
|	=	Backstitch: orange			

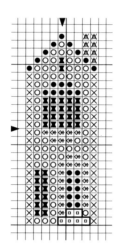

#19

Design size: 9 wide x 24 high

			Anchor	Coats	DMC
▫	=	white	2	1001	blanc
✿	=	pink	26	3126	894
✖	=	rust	352	5471	300
O	=	lt gray	398	8398	415
✕	=	med gray	235	8513	414
●	=	dk gray	236	8514	413
✗	=	black	403	8403	310
|	=	Backstitch:			
		windows—white			
		steps—dk gray			

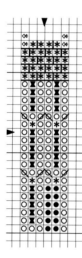

#20

Design size: 6 wide x 25 high

			Anchor	Coats	DMC
O	=	lt green	241	6225	704
✱	=	med green	257	6258	988
●	=	dk green	246	6246	986
✿	=	rust	352	5471	300
✗	=	gray-black	1041	8501	844
|	=	Backstitch:			
		front trim—dk green			
		roof—gray-black			

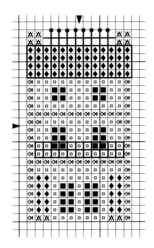

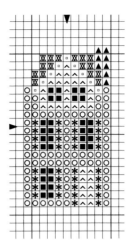

#21

Design size: 13 wide x 24 high

		Anchor	Coats	DMC
⊕ =	med rust	1024	3071	3328
◆ =	blue-gray	1034	7051	931
▫ =	tan	1047	5347	402
✕ =	dk rust	352	5471	300
■ =	black	403	8403	310
• =	French Knots: black			
| =	Backstitch: black			

#22

Design size: 11 wide x 20 high

		Anchor	Coats	DMC
∧ =	turquoise	1038	7169	519
○ =	lt purple	95	4085	554
✳ =	dk purple	99	4092	552
▲ =	rust	351	3340	400
▫ =	lt gray	398	8398	415
✕ =	dk gray	400	8999	414
■ =	black	403	8403	310
| =	Backstitch: lt gray			

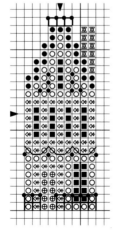

#23

Design size: 9 wide x 24 high

		Anchor	Coats	DMC
⊕ =	pink	31	3127	3708
✕ =	rust	352	5471	300
○ =	lt gray	234	8510	762
⊕ =	med gray	399	8511	318
● =	dk gray	400	8999	414
■ =	black	403	8403	310
• =	French Knots:			
	on front—dk gray			
	widow's walk, fence—black			
| =	Backstitch:			
	awning—lt gray			
	on front—dk gray			
	widow's walk, fence—black			

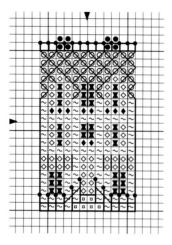

#24

Design size: 12 wide x 22 high

			Anchor	Coats	DMC
□	=	cream	275	2386	3770
~	=	yellow	386	2350	745
◇	=	lt green	256	6267	704
♦	=	med green	258	6268	987
●	=	rust	352	5471	300
○	=	brown	1007	5579	3772
✕	=	gray-black	1041	8501	844
•	=	French Knots: gray-black			
|	=	Backstitch:			
		shutters—cream			
		awnings—med green			
		house—brown			
		railings—gray-black			

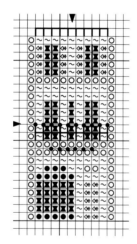

#25

Design size: 11 wide x 24 high

			Anchor	Coats	DMC
~	=	very lt pink	48	3067	818
○	=	lt pink	55	3001	604
✿	=	med pink	42	3154	326
●	=	dk pink	1005	3410	816
✕	=	gray-black	1041	8501	844
•	=	French Knots: dk pink			
|	=	Backstitch:			
		windows—very lt pink			
		railings—dk pink			

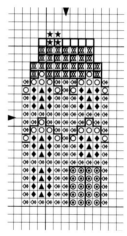

#26

Design size: 11 wide x 22 high

			Anchor	Coats	DMC
⊙	=	med green	242	6225	702
♦	=	dk green	245	6211	986
✿	=	blue	1038	7169	519
★	=	rust	352	5471	300
○	=	lt blue-gray	976	7876	3752
✕	=	med blue-gray	922	7980	930
▲	=	gray-black	1041	8501	844
|	=	Backstitch: gray-black			

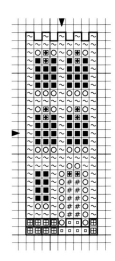

#27

Design size: 9 wide x 25 high

			Anchor	Coats	DMC
▫	=	white	2	1001	blanc
#	=	blue	1038	7169	519
~	=	tan	366	3335	951
O	=	taupe	392	5393	3032
◉	=	brown	1046	5371	435
⊞	=	rust	352	5471	300
■	=	gray-black	1041	8501	844
|	=	Backstitch:			
		outline—brown			
		steps, brick—gray-black			

#28

Design size: 7 wide x 22 high

			Anchor	Coats	DMC
▫	=	lt yellow	301	2289	745
⊠	=	dk yellow	298	2298	725
#	=	turquoise	1039	7168	518
◇	=	lt brown	1007	5579	3772
◆	=	med brown	352	5471	300
		dk brown	360	5476	898
✕	=	gray-black	1041	8501	844
•	=	French Knots: gray-black			
|	=	Backstitch:			
		windows—lt yellow			
		roof—dk brown			
		railing—gray-black			

#29

Design size: 41 wide x 29 high

			Anchor	Coats	DMC
		med red	1024	3071	3328
		dk red	1025	3013	347
×	=	yellow	305	2295	743
◆	=	green	258	6268	987
⊞	=	lt rust	1047	5347	402
■	=	med rust	1048	3336	3776
✳	=	brown	357	5475	801
•	=	French Knots:			
		border—med red			
		roses—dk red			
		lettering—green			
|	=	Backstitch:			
		border—med red			
		lettering—green			

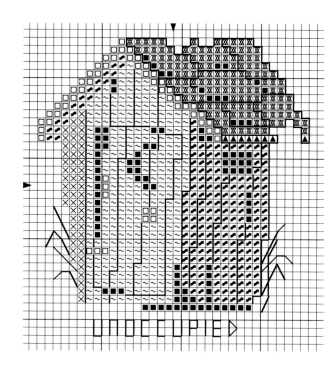

#30

Design size: 34 wide x 37 high

			Anchor	Coats	DMC
		green	243	6239	703
~	=	lt taupe	390	5388	3033
✕	=	med taupe	392	5393	3032
◣	=	dk taupe	1050	5889	3781
□	=	lt blue-gray	274	7225	927
⊠	=	med blue-gray	850	7226	3768
▲	=	dk blue-gray	851	7227	924
■	=	gray-black	1041	8501	844
│	=	Backstitch:			

grass—green
lettering—dk blue-gray
outhouse—gray-black

#31

Design size: 43 wide x 43 high

			Anchor	Coats	DMC
✧	=	lt pink	26	3126	894
⊠	=	dk pink	28	3152	892
♥	=	yellow	305	2295	743
▲	=	green	210	6031	562
♦	=	turquoise	169	7169	3765
∧	=	lt blue-gray	1033	7050	932
●	=	dk blue-gray	1035	7052	930
•	=	French Knots: yellow			

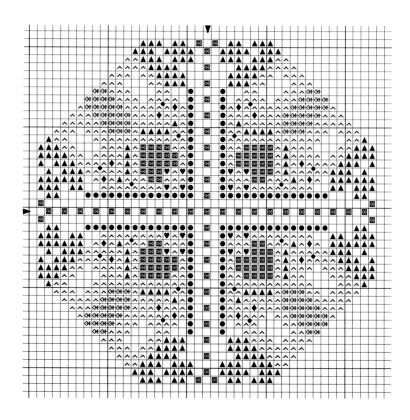

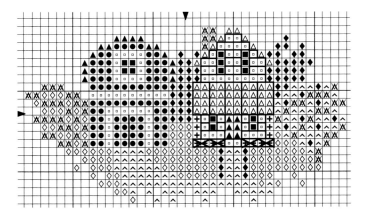

#32

Design size: 40 wide x 22 high

			Anchor	Coats	DMC
▫	=	white	2	1001	blanc
●	=	red	13	3013	347
+	=	yellow	1002	2306	977
◇	=	lt green	265	6266	3348
◆	=	med green	245	6211	986
∧	=	lt brown	378	5578	841
✗	=	med brown	358	5475	433
△	=	lt blue-gray	1033	7050	932
▲	=	dk blue-gray	1035	7052	930
■	=	gray-black	236	8514	3799
|	=	Backstitch:			
		barn door—white			
		roof—dk blue-gray			
		siding, railing—gray-black			

#33

Design size: 39 wide x 23 high

			Anchor	Coats	DMC
∧	=	lt green	259	6250	772
✦	=	med green	257	6258	988
◆	=	dk green	212	6211	561
☆	=	lt blue-gray	1033	7050	932
★	=	dk blue-gray	1034	7051	931
▫	=	tan	1011	2331	948
◞	=	rust	1013	2338	3778
○	=	lt gray	231	8231	453
✗	=	med gray	233	8233	451
●	=	dk gray	401	8999	413
|	=	Backstitch:			
		windows—tan			
		remaining house—dk gray			

#34

Design size: 39 wide x 39 high

			Anchor	Coats	DMC
▫	=	lt pink	24	3173	963
✦	=	dk pink	38	3176	961
○	=	lt orange	1012	2331	754
●	=	dk orange	323	2323	3341
◇	=	lt gold	301	2289	745
◆	=	dk gold	363	5943	436
□	=	lt green	240	6020	966
■	=	med green	243	6239	703
		dk green	245	6211	986
♡	=	lt blue	129	7020	809
♥	=	dk blue	131	7080	798
|	=	Backstitch:			
		on corresponding house—dk orange,			
		dk gold, dk green, dk blue			
		lettering—dk green			

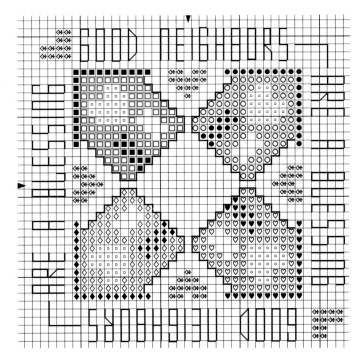

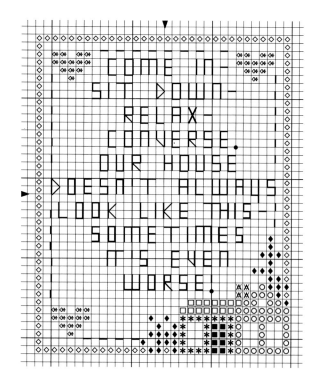

#35

Design size: 32 wide x 40 high

			Anchor	Coats	DMC
✪	=	med pink	38	3176	961
		dk pink	42	3154	326
O	=	yellow	891	5363	676
✱	=	gold	1002	2306	977
◇	=	lt green	265	6266	3348
◆	=	dk green	268	6269	469
✕	=	rust	351	3340	400
□	=	lt brown	369	5347	435
■	=	dk brown	370	5349	434
•	=	French Knots:			
		exclamation point—med pink			
		period—dk brown			
– –	=	Running Stitch: dk pink			
│	=	Backstitch:			
		"worse!"—med pink			
		remaining lettering—dk brown			

#36

Design size: 52 wide x 41 high

			Anchor	Coats	DMC
▫	=	white	2	1001	blanc
⌃	=	yellow	297	2294	726
◇	=	lt green	264	6253	472
◆	=	med green	257	6258	988
◢	=	blue-green	212	6211	561
△	=	med taupe	392	5393	3032
▲	=	dk taupe	905	8500	645
~	=	very lt gray	397	8232	762
□	=	lt gray	398	8398	415
#	=	med gray	235	8513	414
◉	=	dk gray	236	8514	413
■	=	black	403	8403	310
•	=	French Knots: dk gray			
│	=	Backstitch:			
		windows—very lt gray			
		octogonal windows, "Dixieland"—			
		dk gray			
		"land of cotton," pillars, remaining			
		house—med gray			

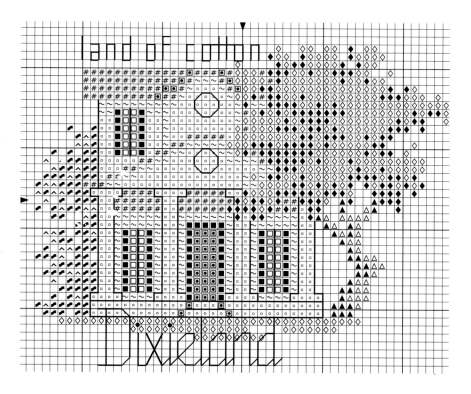

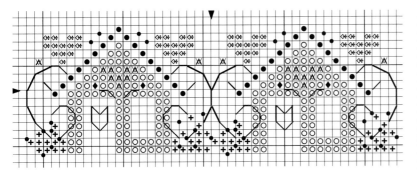

#37

Design size: 46 wide x 16 high

		Anchor	Coats	DMC
✿	= pink	25	3125	3326
	red	43	3044	814
+	= lt green	240	6020	966
♦	= dk green	258	6268	987
⋈	= turquoise	169	7169	3765
O	= lt brown	1008	2337	3773
●	= dk brown	936	5936	632
•	= French Knots:			
	in bushes—red			
	above roofs—turquoise			
|	= Backstitch:			
	hearts—red			
	tendrils—dk green			

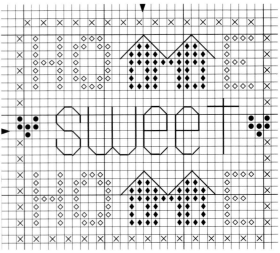

#38

Design size: 32 wide x 28 high

		Anchor	Coats	DMC
	med rose	38	3176	961
●	= dk rose	42	3154	326
✕	= green	243	6239	703
◇	= lt blue-gray	1033	7050	932
♦	= dk blue-gray	1035	7052	930
|	= Backstitch:			
	"sweet"—med rose			
	roofs—dk blue-gray			

#39

Design size: 29 wide x 43 high

		Anchor	Coats	DMC
▫	= white	2	1001	blanc
O	= lt pink	25	3125	3326
	med pink	42	3154	326
	red	1005	3410	816
	yellow	306	2307	725
♦	= green	210	6031	562
	med brown	349	5309	3776
▲	= dk brown	352	5471	300
∧	= lt gray	398	8398	415
⋈	= med gray	235	8513	414
⊞	= dk gray	400	8999	317
■	= gray-black	1041	8501	844
•	= French Knots:			
	rose arbor—red			
	dot on "i"—med brown			
|	= Backstitch:			
	vertical windows—white			
	"Home" & "Heart"—med pink			
	heart string—yellow			
	"is" & "where you hang your"—med brown			
	roof, siding—dk gray			
	octagonal window—gray-black			

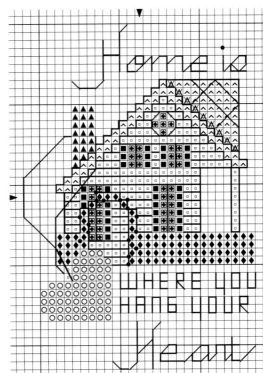

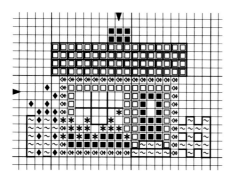

#40

Design size: 23 wide x 16 high

			Anchor	Coats	DMC
~	=	white	2	1001	blanc
✧	=	yellow	301	2289	745
✳	=	orange	323	2323	3341
◆	=	green	246	6246	986
□	=	lt brown	378	5578	841
■	=	dk brown	936	5936	632
|	=	Backstitch: dk brown			

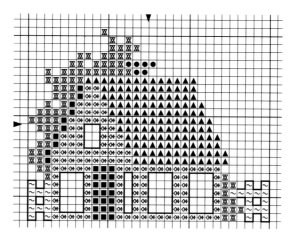

#41

Design size: 30 wide x 24 high

			Anchor	Coats	DMC
~	=	white	2	1001	blanc
⊠	=	green	267	6267	3346
✧	=	blue	129	7020	809
▲	=	med blue-gray	1034	7051	931
■	=	dk blue-gray	1035	7052	930
●	=	rust	1004	3337	920
|	=	Backstitch:			
		windows—med blue-gray			
		corner of house—dk blue-gray			
		fence—rust			

#42

Design size: 43 wide x 47 high

			Anchor	Coats	DMC
▫	=	white	2	1001	blanc
✧	=	pink	26	3126	894
●	=	red	42	3154	326
◇	=	lt green	264	6253	472
⊠	=	med green	266	6010	3347
◆	=	dk green	268	6269	469
#	=	med blue-green	211	6213	562
▲	=	dk blue-green	683	6880	890
~	=	lt blue	129	7020	809
⊕	=	med blue	978	7978	312
^	=	lt purple	95	4085	554
✳	=	dk purple	98	4097	553
□	=	lt gray	234	8510	762
⊠	=	med gray	235	8513	414
		dk gray	236	8514	413
■	=	black	403	8403	310
|	=	Backstitch:			
		2nd floor shutters—white			
		remaining outlines—dk gray			

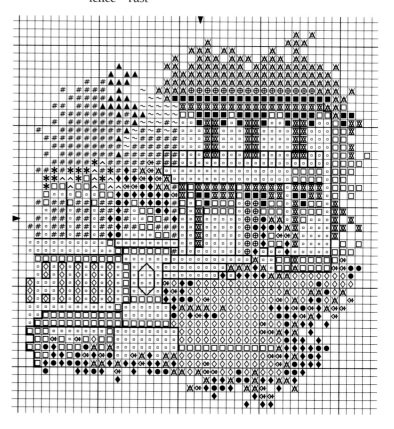

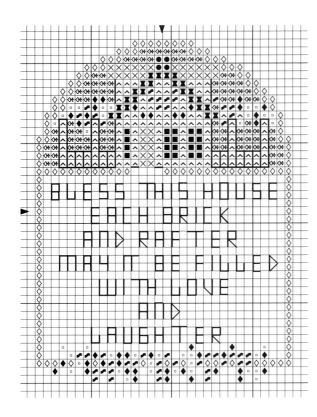

#43

Design size: 32 wide x 43 high

			Anchor	Coats	DMC
□	=	lt pink	31	3127	3708
➴	=	dk pink	39	3154	309
●	=	red	43	3044	814
∧	=	yellow	891	5363	676
◇	=	lt green	265	6266	3348
◆	=	dk green	212	6211	561
✛	=	blue	1031	7031	3753
✕	=	med brown	379	5379	840
✠	=	dk brown	360	5476	898
■	=	brown-black	381	5381	938
|	=	Backstitch:			
		lettering—dk green			
		house, porch—dk brown			

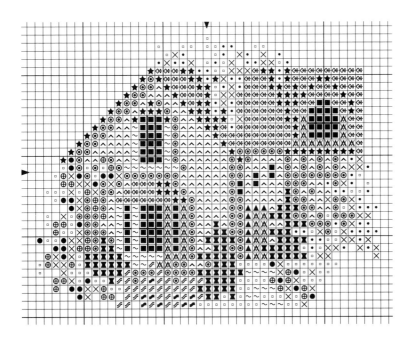

#44

Design size: 43 wide x 34 high

			Anchor	Coats	DMC
⊕	=	med red	1024	3071	3328
●	=	dk red	1005	3410	816
•	=	yellow	305	2295	743
□	=	lt yellow-green	265	6266	3348
✕	=	med yellow-green	268	6269	469
⌇	=	lt green	242	6225	702
➴	=	med green	245	6258	986
✠	=	dk green	212	6211	561
✛	=	med blue-gray	920	7050	932
★	=	dk blue-gray	1035	7052	930
~	=	lt brown	376	5576	950
✕	=	med brown	1007	5579	3772
▲	=	dk brown	360	5476	898
∧	=	lt gray	398	8398	415
⊙	=	med gray	235	8513	414
■	=	gray-black	1041	8501	844
|	=	Backstitch: lt brown			

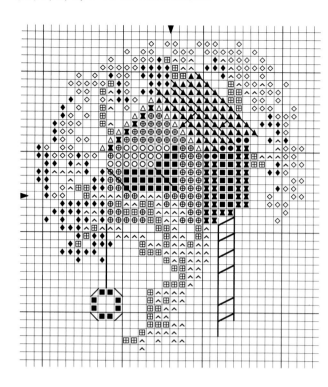

#45

Design size: 34 wide x 39 high

		Anchor	Coats	DMC	
O	= lt red	1021	3068	761	
⊕	= med red	1024	3071	3328	
✖	= dk red	1006	3401	304	
●	= very dk red	43	3044	814	
◇	= lt green	243	6239	703	
◆	= dk green	246	6246	986	
△	= lt blue-gray	1032	7876	3752	
▲	= dk blue-gray	1034	7051	931	
∧	= lt brown	1007	5579	3772	
⊞	= dk brown	360	5476	898	
■	= black	403	8403	310	
\	= Straight Stitch: awning supports—lt red				
|	= Backstitch:				
	tire rope, ladder—dk brown				
	roof—black				
	tire—black (2 strands)				

#46

Design size: 44 wide x 32 high

		Anchor	Coats	DMC
~	= cream	1009	3334	3770
O	= lt pink	25	3125	3326
⊕	= med pink	38	3176	961
●	= red	43	3044	814
∧	= lt yellow-green	265	6266	3348
◇	= med yellow-green	257	6258	988
#	= med green	208	6210	563
◆	= dk green	212	6211	561
△	= lt blue-gray	848	6006	927
✖	= med blue-gray	850	7226	3768
▲	= dk blue-gray	922	7980	930
+	= tan	368	5345	437
▫	= lt gray	231	8231	453
ω	= med gray	233	8233	451
■	= gray-black	1041	8501	844
|	= Backstitch: cream			

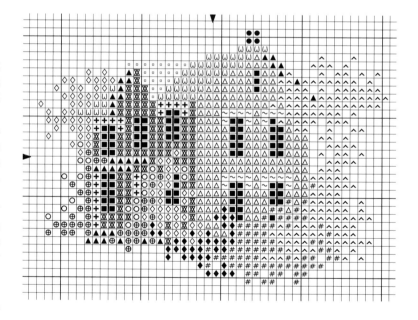

#47

Design size: 24 wide x 49 high

		Anchor	Coats	DMC
❖ =	lt pink	24	3173	963
▨ =	med pink	27	3127	899
	dk pink	42	3154	326
✳ =	lt purple	96	4104	3609
▲ =	dk purple	100	4107	327
○ =	lt brown	1007	5579	3772
⊕ =	med brown	936	5936	632
● =	dk brown	360	5476	898
~ =	lt gray	398	8398	415
× =	med gray	235	8513	414
	gray-black	1041	8501	844
• =	French Knots: gray-black			
	=	Backstitch:			

windows—dk pink

widow's walk, trim, stonework—gray-black

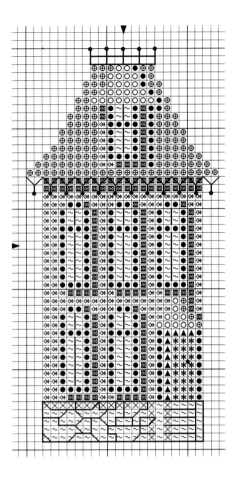

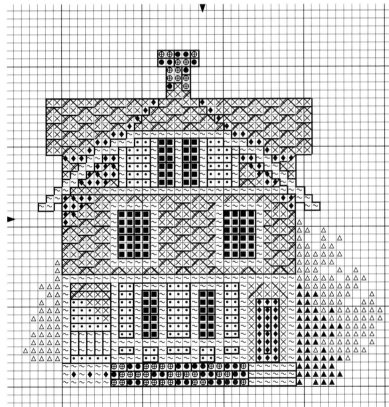

#48

Design size: 45 wide x 42 high

		Anchor	Coats	DMC
⊕ =	lt plum	1017	3081	316
● =	dk plum	1028	3089	3685
△ =	lt blue-green	1042	6875	504
▲ =	med blue-green	210	6031	562
• =	very lt tan	1009	3334	3770
× =	med tan	1008	2337	3773
~ =	lt brown	368	5345	437
◆ =	med brown	351	3340	400
	dk brown	358	5475	433
■ =	brown-black	381	5381	938
	=	Backstitch:			

windows, door—very lt tan

roof, chimney, siding, stone wall—dk brown

#49

Design size: 34 wide x 59 high

		Anchor	Coats	DMC
	white	2	1001	blanc
▫ =	lt pink	25	3125	3326
✵ =	med pink	28	3152	892
♥ =	red	47	3047	321
✳ =	yellow	305	2295	743
△ =	lt green	253	6253	472
⊙ =	med green	257	6258	988
▲ =	dk green	246	6246	986
☆ =	lt turquoise	1038	7169	519
★ =	dk turquoise	169	7162	517
○ =	lt blue-gray	1033	7050	932
	med blue-gray	1034	7051	931
● =	dk blue-gray	1035	7052	930
∧ =	lt gray	398	8398	415
⋈ =	med gray	235	8513	414
⊠ =	dk gray	400	8999	317
■ =	gray-black	1041	8501	844
⎮ =	Backstitch:			

red banner—white
diagonal window panes—lt green
iron gate—med blue-gray
outline of turrets—dk gray
flagpoles, roofs, steps—gray-black

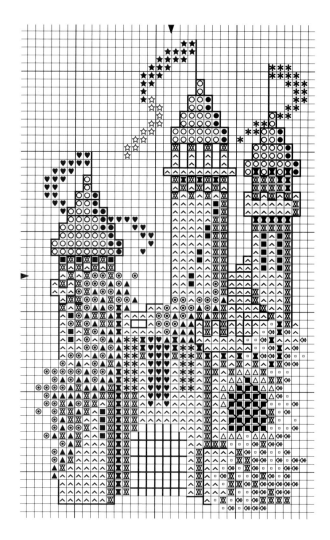

#50

Design size: 28 wide x 35 high

		Anchor	Coats	DMC
~ =	yellow	386	2386	745
✵ =	lt pink	25	3125	3326
⊞ =	med pink	38	3176	961
◇ =	lt green	259	6250	772
⋈ =	med green	253	6253	472
◣ =	dk green	243	6239	703
♦ =	very dk green	212	6211	561
	turquoise	169	7169	3765
○ =	lt purple	108	4302	209
● =	dk purple	111	4300	553
♡ =	lt brown	368	5345	437
✕ =	med brown	379	5379	840
♥ =	dk brown	370	5356	434
	gray-brown	1050	5889	3781
■ =	gray-black	1041	8501	844
• =	French Knots: turquoise			
⎮ =	Backstitch:			

vine—dk green
heart string—turquoise
roof, siding—gray-brown

50
Profession
Designs

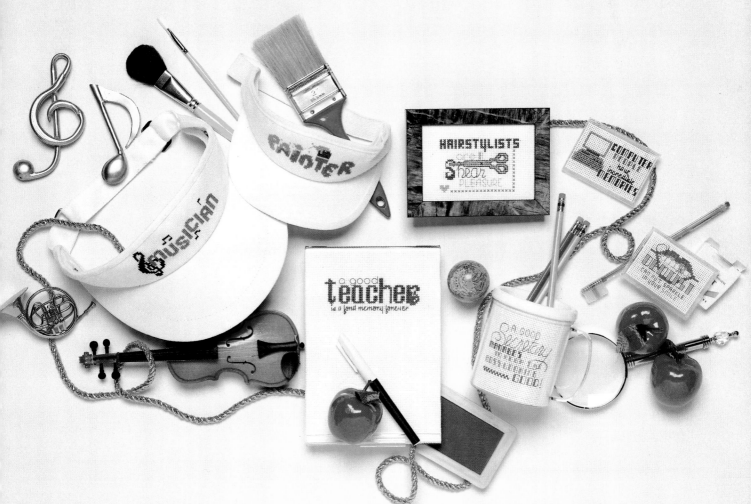

From attorney to clergyman, here are wonderful designs for special people:
teachers, nurses, musicians, pilots, baby sitter—even the professionally retired.

RECEPTIONIST
=a very pleasant=
FIRST AND LAST
IMPRESSION

Professional
HOMEMAKER!
long hours~heavy work load
GREAT BENEFITS

engineers
"practical ends are achieved through
the application of scientific principles"

PEDIATRICIAN
LOVING•CONSOLING•CARING•COMPASSIONATE

me AND my
PET ♥
OUR **VET**
CHIRP CHIRP•BOW•WOW~MEOW MEOW

Professional
QUILTER
goes to pieces
and loves it

Clergy

don't *Professors*
always go by
THE **BOOK**

anyone can cook
BUT IT TAKES A SEARING
DESIRE AND A PORTION
OF TALENT TO BE A
CHEF

SOLDIER
DEDICATED TO DEFENDING OUR
FREEDOM

JENNIFER COLER
BabySiTTer
WE OFTEN NEGLECT TO SAY
HOW MUCH YOU ARE APPRECIATED

ONCE A
MARINE
ALWAYS A MARINE

**PROFESSIONAL
STUDENT**
•HISTORY• •SOCIOLOGY-ART~BUSINESS• •CHEMISTRY•

Supermarket
CASHIERS
HANDLE FOOD AND MONEY ALL DAY
YET NEVER GAIN WEIGHT OR EVER GET RICH

a **GOOD**
WAITRESS
serves, caters, and pampers us
AND GRATEFULLY ACCEPTS ANY
TIPS we may offer

**PROFESSIONALLY
RETIRED**
NO BOSS - NO CLOCK - NO MONEY

EXECUTIVE
always **MANAGING** to get by

ATTORNEY
W.R. HUMPHREY

professional
GRANDPARENTS
⚘ highly skilled at ⚘
LOVING

wings of **VICTORY**
AIRFORCE

**POLICE
OFFICERS**
never **COP** out

**TRUCKERS
ALWAYS
HAVE
IT IN
GEAR**

ACCOUNTANT
= OF THE YEAR =
presented for outstanding
contributions to vast
numbers
throughout the year
JOHN CARL

COACH

PET
GROOMER

+
PARAMEDIC

PHYSICIANS
HAVE LOTS OF
PATIENCE

MANICURISTS
are good therapists:
they hold your hand while listening
to your problems!

FIREFIGHTER
"ABOVE AND BEYOND THE CALL OF DUTY"

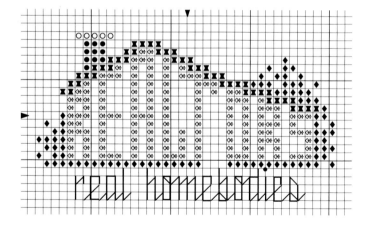

#1

Design size: 38 wide x 21 high

		Anchor	Coats	DMC
O =	lt rose	895	3071	3722
● =	dk rose	897	3243	3721
♦ =	green	243	6239	703
⬥ =	blue	168	7168	807
⧓ =	blue-gray	922	7980	930
• =	French Knot: dk rose			
| =	Backstitch: dk rose			

#2

Design size: 51 wide x 20 high

		Anchor	Coats	DMC
● =	red	19	3500	321
	gray	400	8999	414
■ =	black	403	8403	310
| =	Backstitch:			
	"RETIRED"—red			
	"no...money"—gray			
	"professionally"—black			

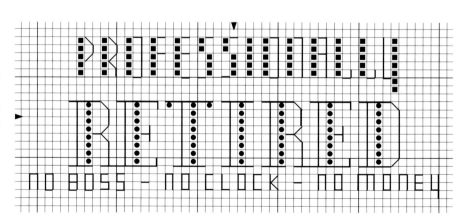

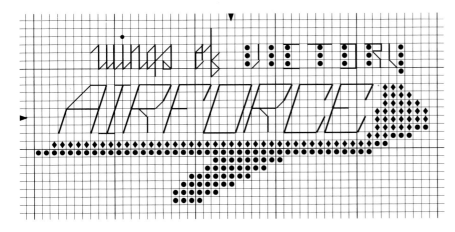

#3

Design size: 49 wide x 22 high

		Anchor	Coats	DMC
● =	red	47	3047	321
	med blue	131	7080	798
◆ =	dk blue	132	7143	797
• =	French Knot: med blue			
	=	Backstitch:			

"wings of," "AIRFORCE"—med blue
"victory"—red

#4

Design size: 41 wide x 21 high

		Anchor	Coats	DMC
○ =	lt blue	131	7080	798
● =	dk blue	133	7100	820
× =	lt gray	398	8398	415
✖ =	dk gray	400	8999	414
	blue-black	152	7160	939
• =	French Knots: blue-black			
	=	Backstitch:			

"people"—lt blue
"computer," "memories"—dk blue
computer—dk gray
"have incredible"—blue-black

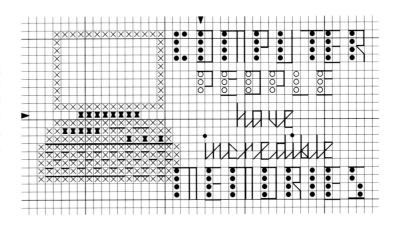

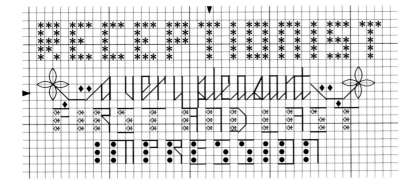

#5

Design size: 43 wide x 18 high

		Anchor	Coats	DMC
	pink	40	3153	335
◆ =	green	243	6239	703
✧ =	blue	131	7080	798
✳ =	lt purple	109	4301	209
● =	dk purple	112	4300	552
◁ =	Lazy Daisies: pink			
	=	Backstitch:			

stems, "a very pleasant"—green
"first and last"—blue
"impression"—dk purple

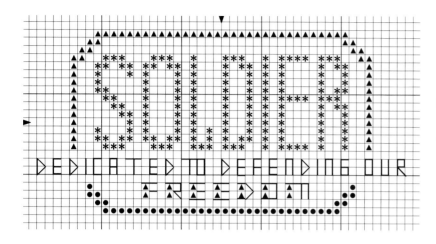

#6

Design size: 46 wide x 23 high

		Anchor	Coats	DMC
●	= red	47	3047	321
✳	= gold	306	2307	725
	green	243	6239	703
▲	= blue	132	7143	797
|	= Backstitch:			

"dedicated...our"—green
"freedom"—blue

#7

Design size: 43 wide x 20 high

		Anchor	Coats	DMC
▫	= white	2	1001	blanc
✧	= pink	26	3126	894
●	= red	47	3047	321
#	= orange	329	2327	3340
~	= peach	6	3006	754
✕	= brown	369	5347	435
✖	= brown-black	381	5381	938
|	= Backstitch: brown-black			

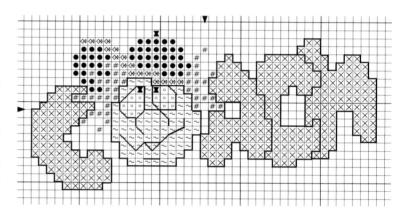

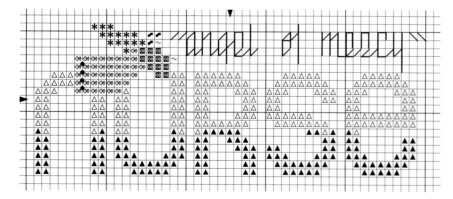

#8

Design size: 49 wide x 19 high

		Anchor	Coats	DMC
✧	= lt pink	50	3151	605
▣	= dk pink	41	3153	335
~	= peach	6	3006	761
✳	= gold	306	2307	725
△	= lt blue	160	7159	3325
▲	= dk blue	162	7162	517
✎	= brown	936	5936	632
•	= French Knots: dk pink			
|	= Backstitch: brown			

#9

Design size: 43 wide x 29 high

		Anchor	Coats	DMC
✪	= pink	52	3152	957
△	= lt blue	130	7021	809
▲	= dk blue	132	7143	797
○	= purple	92	4087	553
■	= dk gray	236	8514	3799
+	= silver metallic			
|	= Backstitch:			

"are a," "pleasure"—lt blue
"shear"—dk blue
scissors—dk gray

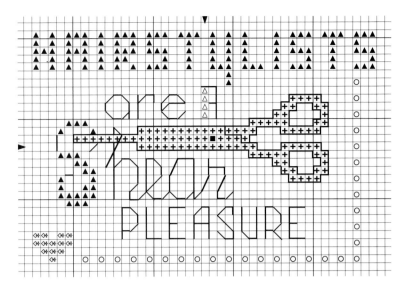

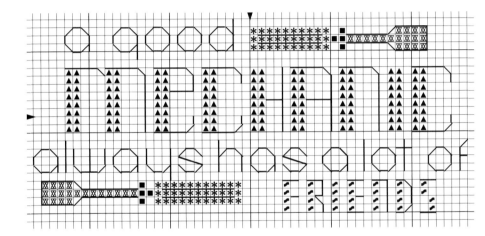

#10

Design size: 54 wide x 24 high

		Anchor	Coats	DMC
	red	19	3500	321
✳	= gold	306	2307	725
▲	= green	245	6211	986
↙	= blue	132	7143	797
⊠	= med gray	399	8511	318
	dk gray	400	8999	414
■	= black	403	8403	310
|	= Backstitch:			

"a good," "always...of"—red
"mechanic"—green
"friends"—blue
screwdriver heads—dk gray
handles—black

#11

Design size: 32 wide x 25 high

		Anchor	Coats	DMC
▫	= white	1	1001	blanc
✪	= pink	52	3152	957
●	= red	19	3500	321
△	= lt blue	167	7167	519
	dk blue	169	7169	3765
	gray	399	8511	318
	silver metallic			
|	= Backstitch:			

"smile"—red
"a," "DENTIST," "can...your"—dk blue
starburst—stitch with dk blue first,
    then with silver metallic
teeth—gray

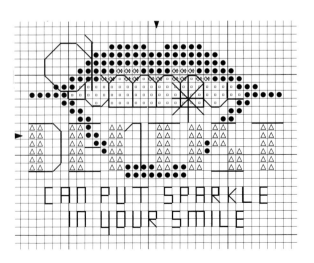

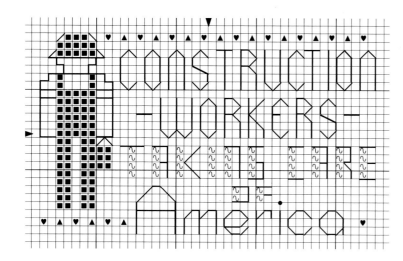

#12

Design size: 42 wide x 25 high

			Anchor	Coats	DMC
♥	=	red	9046	3046	666
▲	=	blue	132	7143	797
∿	=	gray	400	8999	414
■	=	black	403	8403	310
•	=	French Knot: blue			
│	=	Backstitch:			

    "taking...of"—gray
     remaining outlines—black

#13

Design size: 38 wide x 29 high

			Anchor	Coats	DMC
		green	243	6239	703
O	=	lt blue	161	7977	813
●	=	dk blue	162	7162	517
✳	=	purple	110	4301	208
•	=	French Knot: purple			
│	=	Backstitch:			

    "good"—green
    "to...looking"—lt blue
    "a," "manages"—dk blue
    "Secretary," "GOOD!"—purple

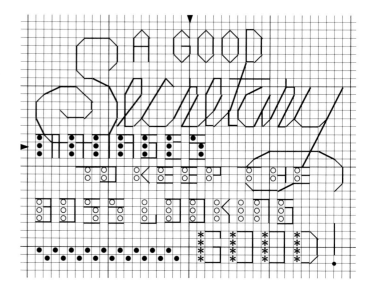

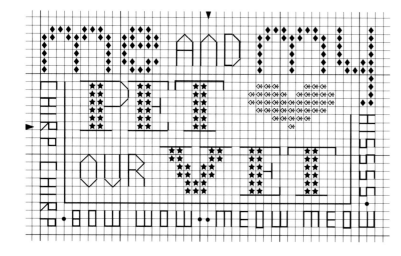

#14

Design size: 42 wide x 25 high

			Anchor	Coats	DMC
✧	=	pink	41	3153	335
♦	=	green	257	6258	988
		blue	162	7162	517
★	=	purple	110	4301	208
		brown	936	5936	632
•	=	French Knots: blue			
│	=	Backstitch:			

    border lettering and line—blue
    "PET," "VET"—purple
    "and," "our"—brown

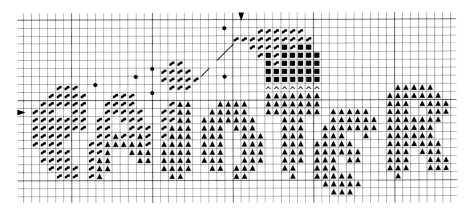

#15

Design size: 52 wide x 21 high

		Anchor	Coats	DMC
✎	= pink	40	3153	335
^	= gold	891	5363	676
▲	= brown	371	5470	434
■	= brown-black	381	5381	938
•	= French Knots: pink			
|	= Backstitch: pink			

#16

Design size: 50 wide x 17 high

		Anchor	Coats	DMC
●	= red	19	3500	321
△	= lt gray	398	8398	415
✕	= med gray	235	8513	414
■	= black	403	8403	310
|	= Backstitch: black			

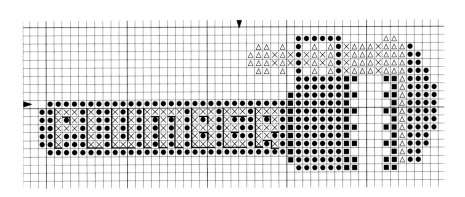

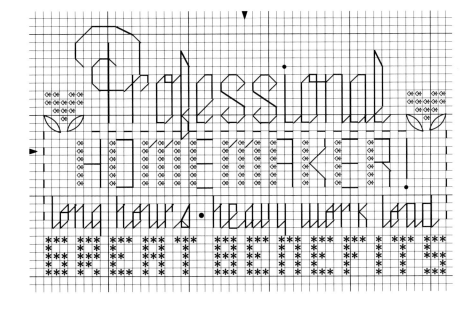

#17

Design size: 50 wide x 31 high

		Anchor	Coats	DMC
✧	= pink	52	3152	957
	green	243	6239	703
✱	= med purple	109	4301	209
	dk purple	110	4302	208
●	= rust	351	3340	400
◯	= Lazy Daisies: green			
•	= French Knots: to match lettering			
- -	= Running Stitch: green			
|	= Backstitch:			

"HOMEMAKER!"—pink

"Professional"—dk purple

"long...load"—rust

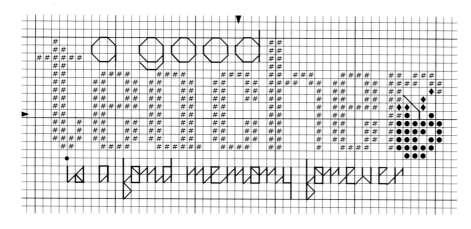

#18

Design size: 51 wide x 21 high

		Anchor	Coats	DMC
●	= red	20	3072	498
◆	= green	245	6211	986
#	= blue-gray	922	7980	930
•	= French Knot: green			
|	= Backstitch:			

    "a good"—red

    stem, "is...forever"—green

#19

Design size: 49 wide x 25 high

		Anchor	Coats	DMC
○	= lt red	35	3152	3705
⊕	= med red	47	3047	321
●	= dk red	20	3072	498
☆	= lt orange	323	2323	3341
★	= dk orange	326	2326	720
△	= lt yellow	305	2295	743
▲	= med yellow	307	5307	783
	dk yellow	309	5309	781
◇	= lt green	206	6209	955
×	= med green	208	6210	563
◣	= dk green	229	6228	700
■	= very dk green	246	6246	986
∿	= lt brown	379	5379	840
	med brown	936	5936	632
|	= Backstitch:			

    carrot—dk orange

    corn—dk yellow

    cornhusk, "our"—dk green

    "God bless"—med brown

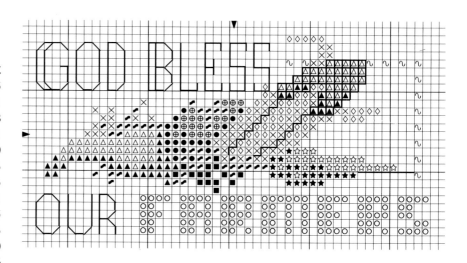

#20

Design size: 50 wide x 16 high

		Anchor	Coats	DMC
■	= blue	164	7182	824
	purple	92	4087	553
⊠	= med gray	235	8513	414
	dk gray	236	8514	3799
•	= French Knots: blue			
|	= Backstitch:			

    "doctor ordered"—blue

    "just...the"—purple

    between mortar & pestle—dk gray

#21

Design size: 50 wide x 19 high

		Anchor	Coats	DMC
	white	1	1001	blanc
♦ =	green	229	6228	700
✢ =	med blue	130	7021	809
▲ =	dk blue	132	7143	797
	brown	371	5470	434

⬭ = Lazy Daisies: dk blue

• = French Knot: brown

| = Backstitch:
   plane wings—white
   "plane people"—green
   "are"—med blue
   "lofty"—dk blue
   "with," "thoughts"—brown

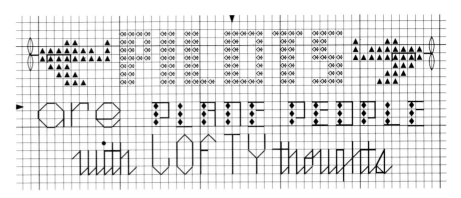

#22

Design size: 66 wide x 19 high

		Anchor	Coats	DMC
	turquoise	187	6187	958
▲ =	green	245	6211	986

| = Backstitch:
   lettering—turquoise
   border—green

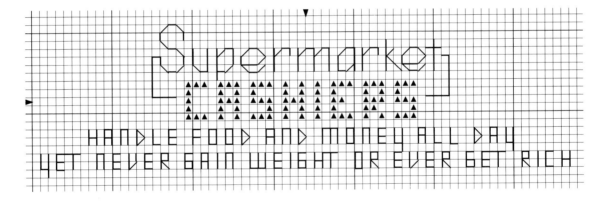

#23

Design size: 51 wide x 21 high

		Anchor	Coats	DMC
○ =	lt brown	378	5578	841
+ =	med brown	936	5936	632
● =	dk brown	360	5476	898

• = French Knots: to match backstitched
   lettering

| = Backstitch:
   "are...everything"—med brown
   "back in place," border—dk brown

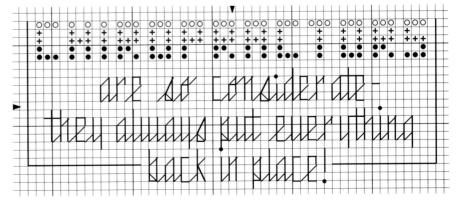

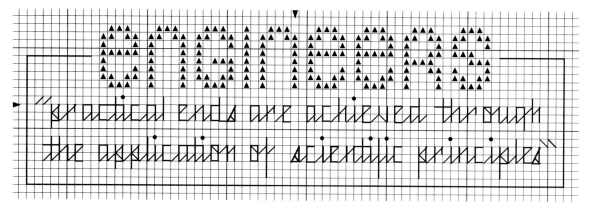

#24

Design size: 67 wide x 20 high

		Anchor	Coats	DMC
▲ =	blue	132	7143	797
	blue-black	152	7160	939
• =	French Knots: blue-black			
│ =	Backstitch: blue-black			

#25

Design size: 50 wide x 16 high

		Anchor	Coats	DMC
◊ =	lt green	256	6267	704
	dk green	245	6211	986
	brown	371	5470	434
│ =	Backstitch:			

"student"—lt green
"PROFESSIONAL"—dk green
border lettering—brown

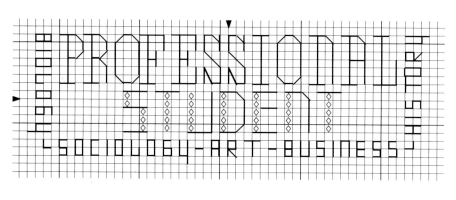

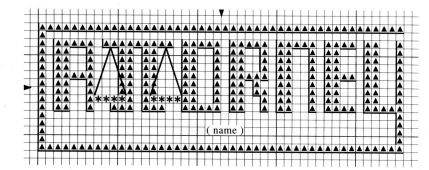

#26

Design size: 46 wide x 16 high

Note: Use the alphabet below to backstitch desired name with black.

		Anchor	Coats	DMC
* =	gold	306	2307	725
▲ =	brown	370	5356	434
	black	403	8403	310
│ =	Backstitch: black			

Alphabet

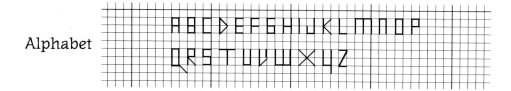

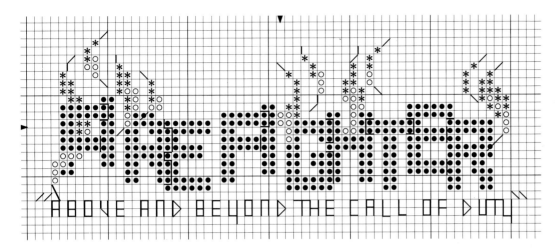

#27

Design size: 61 wide x 24 high

		Anchor	Coats	DMC
	cream	275	2386	3770
●	= red	9046	3046	666
✳	= orange	329	2327	3340
○	= yellow	305	2295	743
	gray-black	236	8514	3799
|	= Backstitch:

    betweeen letters—cream
    tip of flame—orange
    base of flame—yellow
    lettering—gray-black

#28

Design size: 45 wide x 22 high

		Anchor	Coats	DMC
	blue	132	7143	797
✕	= med gray	235	8513	414
	dk gray	400	8999	317
■	= black	403	8403	310
|	= Backstitch:

    "always...the"—blue
    "professors"—med gray
    "don't"—dk gray
    tassel—black

#29

Design size: 31 wide x 13 high

		Anchor	Coats	DMC
○	= lt blue	159	7976	3325
	dk blue	162	7162	517
|	= Backstitch: dk blue

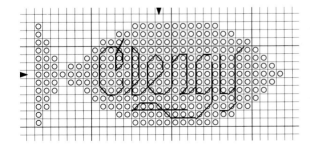

#30

Design size: 72 wide x 33 high

Note: Use the alphabet on page 154 to backstitch desired name with dk green.

			Anchor	Coats	DMC
O	=	pink	26	3126	894
✳	=	orange	329	2327	3340
★	=	yellow	305	2295	743
◇	=	lt green	254	6001	3348
◆	=	dk green	244	6226	702
△	=	lt blue	167	7167	519
✕	=	med blue	169	7169	3765
✔	=	purple	110	4301	208
		gray	400	8999	414
|	=	Backstitch:			

  name—dk green
  "we...appreciated"—med blue
  balloon strings—gray

#31

Design size: 36 wide x 17 high

			Anchor	Coats	DMC
▲	=	med green	257	6258	988
		dk green	246	6246	986
|	=	Backstitch: dk green			

#32

Design size: 31 wide x 22 high

			Anchor	Coats	DMC
✺	=	rose	895	3071	3722
		blue	169	7169	3765
		purple	92	4087	553
•	=	French Knots: to match lettering			
|	=	Backstitch:			

  "QUILTER"—rose
  "Professional"—blue
  "goes...it"—purple

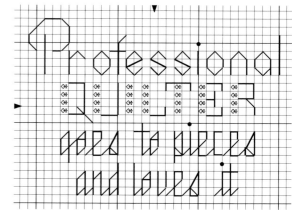

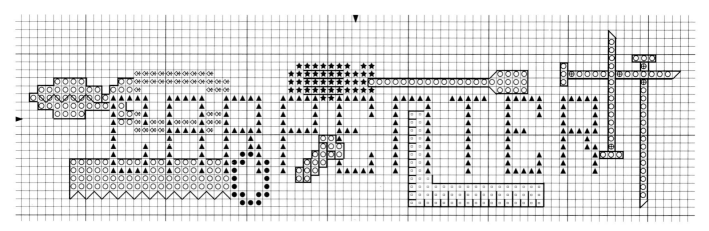

#33

Design size: 81 wide x 22 high

		Anchor	Coats	DMC
	orange	326	2326	720
★ =	yellow	305	2295	743
✥ =	blue	131	7080	798
▫ =	lt rust	347	5347	402
▲ =	dk rust	351	3340	400
● =	brown	936	5936	632

		Anchor	Coats	DMC
O =	lt gray	398	8398	415
⊕ =	med gray	235	8513	414
	dk gray	236	8514	413
❙ =	Backstitch:			
	screwdriver handle—orange			
	remaining outlines—dk gray			

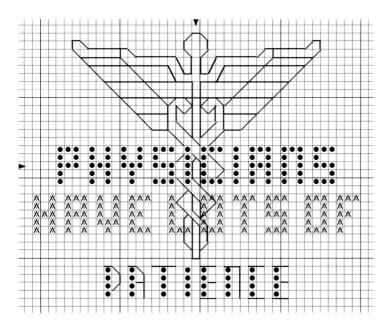

#34

Design size: 41 wide x 33 high

		Anchor	Coats	DMC
	red	19	3500	321
⋈ =	gray	235	8513	414
● =	black	403	8403	310
❙ =	Backstitch:			
	motif—red			
	lettering—black			

#35

Design size: 38 wide x 16 high

		Anchor	Coats	DMC
△ =	lt blue	130	7021	809
▲ =	dk blue	132	7143	797
⋈ =	silver metallic			
• =	French Knot: dk blue			
❙ =	Backstitch:			
	border—lt blue			
	lettering—dk blue			

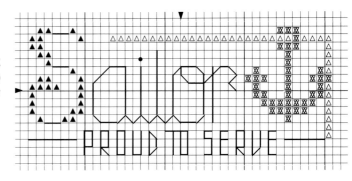

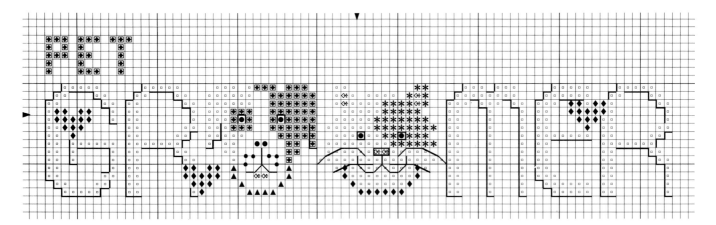

#36

Design size: 78 wide x 20 high

		Anchor	Coats	DMC
✣	= pink	50	3151	605
◆	= red	42	3154	326
✱	= gold	891	5363	676
▲	= blue	131	7080	798
▫	= lt brown	368	5345	437
⊞	= dk brown	370	5356	434
●	= brown-black	381	5381	938
•	= French Knots: brown-black			
│	= Backstitch:			

edges of letters, kitty eyes and whiskers—
dk brown
puppy face—brown-black

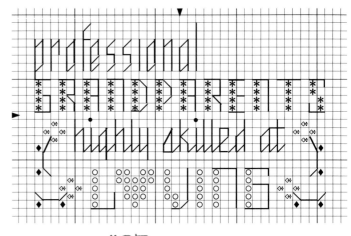

#37

Design size: 36 wide x 23 high

		Anchor	Coats	DMC
○	= pink	895	3071	3722
✱	= gold	306	2307	725
◆	= green	245	6211	986
✣	= blue	168	7168	807
•	= French Knots: green			
│	= Backstitch:			

"loving"—pink
"grandparents"—gold
stems, "highly...at"—green
"professional"—blue

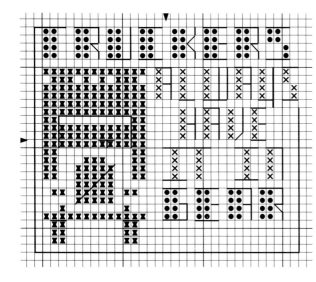

#38

Design size: 33 wide x 28 high

		Anchor	Coats	DMC
●	= red	47	3047	321
×	= gray	400	8999	414
✖	= gray-black	403	8403	310
│	= Backstitch:			

"truckers," "gear," border—red
truck, "Always...in"—gray

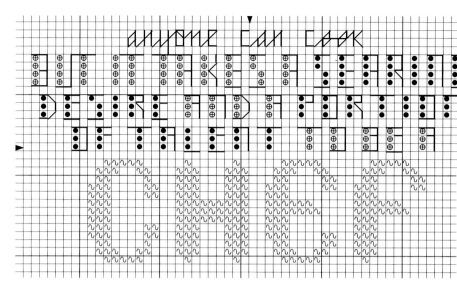

#39

Design size: 54 wide x 29 high

		Anchor	Coats	DMC
∿	= med orange	323	2323	3341
	dk orange	329	2327	3340
⊕	= med purple	109	4301	209
●	= dk purple	112	4300	552
|	= Backstitch:			

"anyone can cook"—dk orange

"but...a," "and a," "to be a"—med purple

remaining lettering—dk purple

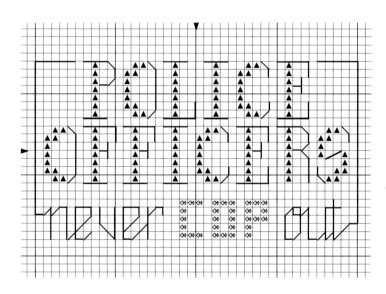

#40

Design size: 40 wide x 22 high

		Anchor	Coats	DMC
▲	= gold	307	5307	783
✧	= lt blue	131	7080	798
	dk blue	132	7143	797
|	= Backstitch:			

"POLICE OFFICERS"—gold

"never," "out," border—dk blue

#41

Design size: 33 wide x 28 high

		Anchor	Coats	DMC
ω	= lt red	35	3152	3705
♥	= med red	47	3047	321
~	= peach	6	3006	754
✱	= yellow	305	2295	743
▲	= green	229	6228	700
	brown	936	5936	632
|	= Backstitch:			

"school bus driver," mouth—med red

"my"—green

eyes, neck and hands—brown

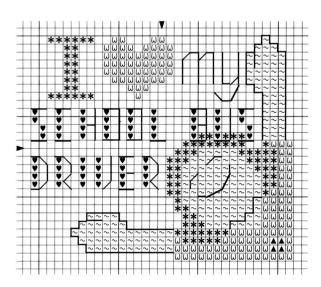

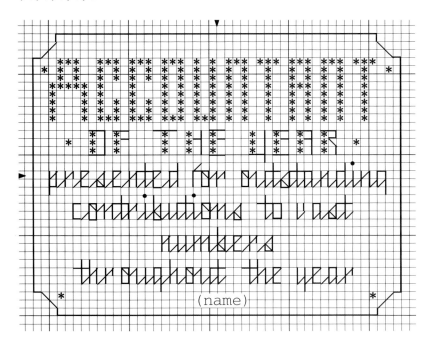

#42

Design size: 46 wide x 35 high

Note: Use the alphabet on page 154 to backstitch desired name with dk gold.

		Anchor	Coats	DMC
✳ =	lt gold	306	2307	725
	dk gold	308	5308	781
	rust	351	3340	400

• = French Knots: rust

| = Backstitch:
  "of the year," name—dk gold
  remaining backstitch—rust

#43

Design size: 42 wide x 19 high

		Anchor	Coats	DMC
☆ =	lt pink	50	3151	605
✧ =	med pink	40	3153	335
▲ =	green	257	6258	988
★ =	purple	110	4301	208
⊠ =	lt gray	399	8511	318
	dk gray	400	8999	414

| = Backstitch:
  "professional"—green
  thread—purple
  needle indentations, eye—dk gray

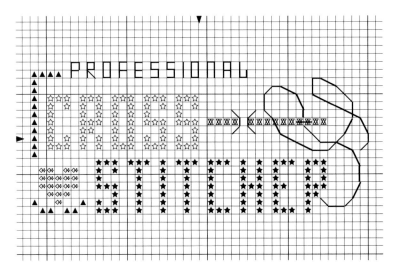

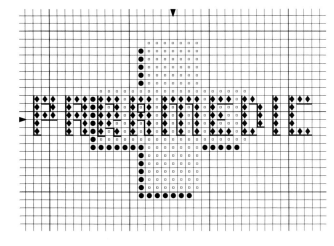

#44

Design size: 35 wide x 20 high

		Anchor	Coats	DMC
▫ =	med red	19	3500	321
● =	dk red	897	3243	3721
◆ =	gray	235	8513	414
	black	403	8403	310

| = Backstitch: black

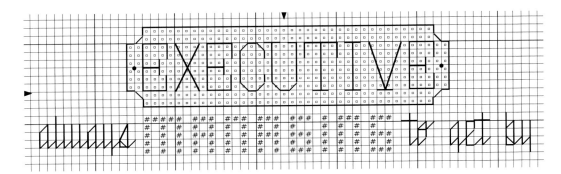

#45

Design size: 61 wide x 16 high

		Anchor	Coats	DMC
□	= gold	891	5363	676
#	= brown	351	3340	400
•	= French Knots: brown			
|	= Backstitch: brown			

#46 ▼

Design size: 56 wide x 23 high

		Anchor	Coats	DMC
⊕	= pink	41	3153	335
×	= green	258	6268	987
	blue	169	7169	3765
	brown	936	5936	632
|	= Backstitch:			

"waitress"—pink
"tips"—green
"a", "serves...us"—blue
"and...any," "we...offer"—brown

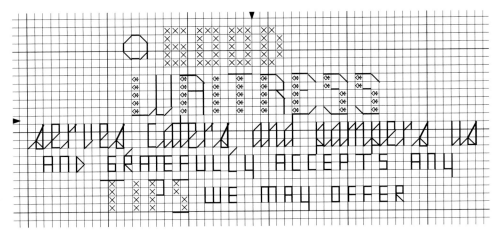

#47

Design size: 58 wide x 24 high

		Anchor	Coats	DMC
✳	= orange	329	2327	3340
★	= yellow	305	2295	743
⋈	= gold	307	5307	783
●	= brown	360	5476	898
|	= Backstitch:			

lettering—orange
light rays—gold

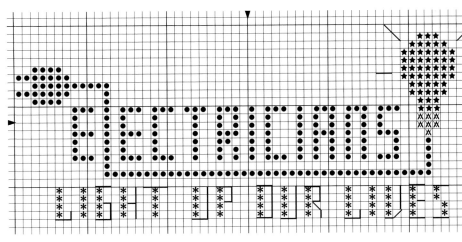

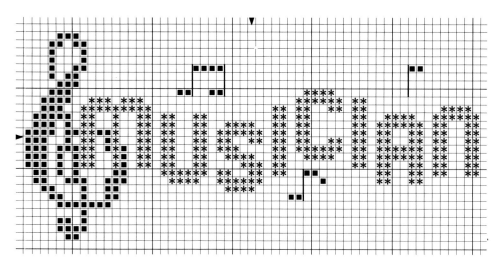

#48

Design size: 57 wide x 26 high

		Anchor	Coats	DMC
✱	= gray	235	8513	414
■	= black	403	8403	310
│	= Backstitch: black			

#49

Design size: 66 wide x 15 high

		Anchor	Coats	DMC
♥	= green	187	6186	958
	purple	94	4089	917
•	= French Knots: purple			
│	= Backstitch: purple			

#50

Design size: 61 wide x 21 high

		Anchor	Coats	DMC
✧	= lt red	35	3152	3705
▲	= dk red	19	3500	321
✗	= gray	235	8513	414
■	= gray-black	236	8514	3799
•	= French Knots: to match lettering			
│	= Backstitch:			

"are good therapists," nail polish
streaks, handle—dk red
"they...problems!"—gray-black

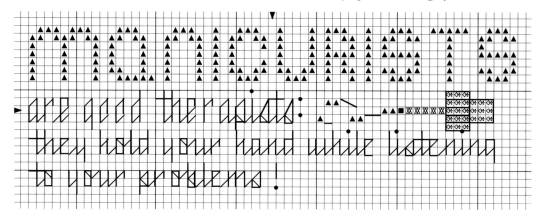

50
House Plant
Designs

If you have fingers that like to stitch, but you don't have a green thumb, here are designs that are great for adding the beauty of nature to your home, and you won't have to worry about overwatering.

Oregano Dill Rosemary Parsley Thyme

Chives

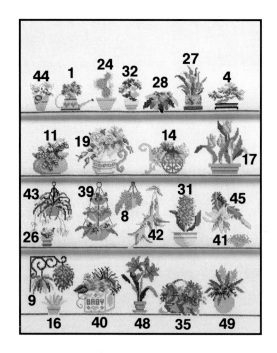

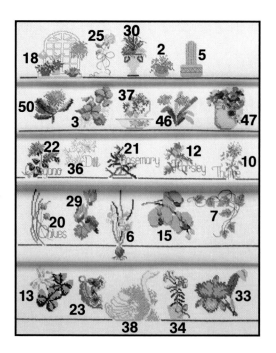

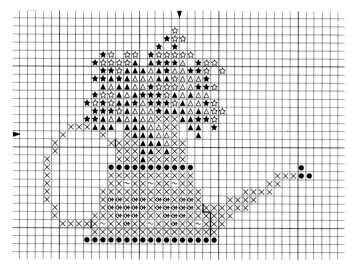

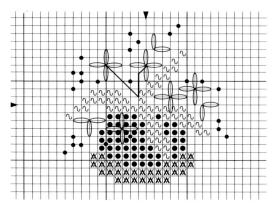

#1

Design size: 34 wide x 27 high

		Anchor	Coats	DMC
✿	= pink	28	3152	892
~	= yellow	289	2288	727
△	= lt green	240	6016	368
▲	= dk green	257	6018	988
☆	= lt blue	145	7021	809
★	= dk blue	147	7181	797
×	= lt blue-gray	343	7876	3752
●	= dk blue-gray	922	7980	930
|	= Backstitch: dk blue-gray			

#2

Design size: 21 wide x 20 high

		Anchor	Coats	DMC
	pink	28	3152	892
↻	= green	243	6018	703
	purple	99	4097	552
✕	= lt brown	347	3336	402
●	= dk brown	349	5309	3776
✛	= Lazy Daisies: pink			
•	= French Knots: purple			
|	= Backstitch: green			

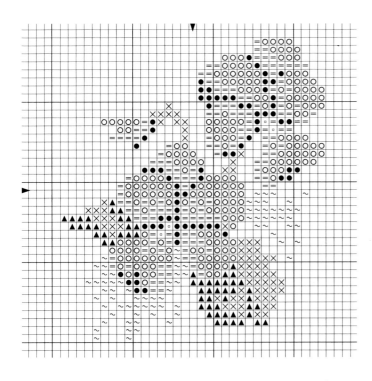

#3

Design size: 33 wide x 38 high

			Anchor	Coats	DMC
▫	=	yellow	289	2288	727
~	=	lt green	259	6250	772
✕	=	med green	255	6256	471
▲	=	dk green	258	6258	987
○	=	lt purple	96	4104	3608
=	=	med purple	98	4097	553
●	=	dk purple	101	4107	327

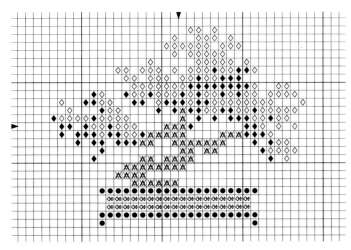

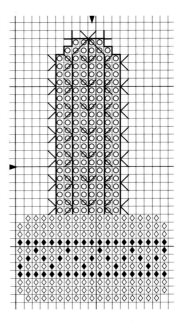

#4

Design size: 32 wide x 25 high

			Anchor	Coats	DMC
◇	=	lt green	214	6875	504
◆	=	dk green	245	6211	986
✤	=	rust	5975	2975	356
✖	=	brown	379	5379	840
●	=	black	403	8403	310

#5

Design size: 19 wide x 34 high

			Anchor	Coats	DMC
○	=	green	260	6266	3364
◇	=	lt brown	9575	3868	3341
◆	=	dk brown	5975	2975	356
		lt gray	399	8511	318
		med gray	235	8399	414
│	=	Backstitch:			
		spines—lt gray			
		vertical lines & outline			
		—med gray			

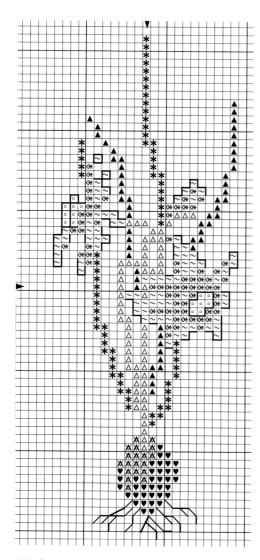

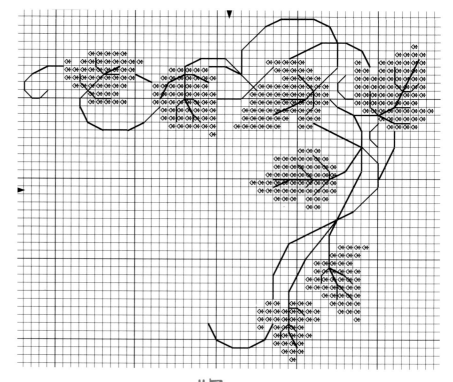

#7

Design size: 51 wide x 43 high

		Anchor	Coats	DMC
✢ =	lt green	241	6238	704
	dk green	245	6211	986
❘ =	Backstitch: dk green			

#6

Design size: 23 wide x 63 high

		Anchor	Coats	DMC
~ =	white	1	1001	blanc
	red	35	3012	3705
▫ =	yellow	289	2288	727
△ =	lt green	240	6016	368
✳ =	med green	242	6225	702
▲ =	dk green	245	6211	986
✢ =	blue	160	7159	519
✕ =	lt brown	369	5347	435
♥ =	med brown	358	5475	433
❘ =	Backstitch:			
	flower centers—red			
	petals—blue			
	roots—med brown			

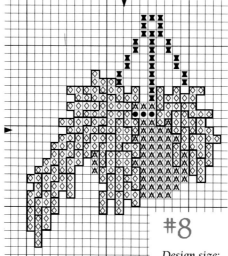

#8

Design size: 24 wide x 29 high

		Anchor	Coats	DMC
◇ =	lt green	260	6266	3364
	dk green	244	6226	702
✕ =	lt brown	9575	3868	3341
● =	dk brown	5975	2975	356
⌧ =	gray	235	8399	414
❘ =	Backstitch: dk green			

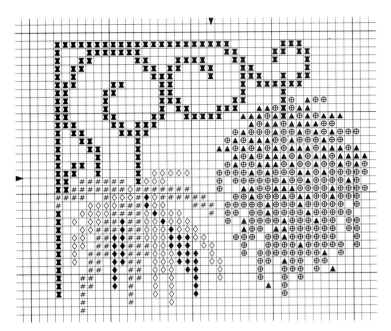

#9

Design size: 39 wide x 34 high

			Anchor	Coats	DMC
◇	=	lt green	240	6016	368
#	=	med green	257	6018	988
◆	=	dk green	245	6211	986
⊕	=	blue-green	877	6876	502
▲	=	purple	96	4104	3608
⏣	=	gray	400	8999	414

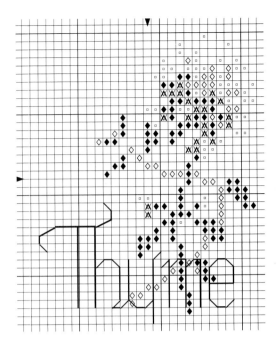

#10

Design size: 27 wide x 36 high

			Anchor	Coats	DMC
▫	=	lt pink	26	3126	894
⋇	=	med pink	28	3152	892
◇	=	lt green	253	6253	472
◆	=	dk green	256	6267	704
		brown	370	5349	975
|	=	Backstitch: brown			

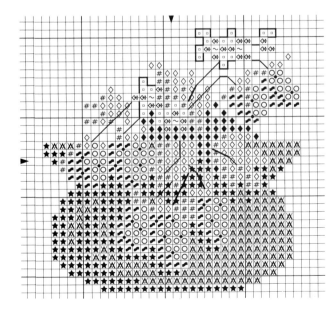

#11

Design size: 32 wide x 33 high

			Anchor	Coats	DMC
▫	=	white	1	1001	blanc
⋇	=	pink	26	3126	894
○	=	lt red	46	3046	666
◗	=	dk red	20	3072	498
~	=	yellow	305	2295	743
◇	=	lt green	240	6016	368
#	=	med green	245	6211	986
◆	=	dk green	878	6878	501
⋈	=	med gold	306	2307	725
★	=	dk gold	308	5308	782
•	=	French Knots: yellow			
|	=	Backstitch: flowers—pink stems— med green			

XXXXXXXXXXXXXXXXXXXXXXXXXXXX 169 XXXXXXXXXXXXXXXXXXXXXXXXXX

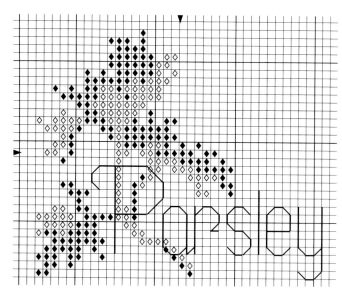

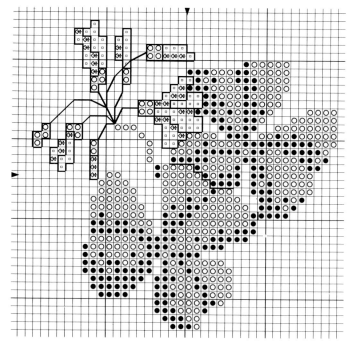

#12

Design size: 36 wide x 31 high

			Anchor	Coats	DMC
◇	=	lt green	260	6266	3364
◆	=	dk green	257	6018	988
		brown	352	5471	300
│	=	Backstitch: brown			

#13

Design size: 38 wide x 39 high

			Anchor	Coats	DMC
▫	=	white	1	1001	blanc
○	=	lt green	241	6238	704
●	=	dk green	218	6880	500
✣	=	blue	160	7159	519
│	=	Backstitch: stems—lt green flowers—blue			

#14

Design size: 45 wide x 30 high

			Anchor	Coats	DMC
✣	=	lt pink	24	3173	963
▩	=	med pink	27	3127	893
●	=	red	35	3012	3705
∧	=	lt yellow-green	253	6253	472
★	=	dk yellow-green	255	6256	471
◇	=	lt green	214	6875	504
⊕	=	med green	876	6879	503
■	=	dk green	878	6878	501
△	=	lt blue	145	7021	809
▲	=	dk blue	147	7181	797
✳	=	lt purple	96	4104	3608
◣	=	dk purple	99	4097	552
∿	=	tan	362	5942	729
◆	=	brown	370	5349	434

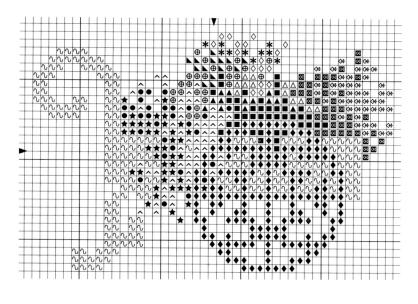

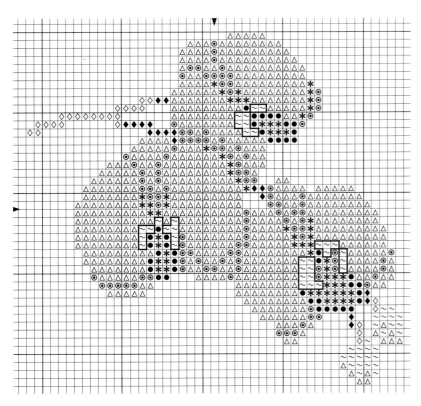

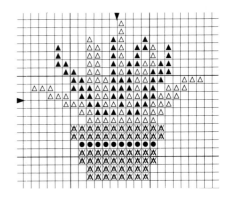

#15

Design size: 47 wide x 44 high

			Anchor	Coats	DMC
◇	=	lt green	215	6879	503
◆	=	dk green	879	6880	500
~	=	very lt purple	95	4104	554
△	=	lt purple	85	4085	3609
⊙	=	med purple	98	4097	553
✳	=	dk purple	94	4089	917
●	=	very dk purple	102	4101	550
|	=	Backstitch: very dk purple			

#16

Design size: 22 wide x 20 high

			Anchor	Coats	DMC
△	=	lt green	253	6253	472
▲	=	med green	241	6238	704
✺	=	lt brown	347	3336	402
●	=	dk brown	370	5349	975

#17

Design size: 48 wide x 48 high

			Anchor	Coats	DMC
▫	=	lt pink	25	3125	3326
◣	=	dk pink	28	3152	892
△	=	lt green	240	6016	368
✳	=	med green	257	6018	988
▲	=	dk green	245	6211	986
✕	=	lt rust	337	2338	3776
●	=	dk rust	351	3340	400

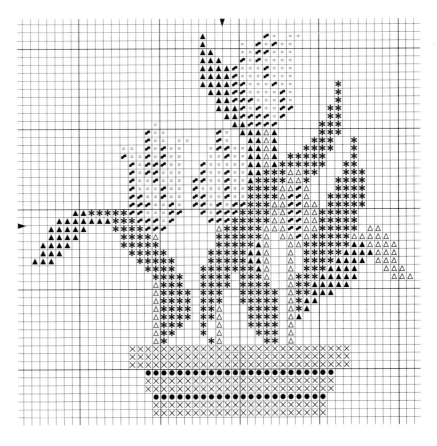

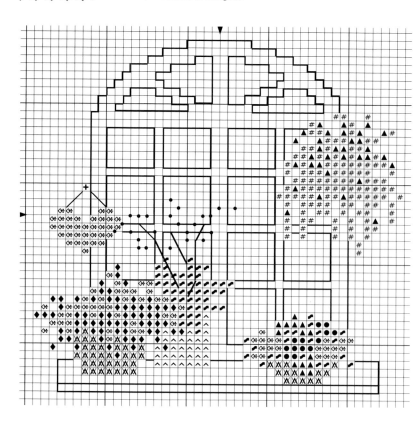

#18

Design size: 46 wide x 44 high

			Anchor	Coats	DMC
✧	=	pink	26	3126	894
⌃	=	yellow	891	2874	676
#	=	med yellow-green	255	6256	471
⬎	=	dk yellow-green	258	6258	987
◆	=	green	245	6211	986
▲	=	blue	145	7021	809
●	=	purple	98	4097	553
✛	=	med brown	349	5309	3776
⋈	=	dk brown	351	3340	400
•	=	French Knots: purple			
|	=	Backstitch:			

stems—dk yellow-green
heart hanger & window outline
   —med brown

#19

Design size: 51 wide x 44 high

			Anchor	Coats	DMC
⌃	=	lt cream	386	2386	745
⊥	=	med cream	891	2874	676
~	=	yellow	301	2296	744
△	=	med gold	307	5307	783
▲	=	dk gold	309	5309	781
▫	=	lt pink	23	3068	3713
⋈	=	med pink	27	3127	893
●	=	dk pink	29	3500	891
◇	=	lt green	259	6250	772
#	=	med green	257	6018	988
◆	=	dk green	245	6211	986
✕	=	blue-gray	976	7876	3752
✱	=	purple	98	4097	553
|	=	Backstitch: med green			

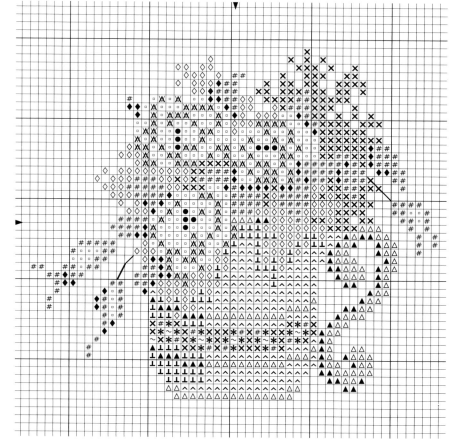

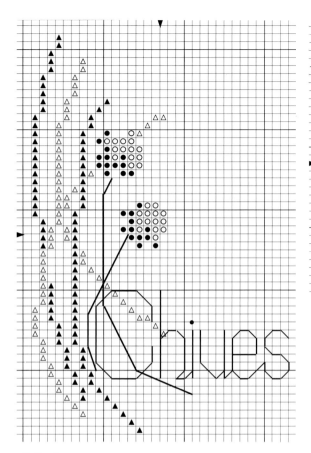

#20

Design size: 32 wide x 50 high

		Anchor	Coats	DMC
△	= lt green	215	6879	503
▲	= dk green	216	6876	502
○	= lt purple	96	4104	3608
●	= dk purple	99	4097	552
	rust	351	3340	400
•	= French Knot: rust			
		= Backstitch:			
	stems—dk green			
	lettering—rust			

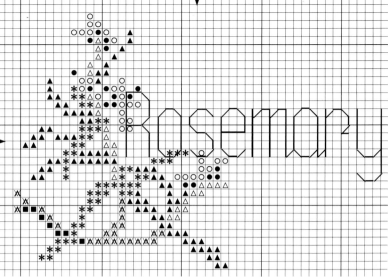

#21

Design size: 46 wide x 32 high

		Anchor	Coats	DMC
△	= lt green	260	6266	3364
✳	= med green	244	6226	702
▲	= dk green	879	6880	500
○	= lt blue	145	7021	809
●	= dk blue	147	7181	797
	rust	351	3340	400
✕	= lt brown	379	5379	840
■	= dk brown	936	5936	632
		= Backstitch: rust			

#22

Design size: 35 wide x 35 high

		Anchor	Coats	DMC
☆	= lt green	241	6238	704
★	= dk green	923	6228	699
△	= lt purple	97	4104	554
▲	= dk purple	100	4107	327
✕	= lt brown	349	5309	3776
	dk brown	352	5471	300
		= Backstitch: dk brown			

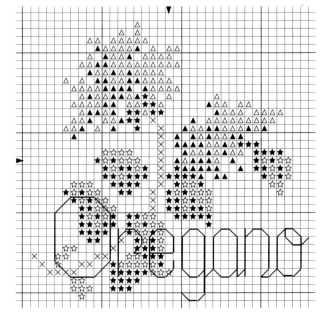

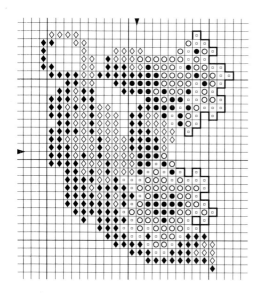

#23

Design size: 24 wide x 30 high

			Anchor	Coats	DMC
▫	=	white	1	1001	blanc
○	=	lt red	35	3012	3705
●	=	dk red	22	3021	814
◇	=	lt green	260	6266	3364
◆	=	dk green	257	6018	988
		gray	399	8511	318
❘	=	Backstitch: gray			

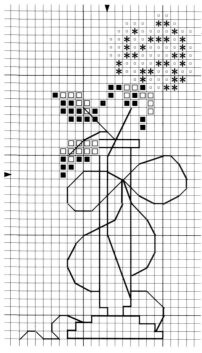

#24

Design size: 21 wide x 36 high

			Anchor	Coats	DMC
~	=	yellow	289	2288	727
◇	=	lt green	253	6253	472
⊕	=	med green	256	6267	704
◆	=	dk green	258	6258	987
⋇	=	lt rust	9575	3868	3341
●	=	dk rust	5975	2975	356
		lt gray	399	8511	318
		dk gray	400	8999	414
❘	=	Backstitch:			
		flower—lt rust			
		outer cactus spines—lt gray			
		inner cactus spines—dk gray			

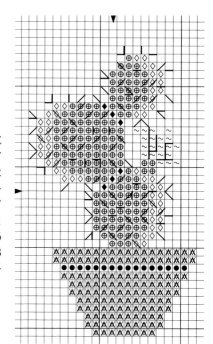

#25

Design size: 22 wide x 41 high

			Anchor	Coats	DMC
▫	=	yellow	301	2296	744
✶	=	gold	306	2307	725
☐	=	lt green	254	6001	3348
■	=	dk green	257	6018	988
		lt blue	160	7159	519
		dk blue	162	7162	517
❘	=	Backstitch:			
		stems—dk green			
		vase—lt blue			
		ribbon—dk blue			

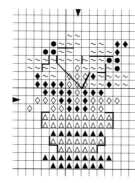

#26

Design size: 13 wide x 17 high

			Anchor	Coats	DMC
~	=	yellow	289	2288	727
◇	=	lt green	241	6238	704
◆	=	dk green	245	6211	986
△	=	lt blue	159	7976	800
▲	=	dk blue	146	7080	798
●	=	brown	936	5936	632
❘	=	Backstitch:			
		stems—dk green			
		pot—dk blue			
		flowers—brown			

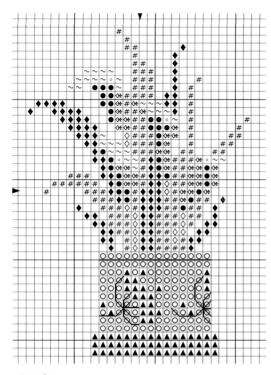

#27

Design size: 28 wide x 41 high

			Anchor	Coats	DMC
~	=	lt pink	24	3173	963
⊛	=	med pink	27	3127	893
●	=	dk pink	29	3500	891
□	=	yellow	305	2295	743
◇	=	lt green	253	6253	472
#	=	med green	257	6018	988
◆	=	dk green	245	6211	986
○	=	lt blue-gray	343	7876	3752
▲	=	med blue-gray	922	7980	930
│	=	Backstitch: med blue-gray			

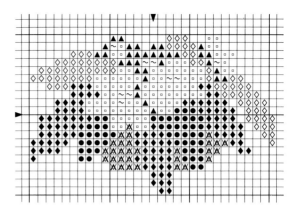

#28

Design size: 31 wide x 20 high

			Anchor	Coats	DMC
~	=	yellow	289	2288	727
◇	=	lt green	240	6016	368
●	=	med green	244	6226	702
◆	=	dk green	923	6228	699
□	=	lt blue	145	7021	809
▲	=	dk blue	147	7181	797
✖	=	tan	362	5942	729

#29

Design size: 22 wide x 45 high

			Anchor	Coats	DMC
∧	=	very lt green	214	6875	504
◇	=	lt green	215	6879	503
#	=	med green	877	6876	502
◆	=	dk green	879	6880	500
△	=	lt purple	85	4085	3609
+	=	med purple	97	4104	553
▲	=	dk purple	100	4107	327
✖	=	rust	349	5309	3776
│	=	Backstitch: med green			

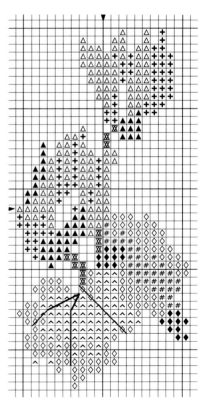

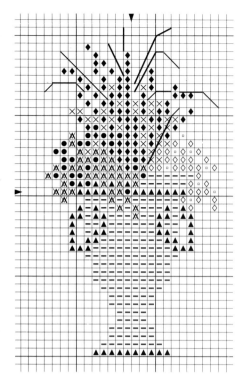

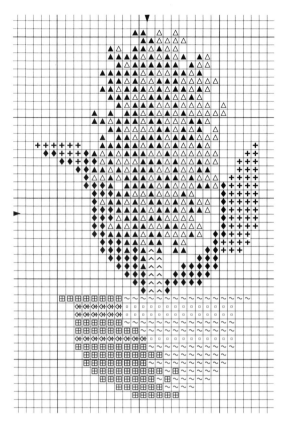

#30

Design size: 22 wide x 41 high

		Anchor	Coats	DMC
●	= red	47	3047	304
▫	= yellow	301	2296	744
◇	= lt green	241	6238	704
◆	= dk green	245	6211	986
✕	= lt yellow-green	254	6001	3348
✕	= med yellow-green	257	6018	988
─	= lt gray	234	8398	762
▲	= dk gray	400	8999	414
│	= Backstitch: dk green			

#31

Design size: 28 wide x 46 high

		Anchor	Coats	DMC
▫	= lt pink	27	3127	893
✧	= dk pink	28	3152	892
∧	= lt green	254	6001	3348
+	= med green	257	6018	988
◆	= dk green	245	6211	986
△	= lt blue	159	7976	800
▲	= med blue	146	7080	798
~	= lt tan	386	2386	745
⊞	= med tan	891	2874	676

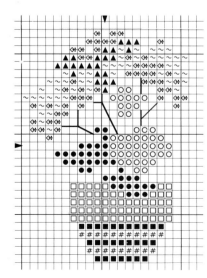

#32

Design size: 21 wide x 29 high

		Anchor	Coats	DMC
☐	= lt pink	23	3068	3713
■	= dk pink	25	3125	3326
○	= lt green	214	6875	504
●	= dk green	218	6880	500
~	= lt blue	159	7976	3325
✧	= med blue	162	7162	517
▲	= dk blue	148	7182	312
#	= rust	5975	2975	356
│	= Backstitch: dk green			

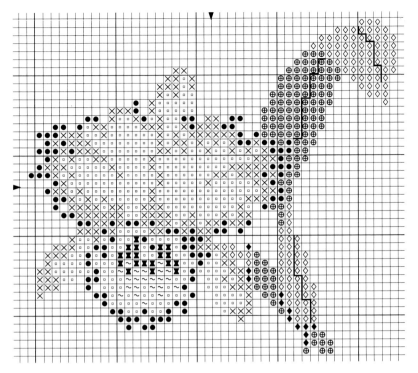

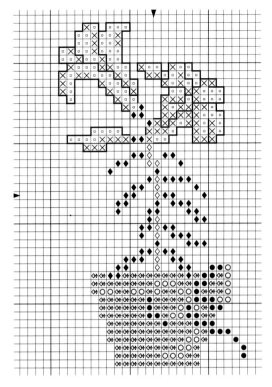

#33

Design size: 46 wide x 42 high

		Anchor	Coats	DMC
~	= yellow	301	2296	744
✗	= gold	306	2307	725
◇	= lt green	253	6253	472
⊕	= med green	257	6018	988
◆	= dk green	245	6211	986
▫	= lt purple	85	4085	3609
✕	= med purple	88	4092	718
●	= dk purple	94	4089	917
|	= Backstitch: dk green			

#34

Design size: 24 wide x 43 high

		Anchor	Coats	DMC
▫	= white	1	1001	blanc
✸	= pink	24	3173	963
◇	= lt green	242	6225	702
◆	= dk green	245	6211	986
✕	= blue	161	7977	813
○	= lt purple	96	4104	3608
●	= dk purple	99	4097	552
|	= Backstitch: blue			

#35

Design size: 42 wide x 32 high

		Anchor	Coats	DMC
~	= yellow	305	2295	743
◇	= lt green	260	6266	3364
+	= med green	257	6018	988
☆	= lt blue	160	7159	519
★	= dk blue	162	7162	517
△	= lt purple	96	4104	3608
○	= med purple	99	4097	552
▲	= dk purple	101	4107	550
✶	= lt brown	378	5578	841
●	= dk brown	936	5936	632

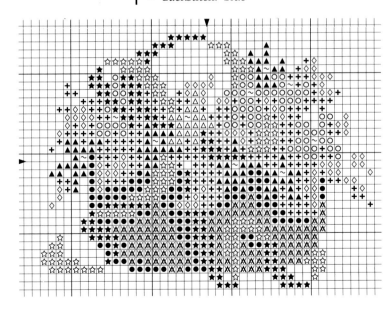

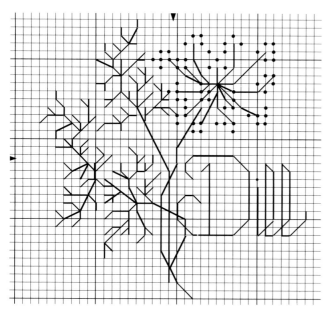

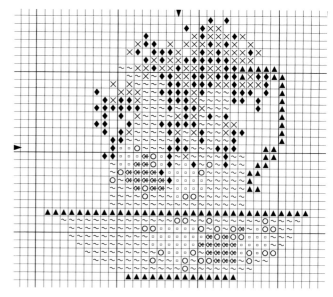

#36

Design size: 33 wide x 35 high

	Anchor	Coats	DMC
yellow	291	2298	444
green	255	6256	471
brown	370	5349	975

- • = French Knots:
  flower—yellow
  lettering—brown
- | = Backstitch:
  stems—green
  lettering—brown

#37

Design size: 33 wide x 33 high

			Anchor	Coats	DMC
□	=	lt pink	25	3125	3326
✳	=	med pink	27	3127	893
~	=	yellow	386	2386	745
▲	=	gold	306	2307	725
○	=	lt green	255	6256	471
◆	=	dk green	258	6258	987
×	=	blue	160	7159	519

#38

Design size: 49 wide x 45 high

			Anchor	Coats	DMC
~	=	white	1	1001	blanc
✳	=	pink	26	3126	894
✳	=	green	260	6266	3364
◊	=	lt blue	159	7976	800
		med blue	160	7159	519
		=	Backstitch: med blue			

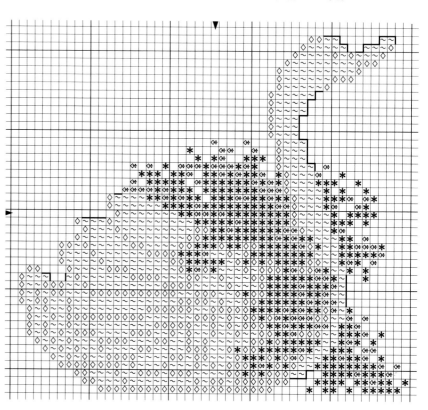

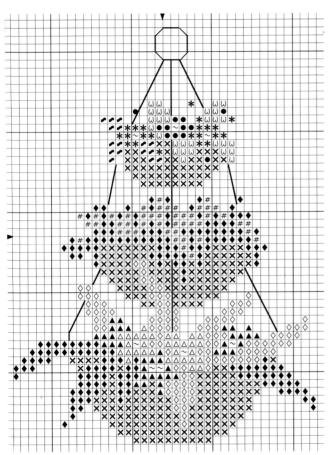

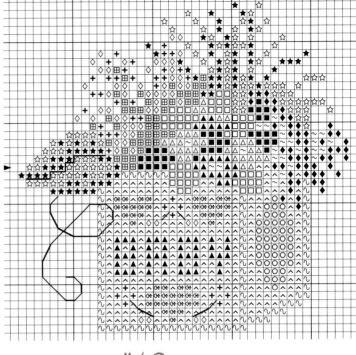

#39

Design size: 38 wide x 52 high

		Anchor	Coats	DMC
#	= pink	25	3125	3326
~	= yellow	302	2303	742
◇	= med green	240	6016	368
◆	= dk green	257	6018	988
ω	= med blue-green	877	6876	502
✎	= dk blue-green	878	6878	501
△	= lt blue	145	7021	809
▲	= dk blue	147	7181	797
✳	= lt purple	96	4104	3608
●	= dk purple	99	4097	552
✕	= brown	338	3337	922
	black	403	8403	310
❘	= Backstitch: black			

#40

Design size: 42 wide x 41 high

		Anchor	Coats	DMC
∧	= white	1	1001	blanc
◈	= pink	25	3125	3326
~	= yellow	289	2288	727
□	= lt yel-green	254	6001	3348
■	= dk yel-green	257	6018	988
◇	= lt green	240	6016	368
⊞	= med green	242	6225	702
◆	= dk green	245	6211	986
	very dk green	923	6228	699
☆	= med blue-green	216	6876	502
★	= dk blue-green	218	6880	500
○	= lt blue	159	7976	800
+	= med blue	146	7080	798
△	= lt purple	96	4104	3608
▲	= dk purple	99	4097	552
∿	= tan	347	3336	402
❘	= Backstitch:			
	leaf stems—lt green			
	leaf vein & vine—very dk green			

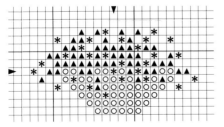

#41

Design size: 21 wide x 11 high

		Anchor	Coats	DMC
▲	= green	241	6238	704
✳	= purple	98	4097	553
○	= tan	362	5942	729

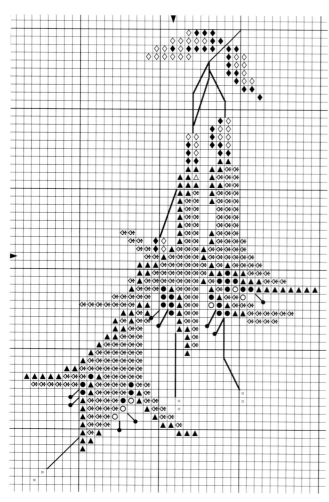

#42

Design size: 37 wide x 57 high

		Anchor	Coats	DMC
⚘ =	lt pink	25	3125	3326
▲ =	dk pink	29	3500	891
▫ =	yellow	301	2296	744
◇ =	lt green	254	6001	3348
◆ =	dk green	256	6267	704
○ =	lt purple	97	4104	554
● =	dk purple	100	4107	327
• =	French Knots: yellow			
│ =	Backstitch: dk green			

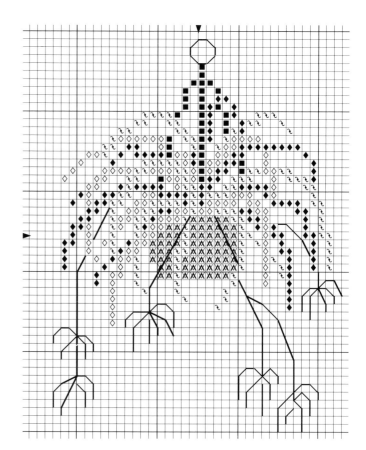

#43

Design size: 36 wide x 49 high

		Anchor	Coats	DMC
◇ =	lt green	254	6001	3348
~ =	med green	244	6226	702
◆ =	dk green	878	6878	501
⋈ =	brown	349	5309	3776
■ =	black	403	8403	310
│ =	Backstitch:			
	stems—med green			
	hook—black			

#44

Design size: 20 wide x 27 high

		Anchor	Coats	DMC
~ =	lt pink	24	3173	963
⧓ =	dk pink	27	3127	893
□ =	lt green	214	6875	504
■ =	dk green	878	6878	501
⋈ =	lt blue-gray	343	7876	3752
● =	dk blue-gray	922	7980	930
• =	French Knots: dk pink			
│ =	Backstitch: dk green			

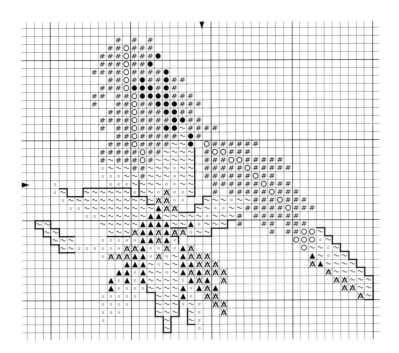

#45

Design size: 42 wide x 37 high

		Anchor	Coats	DMC
~	= very lt pink	23	3068	3713
□	= lt pink	25	3125	3326
◈	= med pink	27	3127	893
▲	= dk pink	29	3500	891
O	= lt green	240	6016	368
✳	= med green	216	6876	502
●	= dk green	218	6880	500
|	= Backstitch: med pink			

#46

Design size: 35 wide x 33 high

		Anchor	Coats	DMC
☆	= lt orange	328	2323	3341
★	= dk orange	332	2330	946
✳	= yellow-green	253	6253	472
^	= lt green	240	6016	368
⋈	= med green	243	6018	703
▲	= dk green	245	6211	986

#47

Design size: 35 wide x 39 high

		Anchor	Coats	DMC
O	= med red	9046	3047	666
●	= dk red	20	3072	498
#	= orange	332	2330	946
□	= yellow	289	2288	727
△	= lt green	254	6001	3348
✕	= med green	243	6018	703
▲	= dk green	923	6228	699
■	= very dk green	878	6878	501
⋈	= lt gray	234	8398	762
★	= med gray	399	8511	318
	dk gray	400	8999	414
|	= Backstitch: dk gray			

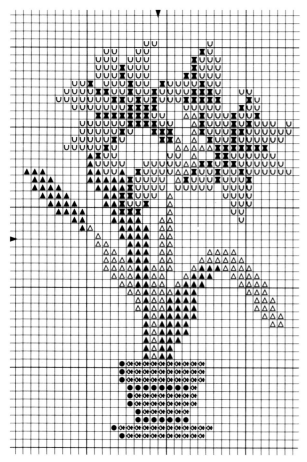

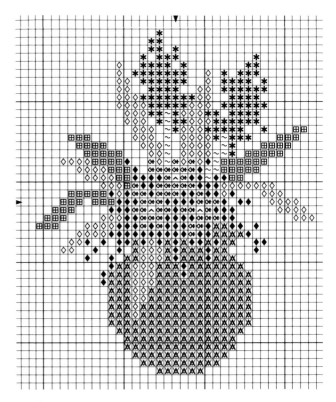

#48

Design size: 34 wide x 50 high

			Anchor	Coats	DMC
U	=	lt red	35	3012	3705
ⵣ	=	dk red	20	3072	498
△	=	lt green	242	6225	702
▲	=	dk green	923	6228	699
⋇	=	lt brown	338	3337	3776
●	=	dk brown	351	3340	400

#49

Design size: 35 wide x 43 high

			Anchor	Coats	DMC
∧	=	cream	386	2386	745
◇	=	lt green	257	6018	988
⊞	=	med green	244	6226	702
◆	=	dk green	218	6880	500
~	=	yellow-green	260	6266	3364
⟡	=	blue	161	7977	813
✳	=	purple	96	4104	3608
⋊	=	brown	347	3336	402

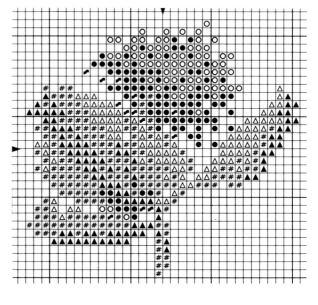

#50

Design size: 34 wide x 32 high

			Anchor	Coats	DMC
○	=	lt orange	328	2323	3341
●	=	med orange	35	3012	3705
◣	=	dk orange	19	3500	321
△	=	lt green	260	6266	3364
#	=	med green	244	6226	702
▲	=	dk green	879	6880	500

50
Patriotic
Designs

Show your true colors by stitching these patriotic designs—from cute teddy bears and patriotic hearts to humorous sayings and military insignias.

MILITARY FAMILY

GOD BLESS AMERICA

"LET FREEDOM RING"

I ♥ America

America is... where I hang ...my ♥

Proud to be an American

America -
God Shed his
grace on thee

THESE COLORS DON'T RUN

KP DUTY

Land of the free
Home of the brave

Home Sweet America ♥

USA

MESS HALL

U.S. ARMY

READY, WILLING, ABLE

U.S. MARINES

A FEW GOOD MEN

U.S. AIR FORCE

WINGS OF VICTORY

U.S. NAVY

PROUD TO SERVE

#1

Design size: 32 wide x 29 high

		DMC	Anchor	Coats
▫ =	cream	746	386	2386
✧ =	pink	776	24	3125
© =	lt red	352	8	3008
	med red	350	11	3111
● =	dk red	304	47	3410
~ =	peach	754	778	3146
○ =	yellow	725	306	2307
★ =	blue	825	162	7979
☐ =	tan	712	387	5387
■ =	gray-black	3799	236	8999
✳ =	French Knots: dk red			
⏐ =	Backstitch:			
	lettering—dk red			
	hair—med red			
	angel—gray-black			

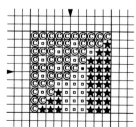

#2

Design size: 10 wide x 10 high

		DMC	Anchor	Coats
▫ =	white	blanc	2	1001
★ =	red	321	9046	3500
© =	blue	825	162	7979

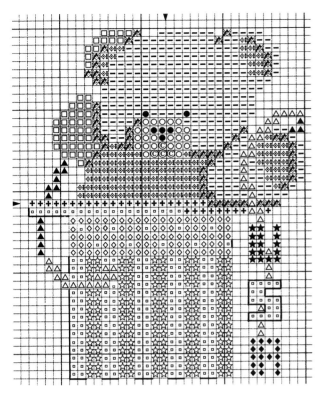

#3

Design size: 34 wide x 43 high

		DMC	Anchor	Coats
□	= white	blanc	2	1001
☆	= lt red	321	9046	3500
★	= dk red	815	43	3073
△	= yellow	726	295	2295
▲	= gold	783	307	5309
◇	= lt blue	809	130	7021
◆	= dk blue	797	132	7100
O	= lt tan	739	387	5387
✤	= med tan	436	363	5943
©	= dk tan	434	309	5365
−	= very lt brown	437	362	5942
□	= lt brown	435	369	5371
✘	= med brown	433	371	5471
●	= dk brown	838	380	5381
+	= gray	318	399	8511
		= Backstitch: gray			

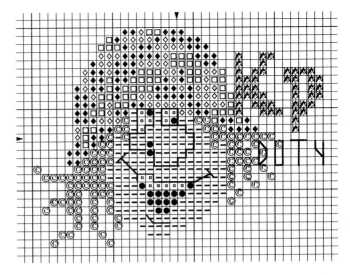

#4

Design size: 36 wide x 27 high

		DMC	Anchor	Coats
□	= white	blanc	2	1001
©	= red	347	13	3013
−	= lt peach	754	778	3146
	dk peach	352	8	3008
◇	= lt green	772	264	6253
◆	= dk green	3363	861	6269
□	= lt brown	3772	679	5579
✘	= dk brown	632	936	5936
●	= very dk brown	838	380	5381
		= Backstitch:
		nose—dk peach
		eyes, mouth & chin—very dk brown
		lettering—very dk brown (2 strands)

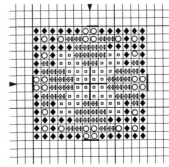

#5

Design size: 14 wide x 14 high

		DMC	Anchor	Coats
O	= cream	746	386	2386
✤	= med red	321	9046	3500
	dk red	815	43	3073
□	= lt blue	813	160	7161
◆	= dk blue	824	164	7182
		= Backstitch:
		inside lines—dk red
		outside edges—dk bue

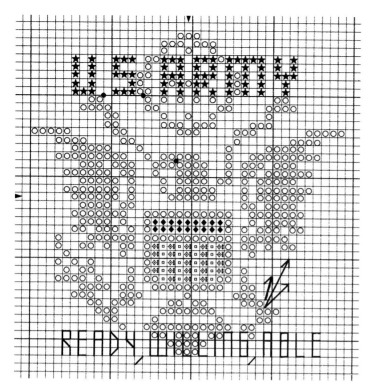

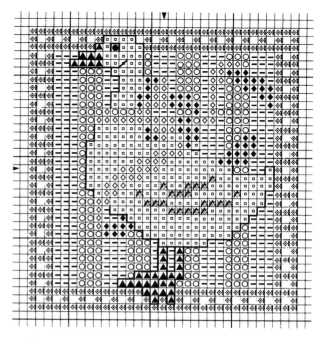

#6

Design size: 39 wide x 41 high

			DMC	Anchor	Coats
□	=	white	blanc	2	1001
✳	=	red	321	9046	3500
O	=	gold	725	306	2307
◆	=	lt blue	809	130	7021
★	=	dk blue	797	132	7100
•	=	French Knots:			
		after "U" & bird's eye—dk blue			
		after "S"—gold			
│	=	Backstitch:			
		arrows—gold			
		lettering—dk blue			

#7

Design size: 33 wide x 35 high

			DMC	Anchor	Coats
□	=	white	blanc	2	1001
O	=	cream	746	386	2386
—	=	pink	776	24	3125
◇	=	lt red	3688	66	3087
◆	=	dk red	3685	70	3089
▲	=	orange	3341	328	2323
✳	=	blue	826	161	7180
⋈	=	gray	318	399	8511
●	=	gray-black	3799	236	8999
│	=	Backstitch: gray			

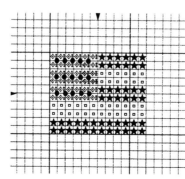

#8

Design size: 12 wide x 10 high

			DMC	Anchor	Coats
□	=	white	blanc	2	1001
★	=	red	304	47	3410
✳	=	blue	826	161	7180
•	=	French Knots: white			

#9

Design size: 30 wide x 42 high

		DMC	Anchor	Coats
□	= white	blanc	2	1001
~	= med peach	754	778	3146
	dk peach	351	11	3011
◆	= red	304	47	3410
☆	= blue	825	162	7979
©	= med gray	318	399	8511
	dk gray	414	400	8399
■	= black	310	403	8403
|	= Backstitch:			

mouth & nose—dk peach
hat brim & beard—dk gray
eyes—black

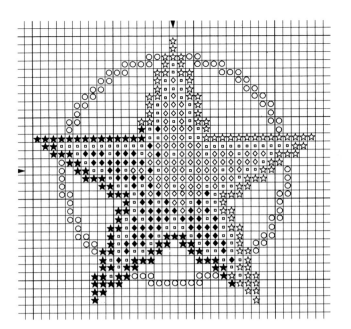

#10

Design size: 35 wide x 33 high

		DMC	Anchor	Coats
□	= white	blanc	2	1001
☆	= lt red	321	9046	3500
★	= dk red	815	43	3073
O	= yellow	725	306	2307
◇	= lt blue	809	130	7021
◆	= dk blue	797	132	7100

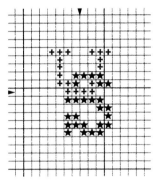

#11

Design size: 8 wide x 11 high

		DMC	Anchor	Coats
+	= pink	3712	9	3071
★	= blue	826	161	7180

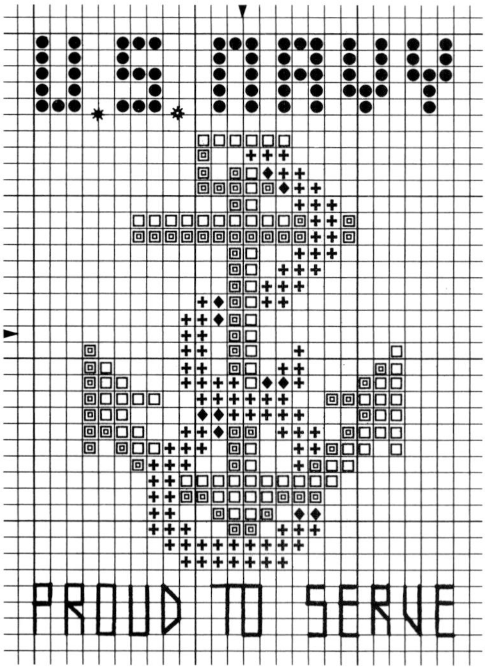

#12

Design size: 26 wide x 37 high

			DMC	Anchor	Coats
□	=	med gold	725	306	2307
▣	=	dk gold	783	307	5309
●	=	blue	797	132	7100
✚	=	rust	400	352	3340
◆	=	brown	838	380	5381
✵	=	French Knots: blue			
|	=	Backstitch: blue			

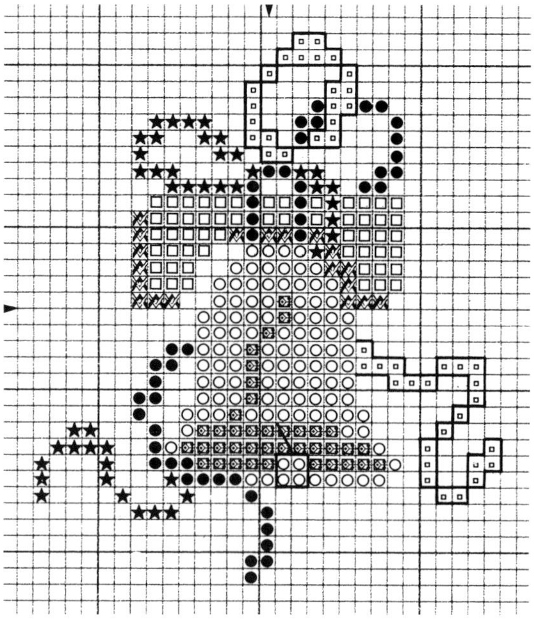

#13

Design size: 29 wide x 34 high

			DMC	Anchor	Coats
▫	=	white	blanc	2	1001
●	=	red	347	13	3013
★	=	blue	825	162	7979
□	=	lt brown	435	369	5371
▩	=	med brown	433	371	5471
○	=	lt blue-gray	932	920	7050
▣	=	dk blue-gray	930	922	7980
|	=	Backstitch: dk blue-gray			

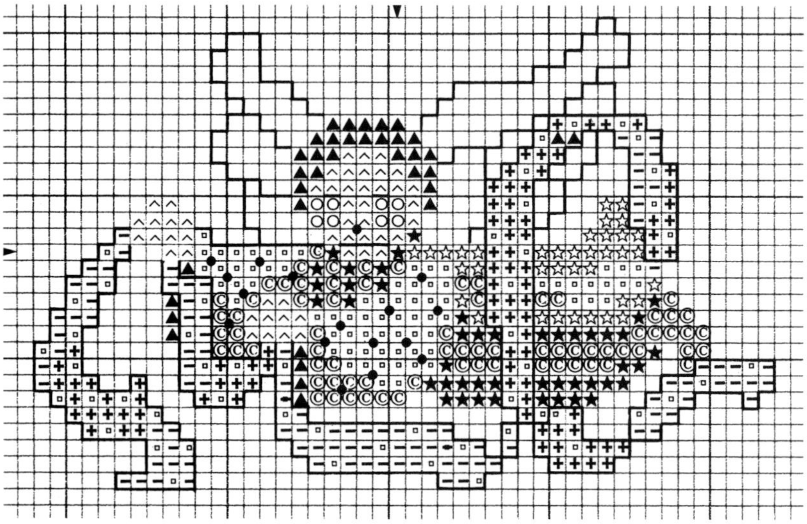

#14

Design size: 20 wide x 14 high

			DMC	Anchor	Coats
▫	=	white	blanc	2	1001
☆	=	red	347	13	3013
○	=	lt blue	826	1621	7180
◆	=	dk blue	824	164	7182
◈	=	tan	738	372	5372

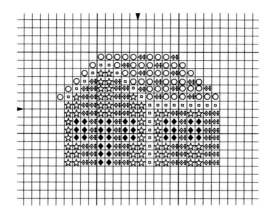

#15

Design size: 46 wide x 29 high

			DMC	Anchor	Coats
▫	=	white	blanc	2	1001
O	=	med pink	776	24	3125
☆	=	dk pink	335	41	3153
★	=	red	815	43	3073
∧	=	peach	754	778	3146
		gold	742	303	2303
−	=	lt blue	813	160	7161
+	=	med blue	825	162	7979
		dk blue	824	164	7182
©	=	lt brown	841	378	5578
▲	=	dk brown	632	936	5936
•	=	French Knots: red			
|	=	Backstitch:			

wings—gold
ribbon—dk blue
sleeve & neck—lt brown
eyes—dk brown

#16

Design size: 32 wide x 35 high

			DMC	Anchor	Coats
▫	=	white	blanc	2	1001
✳	=	pink	3712	9	3071
◉	=	lt red	347	13	3013
●	=	dk red	815	43	3073
□	=	lt yellow	744	301	2296
▣	=	med yellow	725	306	2307
▲	=	green	905	258	6239
☆	=	lt blue	809	130	7021
◆	=	dk blue	797	132	7100
×	=	lt brown	437	362	5942
✖	=	med brown	435	369	5371
■	=	dk brown	300	352	5471
−	=	lt gray	415	398	8398
+	=	med gray	414	400	8399
|	=	Backstitch:			

stems—green
lettering—dk blue
body—med brown
mouth—dk brown
hat—med gray

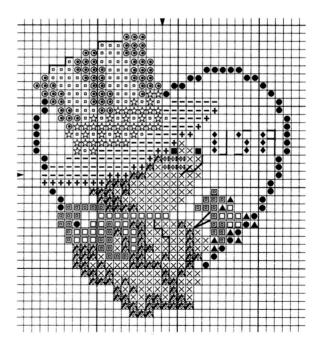

#17

Design size: 15 wide x 11 high

		DMC	Anchor	Coats
★	= red	815	43	3073
✿	= blue	797	132	7100
•	= French Knots: red			
│	= Backstitch:			
	"Born" & "U.S.A."—red			
	"in the"—blue			

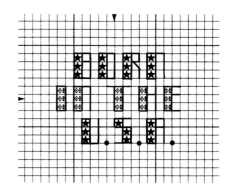

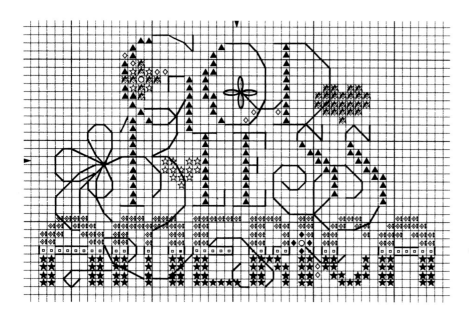

#18

Design size: 49 wide x 31 high

		DMC	Anchor	Coats
▫	= white	blanc	2	1001
☆	= lt pink	776	24	3125
✖	= dk pink	335	41	3153
★	= red	304	47	3410
○	= gold	742	303	2303
◇	= green	702	239	6226
✿	= blue	798	137	7080
	blue-gray	932	920	7050
◆	= purple	553	98	4097
▲	= brown	632	936	5936
✛	= Lazy Daisy: purple			
│	= Backstitch:			
	bow—gold			
	stems—green			
	"America"—blue-gray			
	lettering—brown			

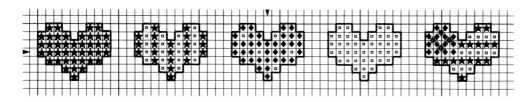

#19

Design size: 57 wide x 7 high

		DMC	Anchor	Coats
▫	= white	blanc	2	1001
★	= red	321	9046	3500
◆	= blue	797	132	7100
	blue-gray	931	921	7052
✳	= French Knots: white			
│	= Backstitch: blue-gray			

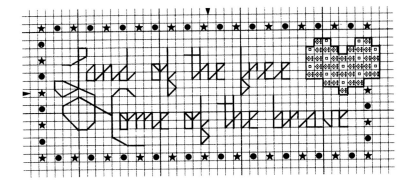

#20

Design size: 42 wide x 17 high

			DMC	Anchor	Coats
▫	=	white	blanc	2	1001
●	=	red	321	9046	3500
◈	=	lt blue	798	137	7080
★	=	dk blue	797	132	7100
		brown	632	936	5936
		= Backstitch:			
		lettering—brown			
		heart—lt blue			

#21

Design size: 52 wide x 13 high

			DMC	Anchor	Coats
▫	=	white	blanc	2	1001
★	=	med red	347	13	3013
		dk red	815	43	3073
◆	=	blue	826	161	7180
◈	=	lt brown	407	914	3883
✖	=	dk brown	632	936	5936
		= Backstitch:			
		hearts—red			
		lt brown lettering—lt brown			
		dk brown lettering—dk brown			

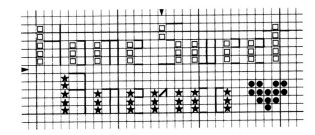

#22

Design size: 31 wide x 11 high

			DMC	Anchor	Coats
●	=	red	304	47	3410
★	=	blue	826	161	7180
□	=	brown	434	309	5365
		= Backstitch:			
		blue lettering—blue			
		brown lettering—brown			

xxxxxxxxxxxxxxxxxxxxxxxxx 193 xxxxxxxxxxxxxxxxxxxxxxxx

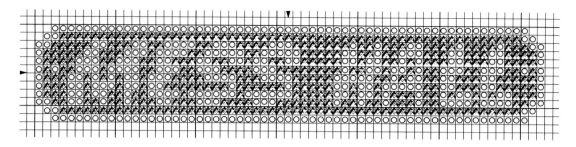

#23

Design size: 63 wide x 12 high

		DMC	Anchor	Coats
O =	gold	744	301	2296
✗ =	brown	433	371	5471

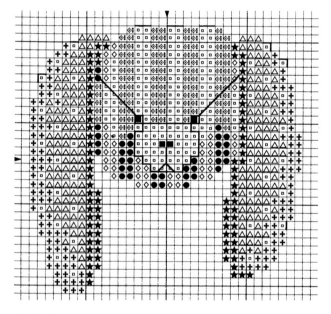

#24

Design size: 34 wide x 33 high

		DMC	Anchor	Coats
▫ =	white	blanc	2	1001
✾ =	med red	321	9046	3500
● =	dk red	815	43	3073
△ =	lt blue	827	159	7159
+ =	med blue	826	161	7180
★ =	dk blue	824	164	7182
◇ =	tan	739	387	5387
■ =	black	310	403	8403
	=	Backstitch:			

ears & top of head—med blue
face—black

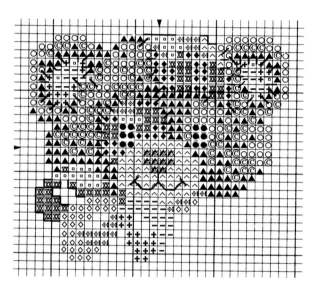

#25

Design size: 32 wide x 28 high

		DMC	Anchor	Coats
▫ =	white	blanc	2	1001
^ =	cream	739	387	5387
◇ =	lt red	3712	9	3071
✾ =	med red	304	47	3410
◆ =	dk red	815	43	3073
– =	lt blue	809	130	7021
+ =	dk blue	797	132	7100
O =	lt brown	437	362	5942
© =	med brown	435	369	5371
▲ =	dk brown	300	352	5471
✗ =	very dk brown	433	371	5374
● =	brown-black	3371	382	5382
✗ =	lt gray	415	398	8398
	med gray	414	400	8399
	=	Backstitch:			

ribbon—med gray
mouth—very dk brown
stitching—brown-black (2 strands)

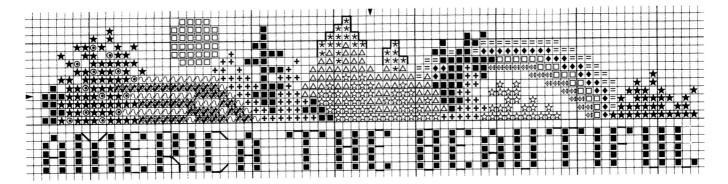

#26

Design size: 81 wide x 19 high

		DMC	Anchor	Coats
★	= white	blanc	2	1001
⊕	= lt red	3712	9	3071
⊙	= dk red	304	47	3410
□	= yellow	726	295	2295
∿	= lt yellow-green	704	256	6238
☆	= med yellow-green	905	258	6239
+	= med green	702	239	6226
★	= dk green	700	229	6227
■	= very dk green	890	879	6021
◆	= blue	809	130	7021
△	= blue-gray	930	922	7980
=	= purple	554	96	4104
✖	= rust	400	352	3340
|	= Backstitch: very dk green			

#27

Design size: 50 wide x 43 high

		DMC	Anchor	Coats
▫	= cream	746	386	2386
☆	= lt rose	3688	66	3087
★	= dk rose	3685	70	3089
◇	= lt blue	809	130	7021
◆	= dk blue	797	132	7100
⊕	= tan	738	372	5372
|	= Backstitch: lt blue			

#28

Design size: 42 wide x 49 high

		DMC	Anchor	Coats
O	= gold	725	306	2307
★	= blue	797	132	7100
•	= French Knots: blue			
│	= Backstitch: blue			

#29

Design size: 19 wide x 22 high

		DMC	Anchor	Coats
☆	= pink	335	41	3153
	red	815	43	3073
	blue	797	132	7100
•	= French Knots: to match lettering			
│	= Backstitch:			
	"America" & dashes—red			
	remaining lettering—blue			

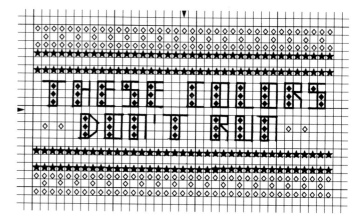

#30

Design size: 37 wide x 21 high

		DMC	Anchor	Coats
★	= red	304	47	3410
◇	= lt blue	826	161	7180
◆	= dk blue	824	164	7182
│	= Backstitch: dk blue			

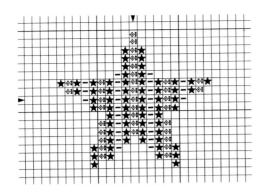

#31

Design size: 19 wide x 17 high

		DMC	Anchor	Coats
★	= red	304	47	3410
✧	= blue	826	161	7180
—	= tan	738	372	5372

#32

Design size: 31 wide x 21 high

		DMC	Anchor	Coats
▫	= white	blanc	2	1001
☆	= lt red	3712	9	3071
+	= dk red	347	13	3013
△	= lt green	772	264	6253
▲	= dk green	3363	861	6269
◇	= lt blue	932	920	7050
✧	= med blue	930	922	7980
—	= brown	300	352	5471

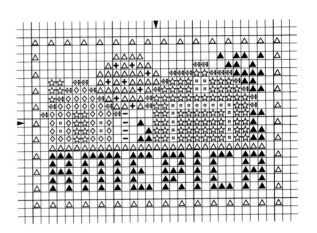

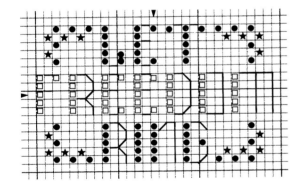

#33

Design size: 29 wide x 17 high

		DMC	Anchor	Coats
●	= red	304	47	3410
□	= lt blue	809	130	7021
★	= dk blue	797	132	7100
|	= Backstitch:			
	blue lettering—lt blue			
	red lettering—red			

#34

Design size: 19 wide x 17 high

		DMC	Anchor	Coats
▫	= white	blanc	2	1001
+	= red	304	47	3410
✧	= blue	813	160	7161
	blue-gray	930	922	7980
|	= Backstitch: blue-gray			

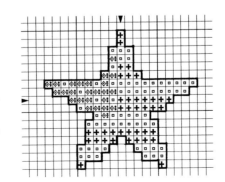

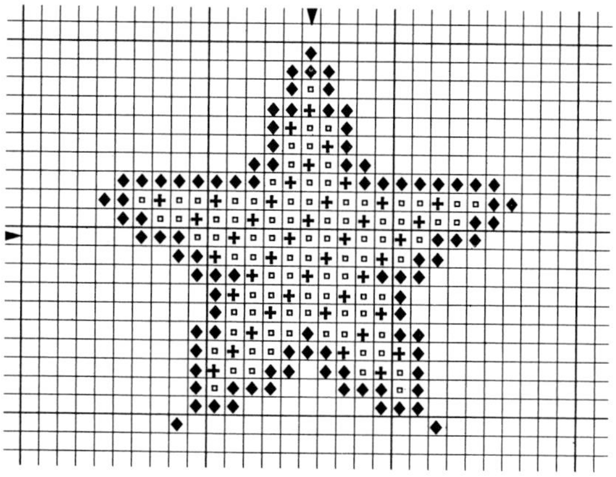

#35

Design size: 23 wide x 21 high

		DMC	Anchor	Coats
▫ =	white	blanc	2	1001
+ =	red	304	47	3410
♦ =	blue	798	137	7080

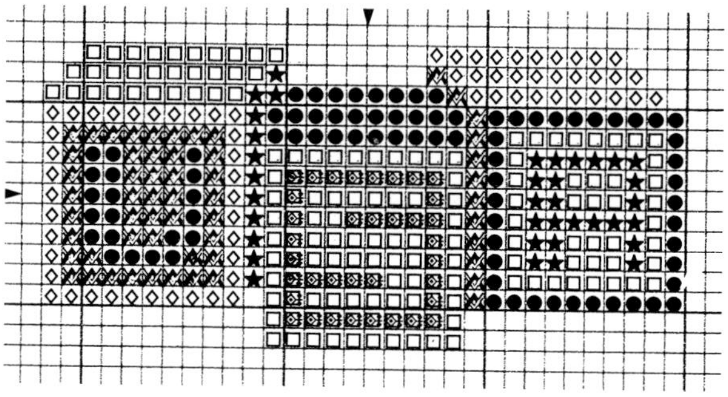

#36

Design size: 32 wide x 15 high

		DMC	Anchor	Coats
⊠ =	pink	335	41	3153
● =	red	815	43	3073
◇ =	lt blue	813	160	7161
★ =	dk blue	825	162	7979
□ =	tan	738	372	5372
✗ =	brown	436	363	5943

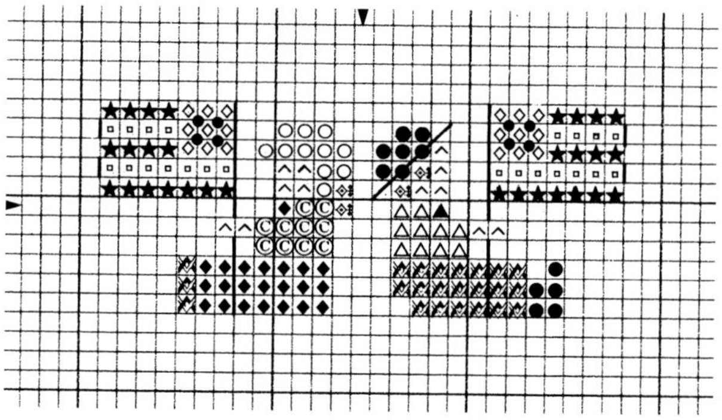

#37

Design size: 27 wide x 11 high

		DMC	Anchor	Coats
▫ =	white	blanc	2	1001
○ =	very lt pink	776	24	3125
© =	lt pink	335	41	3153
♦ =	dk pink	304	47	3410
★ =	red	321	9046	3500
^ =	peach	754	778	3146
◈ =	gold	436	363	5943
◇ =	blue	825	162	7979
△ =	lt blue-gray	932	920	7050
▲ =	med blue-gray	930	922	7980
✗ =	med brown	632	936	5936
● =	dk brown	839	360	5360

• = French Knots: white

| = Backstitch:
flag—lt blue-gray
flag poles & hat—dk brown

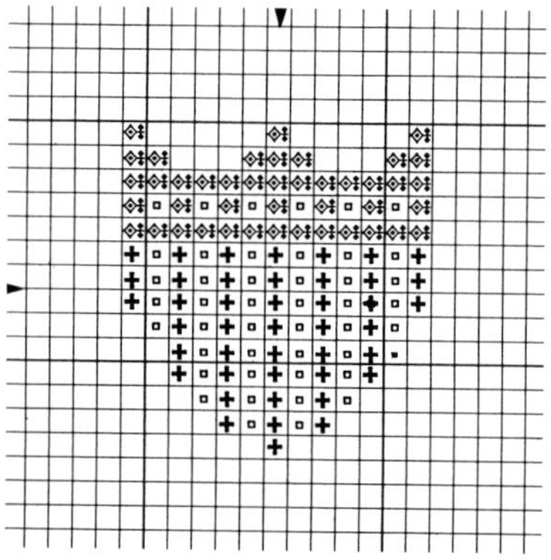

#38

Design size: 13 wide x 14 high

		DMC	Anchor	Coats
▫ =	white	blanc	2	1001
+ =	red	347	13	3013
◈ =	blue	826	161	7180

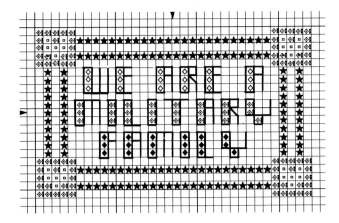

#39

Design size: 34 wide x 21 high

			DMC	Anchor	Coats
□	=	cream	746	386	2386
★	=	red	321	9046	3500
◇	=	lt blue	809	130	7021
✿	=	med blue	798	137	7080
◆	=	dk blue	797	132	7100
|	=	Backstitch:			

1st line—lt blue
2nd line—med blue
3rd line—dk blue

#40

Design size: 35 wide x 13 high

			DMC	Anchor	Coats
✚	=	med red	335	41	3153
★	=	dk red	304	47	3410
✿	=	med blue	813	160	7161
◆	=	dk blue	825	162	7979
□	=	tan	437	362	5942
△	=	brown	434	309	5365

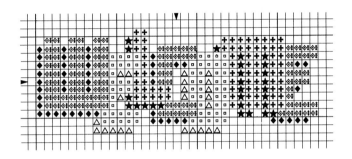

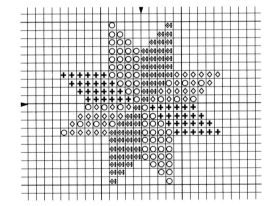

#41

Design size: 20 wide x 20 high

			DMC	Anchor	Coats
✚	=	red	304	47	3410
◇	=	lt blue	813	160	7161
✿	=	med blue	825	162	7979
O	=	tan	437	362	5942

#42

Design size: 40 wide x 17 high

			DMC	Anchor	Coats
‒	=	cream	746	386	2386
★	=	red	304	47	3410
△	=	blue	797	132	7100
		blue-gray	931	921	7052
|	=	Backstitch: blue-gray			

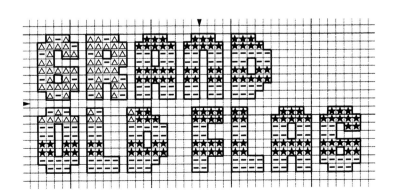

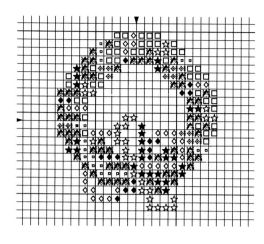

#43

Design size: 20 wide x 22 high

			DMC	Anchor	Coats
▫	=	white	blanc	2	1001
☆	=	lt red	321	9046	3500
★	=	dk red	815	43	3073
◇	=	lt blue	809	130	7021
◆	=	dk blue	798	137	7080
□	=	lt brown	841	378	5578
✖	=	dk brown	839	360	5360
✣	=	gray	415	398	8398

#44

Design size: 39 wide x 22 high

			DMC	Anchor	Coats
☆	=	pink	776	24	3125
		green	703	238	6238
✖	=	brown	3772	936	5579
•	=	French Knot: green			
|	=	Backstitch:			
		"America"—green			
		"I"—brown			

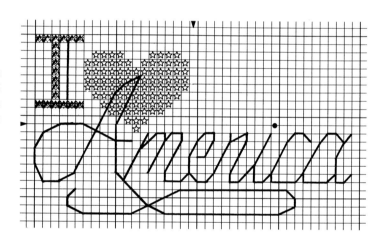

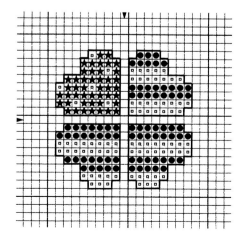

#45

Design size: 17 wide x 17 high

			DMC	Anchor	Coats
▫	=	cream	746	386	2275
●	=	red	304	47	3410
★	=	blue	826	161	7180
		blue-gray	930	922	7980
|	=	Backstitch: blue-gray			

#46

Design size: 27 wide x 27 high

			DMC	Anchor	Coats
★	=	red	321	9046	3500
⬥	=	blue	798	137	5933
△	=	lt taupe	842	376	5379
		med taupe	840	379	5379
▲	=	dk taupe	838	380	5381
|	=	Backstitch: med taupe			

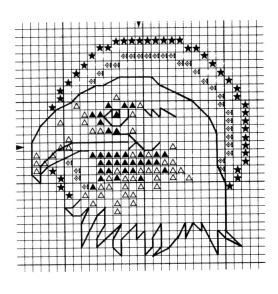

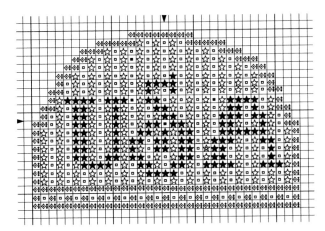

#47

Design size: 33 wide x 22 high

			DMC	Anchor	Coats
▫	=	white	blanc	2	1001
☆	=	lt red	335	41	3153
★	=	dk red	815	43	3073
⬥	=	blue	797	132	7100

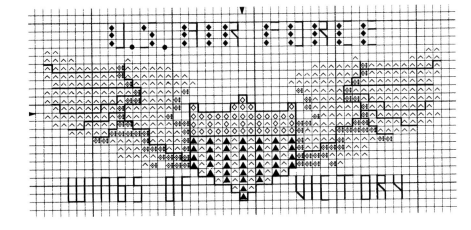

#48

Design size: 49 wide x 22 high

			DMC	Anchor	Coats
▲	=	red	321	9046	3500
◇	=	lt blue	809	130	7021
◆	=	dk blue	797	132	7100
∧	=	lt gray	762	397	8510
⬥	=	med gray	318	399	8511
		dk gray	317	400	8512
•	=	French Knots: dk blue			
|	=	Backstitch:			
		lettering—dk blue			
		wings & emblem—dk gray			

#49

Design size: 38 wide x 26 high

		DMC	Anchor	Coats
◈ =	pink	335	41	3153
	red	815	43	3073
▲ =	green	702	239	6226
	blue	825	162	7979
	brown	632	936	5936

• = French Knots:
  "America"—red
  "is"—brown
  knots on heart—blue

| = Backstitch:
  "America"—red
  bow—blue
  remaining lettering—brown

#50

Design size: 52 wide x 39 high

		DMC	Anchor	Coats
▫ =	white	blanc	2	1001
+ =	lt red	321	9046	3500
★ =	dk red	815	43	3073
◇ =	lt blue	809	130	7021
◆ =	dk blue	797	132	7100
□ =	tan	842	376	5933

50 Santa Designs

From a jolly, rosy-cheeked Santa to a folk-art antique Saint Nicholas, here is a wonderful array of the loveable old elf to decorate everyday items that become Christmas treasures.

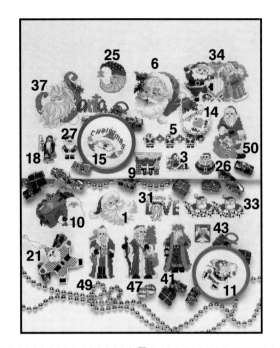

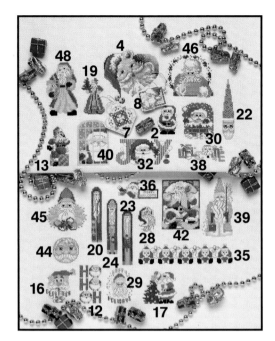

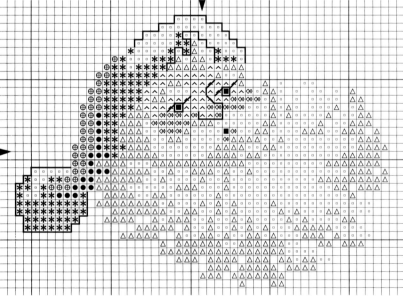

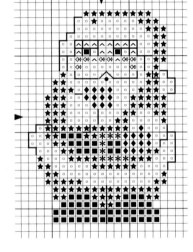

#1

Design size: 47 wide x 34 high

			Anchor	**Coats**	**DMC**
□	=	white	2	1001	blanc
✳	=	cream	386	2386	745
◈	=	pink	36	3125	3326
⊕	=	med red	59	3019	326
●	=	dk red	44	3073	815
⌃	=	peach	1012	2331	754
△	=	lt gray	398	8398	415
		med gray	399	8511	318
■	=	very dk gray	1041	8501	844
|	=	Backstitch: fur, ball on hat—med gray;			
		eyes, nose—very dk gray			

#2

Design size: 19 wide x 28 high

			Anchor	**Coats**	**DMC**
□	=	white	2	1001	blanc
◈	=	pink	1023	3069	3712
★	=	red	1006	3401	304
⌃	=	peach	6	3006	754
◆	=	green	230	6031	699
		gray	235	8513	414
■	=	black	403	8403	310
✳	=	metallic gold			
•	=	French Knot: red			
|	=	Backstitch: between boots—white;			
		eyes, clothing—black;			
		remaining backstitch—gray			

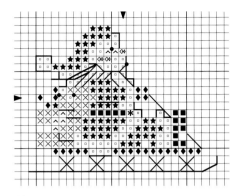

#3

Design size: 25 wide x 19 high

			Anchor	Coats	DMC
▫	=	white	2	1001	blanc
✿	=	pink	894	3069	223
★	=	red	19	3500	321
∧	=	peach	1012	2331	754
◆	=	green	230	6031	699
✕	=	med brown	379	5379	840
		dk brown	936	5936	632
		lt gray	235	8513	414
		dk gray	400	8999	317
■	=	black	403	8403	310
✳	=	metallic gold			
•	=	French Knots: mouth—red; eyes—black			
│	=	Backstitch: bear—dk brown; fur—lt gray;			
		beard—dk gray; rope—black;			
		sled runners—metallic gold			

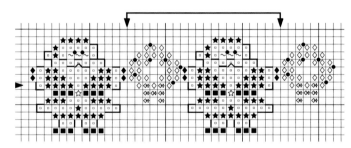

#5

Design size: 20-wide-repeat x 13 high

			Anchor	Coats	DMC
▫	=	white	2	1001	blanc
✿	=	pink	27	3127	899
★	=	red	9046	3046	666
~	=	peach	4146	2336	754
☆	=	yellow	305	2295	743
◇	=	lt green	205	6031	912
◆	=	dk green	228	6228	910
		gray	235	8513	414
■	=	black	403	8403	310
•	=	French Knots: berries—red; eye—black			
│	=	Backstitch: nose—pink; fur—gray; mouth—black			

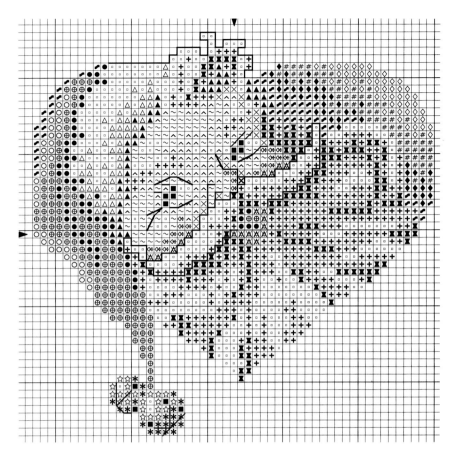

#4

Design size: 53 wide x 53 high

			Anchor	Coats	DMC
▫	=	white	2	1001	blanc
✿	=	lt pink	36	3125	3326
✕	=	med pink	27	3127	899
○	=	lt red	28	3152	892
⊕	=	med red	19	3500	321
●	=	dk red	43	3044	814
~	=	lt peach	4146	2336	754
∧	=	dk peach	868	3868	353
☆	=	yellow	305	2295	743
✳	=	gold	308	5308	781
◇	=	lt green	240	6020	966
#	=	med green	226	6239	702
◆	=	dk green	227	6227	701
◢	=	very dk green	923	6228	699
△	=	lt blue-gray	1034	7051	931
▲	=	med blue-gray	1035	7052	930
✕	=	med brown	883	3883	407
		dk brown	352	5471	300
+	=	lt gray	398	8398	415
⊠	=	med gray	235	8513	414
		dk gray	400	8999	317
■	=	black	403	8403	310
│	=	Backstitch: nose, eyelids, eye creases—			
		dk brown; fur on hat, moustache—			
		dk gray; eyelashes, bells—black			

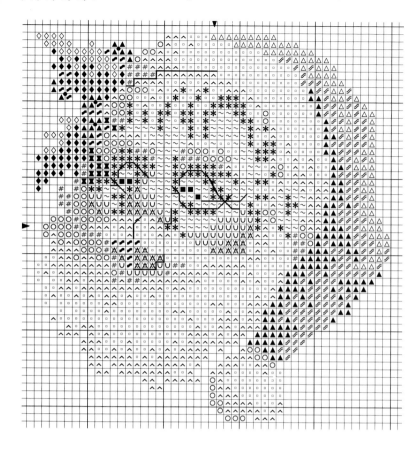

#6

Design size: 47 wide x 51 high

			Anchor	Coats	DMC
▫	=	white	2	1001	blanc
∪	=	lt pink	36	3125	3326
⋈	=	med pink	894	3069	223
△	=	lt red	27	3127	899
⌇	=	med red	29	3047	309
▲	=	dk red	19	3500	321
✐	=	very dk red	44	3073	815
~	=	peach	1012	2331	754
◇	=	lt green	205	6031	912
◆	=	dk green	923	6228	699
✳	=	med rust	347	5347	402
		dk rust	352	5471	300
■	=	brown	381	5381	938
∧	=	very lt gray	234	8510	762
O	=	lt gray	399	8511	318
#	=	med gray	235	8513	414
⊠	=	dk gray	400	8999	317
		very dk gray	1041	8501	844
•	=	French Knots: white			

│ = Backstitch: mouth—very dk red;
     below eyes, nose—dk rust; eyelashes—brown;
     edge of hat—very dk gray

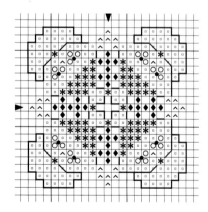

#7

Design size: 21 wide x 21 high

			Anchor	Coats	DMC
▫	=	white	2	1001	blanc
∧	=	med red	28	3152	892
✳	=	dk red	59	3019	326
O	=	peach	1012	2331	754
◆	=	green	217	6211	561
		lt gray	235	8513	414
		dk gray	236	8514	3799
•	=	French Knots: dk gray			

│ = Backstitch: lt gray

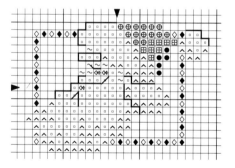

#8

Design size: 24 wide x 17 high

			Anchor	Coats	DMC
▫	=	white	2	1001	blanc
✧	=	pink	1023	3069	3712
⊕	=	med red	35	3152	3705
⊞	=	dk red	19	3500	321
●	=	very dk red	44	3073	815
~	=	peach	6	3006	754
◇	=	lt green	238	6238	703
◆	=	dk green	229	6228	700
∧	=	lt gray	399	8511	318
		dk gray	400	8999	414

│ = Backstitch: edges of white areas—lt gray;
     remaining backstitches—dk gray

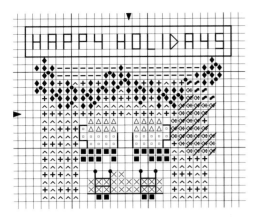

#9

Design size: 27 wide x 23 high

		Anchor	Coats	DMC
□	= white	2	1001	blanc
✿	= lt pink	25	3125	3326
◣	= med pink	27	3127	899
△	= med red	19	3500	321
+	= dk red	44	3073	815
	lt green	226	6227	702
◆	= dk green	230	6031	699
—	= lt brown	368	5345	437
×	= med brown	370	5356	434
^	= med gray	235	8513	414
	dk gray	400	8999	317
■	= black	403	8403	310
•	= French Knots: holly berries—med red; stocking pin, andirons—black			
	= Backstitch: banner edge—med red; stocking stripes—lt green; lettering—lt green (2 strands); boots—dk gray; andirons—black			

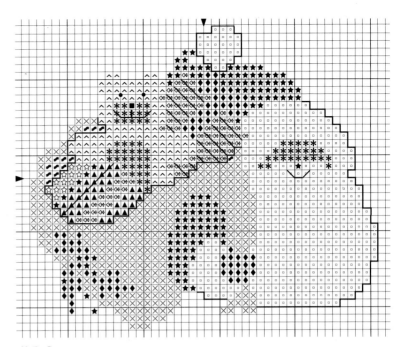

#10

Design size: 46 wide x 40 high

		Anchor	Coats	DMC
□	= white	2	1001	blanc
✿	= pink	27	3127	899
★	= red	59	3019	326
☆	= yellow	291	2298	444
◆	= green	923	6228	699
▲	= turquoise	433	7001	996
✳	= lt tan	368	5345	437
^	= med tan	349	5309	3776
×	= med brown	370	5356	434
◣	= dk brown	359	5472	801
	gray	399	8511	318
■	= black	403	8403	310
•	= French Knots: black			
	= Backstitch: ornament—pink; package—red; inner edge of bag—dk brown; fur—gray; faces—black			

#11

Design size: 30 wide x 31 high

		Anchor	Coats	DMC
□	= white	2	1001	blanc
~	= peach	1012	2331	754
✿	= lt pink	36	3125	3326
×	= med pink	27	3127	899
⊕	= med red	29	3047	309
●	= dk red	43	3044	814
◆	= green	229	6228	700
	lt gray	399	8511	318
	dk gray	400	8999	414
■	= black	403	8403	310
✳	= metallic gold			
•	= French Knots: black			
	= Backstitch: mitten stripes—white; fur—lt gray; beard, candle wick & smoke—dk gray; bell—black			

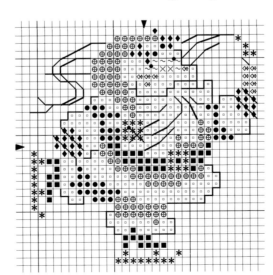

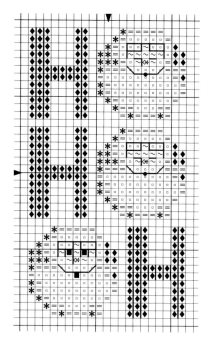

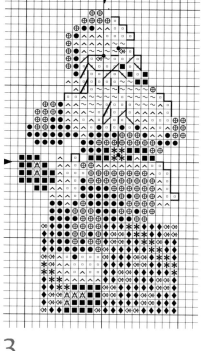

#12

Design size: 21 wide x 38 high

			Anchor	Coats	DMC
□	=	white	2	1001	blanc
✢	=	pink	36	3125	3326
*	=	red	1006	3401	304
~	=	peach	1012	2331	754
◆	=	green	229	6228	700
=	=	lt gray	398	8398	415
		med gray	400	8999	414
■	=	very dk gray	1041	8501	844
•	=	French Knots: red			
|	=	Backstitch: stripes—white; beards—med gray; eyes, eyebrows—very dk gray			

#13

Design size: 22 wide x 40 high

			Anchor	Coats	DMC
□	=	white	2	1001	blanc
✢	=	pink	27	3127	899
⊕	=	med red	1006	3401	304
●	=	dk red	44	3073	815
~	=	peach	6	3006	754
◆	=	green	227	6227	701
∧	=	med gray	235	8513	414
Ж	=	dk gray	401	8999	413
■	=	black	403	8403	310
*	=	metallic gold			
•	=	French Knots: black			
|	=	Backstitch: mouth, nose—med red; fur— med gray; remaining backstitch—dk gray			

#14

Design size: 31 wide x 31 high

			Anchor	Coats	DMC
□	=	white	2	1001	blanc
✢	=	lt pink	894	3069	223
Ж	=	med pink	36	3125	3326
⊕	=	med red	29	3047	309
●	=	dk red	44	3073	815
~	=	peach	1012	2331	754
◆	=	green	230	6031	699
▲	=	blue	147	7181	797
		gray	400	8999	414
|	=	Backstitch: mouth—med red; fur, beard—gray			

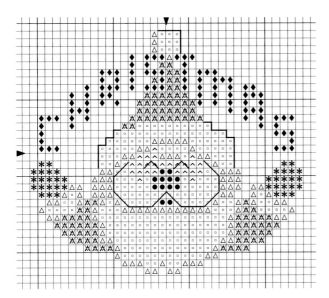

#15

Design size: 36 wide x 32 high

		Anchor	Coats	DMC
□	= white	2	1001	blanc
⋈	= pink	28	3152	892
●	= red	59	3019	326
∧	= peach	4146	2336	754
◆	= green	227	6227	701
✳	= turquoise	186	6186	959
△	= blue	144	7976	800
	black	403	8403	310
│	= Backstitch: fur, beard—blue; eyes—black			

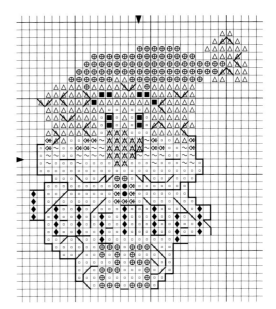

#16

Design size: 29 wide x 34 high

		Anchor	Coats	DMC
□	= white	2	1001	blanc
⟡	= lt pink	894	3069	223
⋈	= med pink	895	3071	3722
⊕	= med red	1025	3013	347
●	= dk red	44	3073	815
~	= peach	4146	2336	754
◆	= green	217	6211	561
△	= lt gray	398	8398	415
	med gray	235	8513	414
■	= dk gray	1041	8501	844
│	= Backstitch: lettering—green; beard outline—med gray; fur, eyes, nose, remaining beard—dk gray			

#17

Design size: 33 wide x 32 high

		Anchor	Coats	DMC
□	= white	2	1001	blanc
⟡	= red	29	3047	309
◤	= dk red	43	3044	814
~	= peach	6	3006	754
◇	= very lt green	240	6020	966
#	= med green	239	6226	702
◆	= dk green	923	6228	699
△	= blue	433	7001	996
	gray	235	8513	414
■	= black	403	8403	310
✳	= metallic gold			
•	= French Knots: black			
│	= Backstitch: between boots—white; sleeve, between legs—dk red; mitten— dk green; fur, hair—gray; eyes, mouth—black			

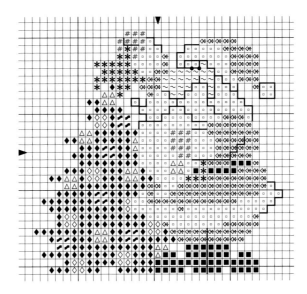

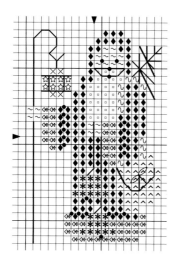

#18

Design size: 18 wide x 28 high

		Anchor	Coats	DMC
▫	= white	2	1001	blanc
	red	59	3019	326
~	= lt peach	4146	2336	754
✢	= dk peach	336	3336	402
☆	= yellow	305	2295	743
	med green	226	6227	702
♦	= dk green	923	6228	699
∧	= lt brown	378	5578	841
∿	= med brown	936	5936	632
	dk brown	381	5381	938
✕	= gray	400	8999	414
✳	= metallic gold			
⊘	= Lazy Daisies: red			
•	= French Knots: mouth—red (1 strand); bell clappers—red (2 strands); sleeves, robe—dk peach; eyes, nose—gray (1 strand)			
│	= Backstitch: bell hangers, streamers on bow—red; pine branch—med green; lantern staff, bag—dk brown; lantern, moustache—gray			

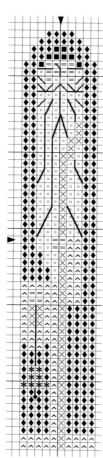

#20 ►

Design size: 10 wide x 55 high

		Anchor	Coats	DMC
▫	= white	2	1001	blanc
=	= peach	4146	2336	754
♦	= green	211	6213	562
∧	= lt brown	883	3883	407
✕	= med brown	352	5471	300
■	= gray	1041	8501	844
✳	= metallic gold			
•	= French Knot: metallic gold			
│	= Backstitch: face, beard—gray; bell rope—metallic gold			

#19

Design size: 22 wide x 36 high

		Anchor	Coats	DMC
▫	= white	2	1001	blanc
✢	= pink	36	3125	3326
○	= lt red	1023	3069	3712
✱	= med red	1025	3013	347
●	= dk red	44	3073	815
~	= peach	4146	2336	754
☆	= med gold	891	5363	676
★	= dk gold	890	2876	729
♦	= green	217	6211	561
✕	= med brown	379	5379	840
	dk brown	936	5936	632
	gray	400	8999	414
⊘	= Lazy Daisies: green			
•	= French Knots: med red			
│	= Backstitch: beard outline—peach; robe edges between red & pink, above & below lower green trim—dk gold; patterned robe trim—green; vertical lines on robe, boots—dk brown; remaining beard—gray; eyes—gray (2 strands)			

#21 ►

Design size: 35 wide x 35 high

		Anchor	Coats	DMC
▫	= white	2	1001	blanc
▲	= red	19	3500	321
~	= peach	6	3006	754
♦	= green	229	6228	700
	gray	400	8999	414
■	= black	403	8403	310
✳	= metallic gold			
•	= French Knot: red			
│	= Backstitch: mouth—red; fur trim, beard, suit—gray; eyes—black			

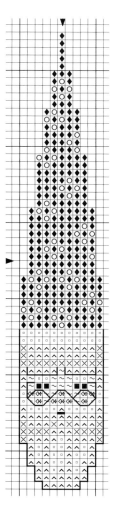

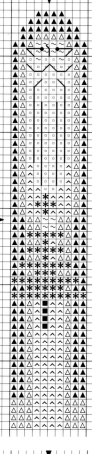

#23

Design size: 10 wide x 55 high

			Anchor	Coats	DMC
□	=	white	2	1001	blanc
~	=	peach	4146	2336	754
✳	=	green	217	6211	561
△	=	lt blue-gray	1034	7051	931
▲	=	dk blue-gray	1035	7052	930
^	=	tan	347	5347	402
■	=	brown	352	5471	300
		gray	1041	8501	844
•	=	French Knots: gray			
│	=	Backstitch: gray			

#22

Design size: 11 wide x 60 high

			Anchor	Coats	DMC
□	=	white	2	1001	blanc
✿	=	lt pink	26	3126	894
O	=	med pink	29	3047	309
~	=	peach	6	3006	754
◆	=	green	215	6879	503
^	=	tan	366	3335	951
X	=	brown	369	5347	435
		gray	400	8999	414
■	=	black	403	8403	310
│	=	Backstitch: mouth—med pink (2 strands); head, beard—brown; eyebrows—gray; glasses—black			

#24

Design size: 10 wide x 55 high

			Anchor	Coats	DMC
□	=	white	2	1001	blanc
⊕	=	pink	27	3127	899
▲	=	rose	43	3044	814
~	=	peach	4146	2336	754
✳	=	yellow	891	5363	676
		brown	349	5309	3776
■	=	gray	1041	8501	844
☆	=	metallic gold			
•	=	French Knots: gold areas—brown; eyes—gray			
│	=	Backstitch: gold areas—brown; face, beard—gray; lantern rope—metallic gold			

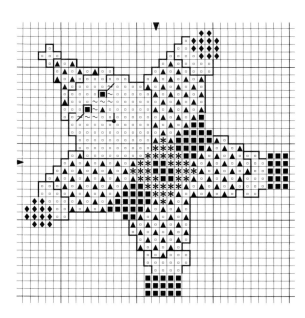

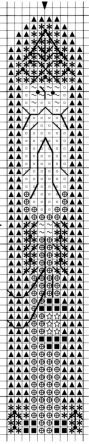

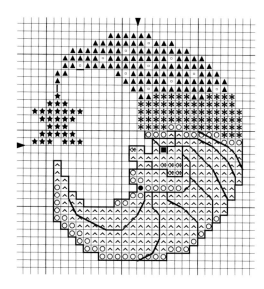

#25

Design size: 28 wide x 30 high

			Anchor	Coats	DMC
▫	=	white	2	1001	blanc
✿	=	pink	6	3006	754
●	=	red	44	3073	815
∧	=	peach	881	2331	3774
▲	=	blue	147	7181	797
○	=	lt rust	347	5347	402
✳	=	med rust	351	3340	400
		dk rust	352	5471	300
■	=	gray	1041	8501	844
★	=	metallic gold			
		=	Backstitch: star hanger—blue; eye—gray; remaining lines—dk rust			

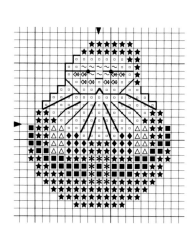

#26

Design size: 19 wide x 22 high

			Anchor	Coats	DMC
▫	=	white	2	1001	blanc
✿	=	pink	895	3071	3722
★	=	red	59	3019	326
~	=	peach	1012	2331	754
◆	=	green	230	6031	699
△	=	blue	144	7976	800
■	=	black	403	8403	310
✳	=	metallic gold			
•	=	French Knots: black			
		=	Backstitch: nose—red; fur, beard outline—blue; remaining beard—black			

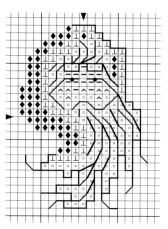

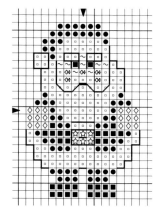

#27

Design size: 15 wide x 23 high

			Anchor	Coats	DMC
▫	=	white	2	1001	blanc
✿	=	pink	36	3125	3326
●	=	red	59	3019	326
~	=	peach	1012	2331	754
◇	=	green	226	6227	702
		gray	235	8513	414
■	=	black	403	8403	310
☆	=	metallic gold			
		=	Backstitch: red (mouth)			
		=	Backstitch: fur, face, beard—gray; eyes, buckle—black			

#28

Design size: 17 wide x 24 high

			Anchor	Coats	DMC
▫	=	white	2	1001	blanc
⊥	=	cream	386	2386	745
∧	=	pink	894	3069	223
		red	19	3500	321
−	=	peach	4146	2336	754
◆	=	green	218	6880	500
		gray	1041	8501	844
•	=	French Knots: gray			
		=	Backstitch: mouth—red (2 strands); hat—green; remaining backstitches—gray			

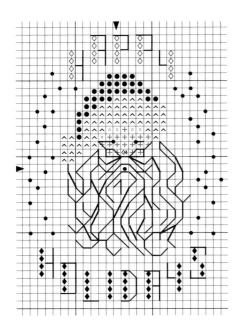

#29

Design size: 25 wide x 35 high

			Anchor	Coats	DMC
□	=	white	2	1001	blanc
✿	=	pink	1023	3069	3712
●	=	red	1025	3013	347
+	=	peach	6	3006	754
◇	=	lt green	226	6227	702
◆	=	dk green	229	6228	700
∧	=	tan	366	3335	951
		gray	235	8513	414
		black	403	8403	310

• = French Knots: mouth—red; scattered pattern— red and lt green, randomly arranged; eyes—gray

| = Backstitch: "happy"—lt green; "holidays"— dk green; facial features, beard—gray; glasses—black

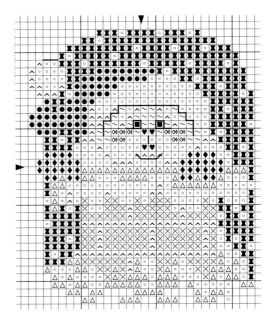

#30

Design size: 30 wide x 36 high

			Anchor	Coats	DMC
□	=	white	2	1001	blanc
✿	=	lt pink	36	3125	3326
♥	=	dk pink	27	3127	899
●	=	red	9046	3046	666
~	=	peach	1012	2331	754
◆	=	green	229	6228	700
△	=	lt blue	144	7976	800
✠	=	dk blue	146	7080	798
×	=	brown	352	5471	300
∧	=	med gray	235	8513	414
		dk gray	401	8999	413
■	=	black	403	8403	310

| = Backstitch: nose, mouth, fur—dk gray; eyes—black

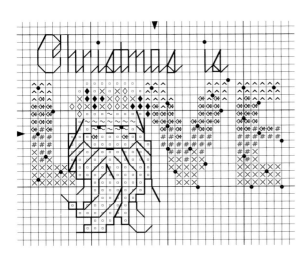

#31

Design size: 33 wide x 26 high

			Anchor	Coats	DMC
□	=	white	2	1001	blanc
∧	=	very lt pink	25	3125	3326
✿	=	lt pink	27	3127	899
#	=	med pink	29	3047	309
×	=	dk pink	59	3019	326
~	=	peach	6	3006	754
◇	=	lt green	205	6031	912
◆	=	dk green	923	6228	699
		gray	1041	8501	844

• = French Knots: lettering—dk pink; on L, V, E—dk green; eyes—gray

❚ = Backstitch: mouth—lt pink

| = Backstitch: nose—lt pink; lettering—dk pink; eyes, beard—gray

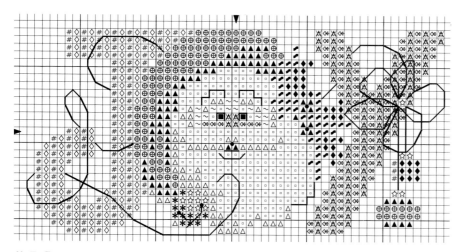

#32

Design size: 55 wide x 27 high

			Anchor	Coats	DMC
▫	=	white	2	1001	blanc
✿	=	lt pink	26	3126	894
✗	=	med pink	29	3047	309
⊕	=	med red	1006	3401	304
▲	=	dk red	44	3073	815
~	=	peach	6	3006	754
☆	=	yellow	305	2295	743
✳	=	gold	308	5308	781
◇	=	lt green	240	6020	966
#	=	med green	227	6227	701
◆	=	dk green	217	6211	561
◣	=	very dk green	923	6228	699
△	=	blue	144	7976	800
		gray	235	8513	414
■	=	black	403	8403	310
		metallic gold			

• = French Knots: holly berries—white;
     mouth, bell—black

| = Backstitch: beard—blue; eyebrows, chin—gray;
     eyes, bell—black; string—metallic gold

#33

Design size: 28-wide-repeat x 23 high

			Anchor	Coats	DMC
▫	=	white	2	1001	blanc
~	=	peach	6	3006	754
✿	=	pink	26	3126	894
♥	=	red	19	3500	321
✳	=	orange	329	2327	3340
☆	=	yellow	291	2298	444
◇	=	lt green	238	6238	703
◆	=	dk green	230	6031	699
△	=	blue	433	7001	996
✗	=	purple	1030	4301	3746
□	=	lt gray	398	8398	415
		dk gray	400	8999	414
■	=	black	403	8403	310

• = French Knots: red

| = Backstitch: fur, beard, hat—dk gray;
     light cord—black

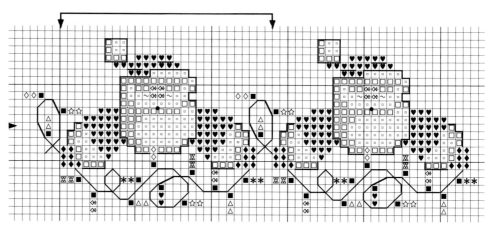

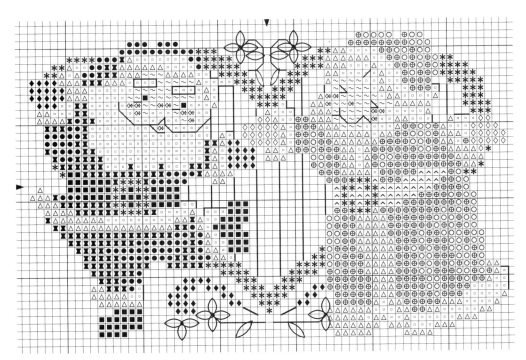

#34

Design size: 63 wide x 40 high

			Anchor	Coats	DMC
▫	=	white	2	1001	blanc
✳	=	pink	36	3125	3326
○	=	lt red	26	3126	894
⊕	=	med red	28	3152	892
●	=	dk red	19	3500	321
⧓	=	very dk red	44	3073	815
~	=	peach	1012	2331	754
◇	=	lt green	226	6227	702
◆	=	dk green	228	6228	910
△	=	blue	144	7976	800
^	=	gray	400	8999	414
■	=	black	403	8403	310
✳	=	metallic gold			
⌀	=	Lazy Daisies: flowers—med red;			
		leaves—dk green			
❘	=	Backstitch: her mouth—med red;			
		stems—dk green; fur—blue;			
		his eyebrows—gray; eyes, moustache—			
		black; lines in heart—metallic gold			

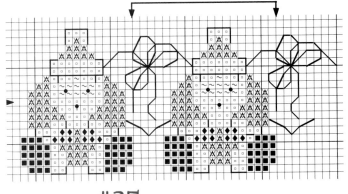

#35

Design size: 19-wide-repeat x 19 high

			Anchor	Coats	DMC
▫	=	white	2	1001	blanc
~	=	peach	6	3006	754
		pink	28	3152	892
⋇	=	red	9046	3046	666
◆	=	green	230	6031	699
		gray	235	8513	414
■	=	black	403	8403	310
•	=	French Knots: mouths—red; eyes—black;			
❘	=	Backstitch: heart—pink; bow—green;			
		fur—gray			

#36

Design size: 40 wide x 18 high

		Anchor	Coats	DMC
□ =	white	2	1001	blanc
♥ =	red	1006	3401	304
~ =	peach	6	3006	754
◇ =	lt green	239	6226	702
♦ =	dk green	923	6228	699
	gray	400	8999	414
	black	403	8403	310

• = French Knot: red

| = Backstitch: mouth, scarf stripes, lettering—red;
fringe of lt green end of scarf—lt green;
fringe of dk green end of scarf—dk green;
fur, face—gray; eyes—black

#37

Design size: 69 wide x 56 high

		Anchor	Coats	DMC
□ =	white	2	1001	blanc
✳ =	lt pink	25	3125	3326
◤ =	med pink	27	3127	899
○ =	med red	28	3152	892
● =	dk red	59	3019	326
∧ =	peach	881	2331	3774
◇ =	lt green	205	6031	912
♦ =	dk green	229	6228	700
✕ =	lt brown	882	3883	758
	med brown	379	5379	840
✳ =	lt gray	234	8510	762
	med gray	235	8513	414
	very dk gray	1041	8501	844
	metallic gold			

| = Backstitch: stripes on letters—white; left
brow, right eye wrinkle, nose—med brown;
hair, beard—med gray; eyes—very
dk gray (2 strands); ribbon—metallic gold

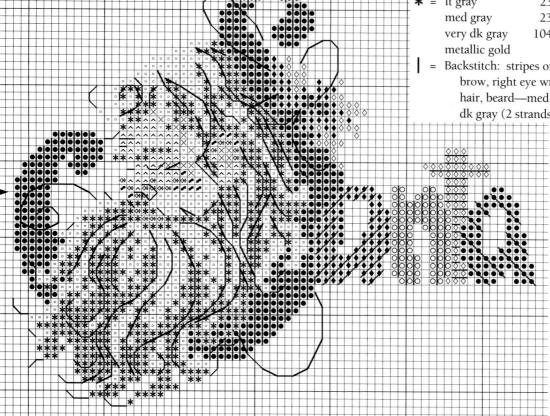

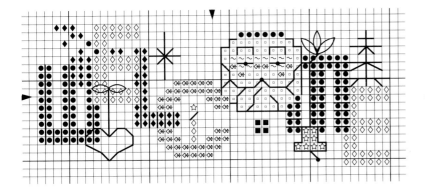

#38

Design size: 44 wide x 18 high

			Anchor	Coats	DMC
▫	=	white	2	1001	blanc
✲	=	pink	36	3125	3326
●	=	red	1006	3401	304
~	=	peach	1012	2331	754
◇	=	lt green	238	6238	703
◆	=	dk green	229	6228	700
		blue	147	7181	797
		gray	400	8999	414
■	=	black	403	8403	310

☆ = metallic gold

✳ = Eyelet: metallic gold

⬭ = Lazy Daisies: bow on package—lt green;
     bow on heart—blue

• = French Knots: mouth—red;
     eyes—black; bell—metallic gold

| = Backstitch: stripes in letters—white;
     bell cord—lt green; pine tree—dk green;
     heart, heart cord—blue; fur, outline of face,
     beard, candle flame—gray; eyes—black;
     bell—metallic gold

#39

Design size: 29 wide x 58 high

			Anchor	Coats	DMC
▫	=	white	2	1001	blanc
∧	=	cream	366	3335	951
✲	=	pink	26	3126	894
★	=	red	1006	3401	304
−	=	peach	6	3006	754
◆	=	green	217	6211	561
△	=	tan	368	5345	437
▲	=	med rust	369	5347	435
✱	=	dk rust	351	3340	400
×	=	brown	359	5472	801

ω = metallic gold

✱ = Eyelet Stitch: metallic gold

• = French Knots: metallic gold

| = Backstitch: edge of beard—cream;
     purse strap—red; robe center—dk rust;
     face, remaining beard—brown

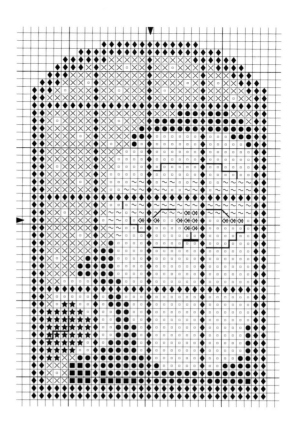

#40

Design size: 31 wide x 47 high

			Anchor	Coats	DMC
□	=	white	2	1001	blanc
✿	=	pink	27	3127	899
●	=	red	9046	3046	666
~	=	peach	6	3006	754
★	=	green	229	6228	700
✕	=	blue	145	7021	809
◆	=	tan	366	3335	951
		gray	400	8999	414
■	=	black	403	8403	310

❘ = Backstitch: mouth—red (2 strands)

❘ = Backstitch: hat, beard—gray;
    eyes, mitten—black

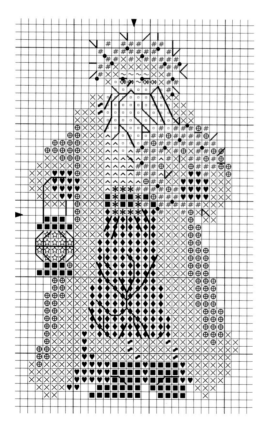

#41

Design size: 28 wide x 48 high

			Anchor	Coats	DMC
□	=	white	2	1001	blanc
✿	=	pink	36	3125	3326
⊕	=	dk red	19	3500	321
♥	=	very dk red	44	3073	815
~	=	peach	4146	2336	754
☆	=	yellow	291	2298	444
#	=	med green	205	6031	912
◆	=	dk green	230	6227	699
^	=	lt brown	347	5347	402
✕	=	med brown	349	5309	3776
✔	=	dk brown	359	5472	801
■	=	black	403	8403	310
✱	=	metallic gold			

• = French Knots: berries—dk red; eyes—black

❘ = Backstitch: boots—white; mouth—dk red;
    evergreens—med green; beard—med brown;
    eyes, nose, lantern, clothing—black

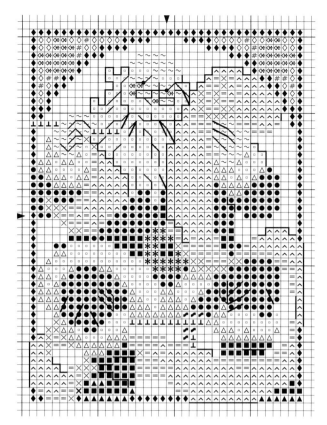

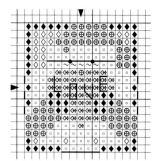

#42

Design size: 36 wide x 49 high

			Anchor	Coats	DMC
□	=	white	2	1001	blanc
✷	=	pink	26	3126	894
●	=	red	1006	3401	304
~	=	peach	6	3006	754
◇	=	lt green	203	6020	564
#	=	med green	227	6227	701
◆	=	dk green	217	6211	561
∧	=	tan	366	3335	951
=	=	lt brown	349	5309	3776
✕	=	med brown	351	3340	400
⊥	=	dk brown	359	5472	801
✒	=	very dk brown	381	5381	938
△	=	lt gray	398	8398	415
▲	=	dk gray	400	8999	414
■	=	black	403	8403	310
✻	=	metallic gold			
•	=	French Knots: black			
│	=	Backstitch: mouth—pink; edges of list—			
		lt brown; hair, fur, boots—lt gray;			
		eyes, beard, hands—dk gray;			
		clothing—black; glasses—metallic gold			

#43

Design size: 15 wide x 17 high

			Anchor	Coats	DMC
□	=	white	2	1001	blanc
✷	=	pink	26	3126	894
⊕	=	med red	19	3500	321
		dk red	43	3044	814
~	=	peach	6	3006	754
◇	=	lt green	204	6210	563
◆	=	dk green	229	6228	700
		gray	1041	8501	844
•	=	French Knots: gray			
│	=	Backstitch: lettering—dk red; outline—			
		dk green; eyeline—gray			

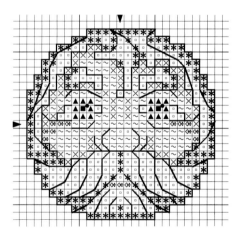

#44

Design size: 25 wide x 25 high

			Anchor	Coats	DMC
□	=	white	2	1001	blanc
✷	=	pink	8	3868	353
~	=	lt peach	881	2331	3774
✕	=	dk peach	883	3883	407
▲	=	blue	146	7080	798
✻	=	lt gray	398	8398	415
		dk gray	235	8513	414
		brown	370	5356	434
◆	=	black	403	8403	310
•	=	French Knots: white			
│	=	Backstitch: face—brown;			
		hair, beard—dk gray			

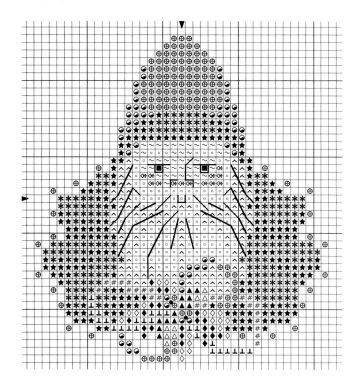

#45

Design size: 39 wide x 43 high

			Anchor	**Coats**	**DMC**
▫	=	white	2	1001	blanc
∧	=	cream	386	2386	745
✤	=	pink	894	3069	223
⊕	=	med red	35	3152	3705
◖	=	dk red	19	3500	321
~	=	peach	4146	2336	754
✳	=	med gold	891	5363	676
★	=	dk gold	890	2876	729
#	=	med green	226	6227	702
⊥	=	dk green	229	6228	700
◇	=	lt blue-green	216	6876	502
◆	=	dk blue-green	218	6880	500
△	=	med brown	378	5578	841
▲	=	dk brown	936	5936	632
■	=	black	403	8403	310
•	=	French Knots: white			
│	=	Backstitch: nose, beard—dk brown; eyes—black			

#46

Design size: 43 wide x 42 high

			Anchor	**Coats**	**DMC**
▫	=	white	2	1001	blanc
✤	=	pink	36	3125	3326
#	=	med rose	1024	3071	3328
		dk rose	43	3044	814
⊕	=	red	19	3500	321
~	=	peach	1012	2331	754
◆	=	green	218	6880	500
∧	=	lt tan	368	5345	437
☆	=	dk tan	349	5309	3776
✕	=	lt brown	883	3883	407
✳	=	med brown	351	3340	400
◣	=	dk brown	359	5472	801
		gray	400	8999	414
■	=	black	403	8403	310
		metallic gold			
•	=	French Knots: red			
│	=	Backstitch: robe—dk rose; paper roll—dk brown; hair, beard, hands—gray; eyes—black; glasses—metallic gold (2 strands)			

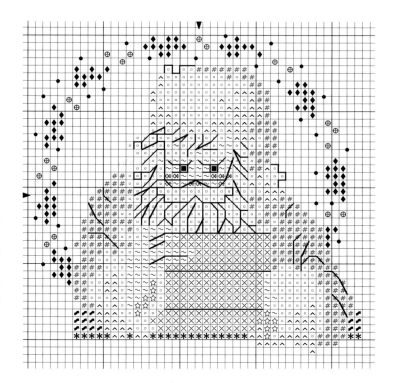

#47

Design size: 36 wide x 52 high

			Anchor	Coats	DMC
▫	=	white	2	1001	blanc
∧	=	cream	386	2386	745
⟡	=	pink	895	3071	3722
⊕	=	med rose	42	3154	326
●	=	dk rose	44	3073	815
−	=	peach	1012	2331	754
✳	=	orange	329	2327	3340
☆	=	yellow	305	2295	743
★	=	gold	890	2876	729
#	=	med green	226	6227	702
		dk green	230	6031	699
△	=	med brown	349	5309	3776
⊠	=	dk brown	352	5471	300
■	=	very dk brown	381	5381	938
		gray	400	8999	414
		black	403	8403	310
•	=	French Knots: black			
│	=	Backstitch: mouth—dk rose (2 strands);			

fur edges, center of robe—gold;
tree—dk green; beard—gray;
eyes, remaining robe—black

#48

Design size: 30 wide x 52 high

			Anchor	Coats	DMC
▫	=	white	2	1001	blanc
∧	=	cream	366	3335	951
⟡	=	lt pink	6	3006	754
✕	=	dk pink	26	3126	894
●	=	red	59	3019	326
~	=	peach	881	2331	3774
✳	=	orange	323	2323	3341
☆	=	gold	891	5363	676
◇	=	green	226	6227	702
△	=	blue	145	7021	809
⊕	=	tan	368	5345	437
ω	=	med brown	883	3883	407
✕	=	dk brown	352	5471	300
■	=	very dk brown	381	5381	938
		gray	400	8999	414
		black	403	8403	310
★	=	metallic gold			
•	=	French Knots: clown's nose—red; eyes—black			
│	=	Backstitch: mouth—red; edges of robe,			

inner edge of bag—med brown;
remaining bag—dk brown;
beard—gray; remaining robe—black

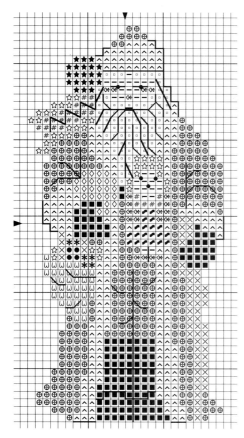

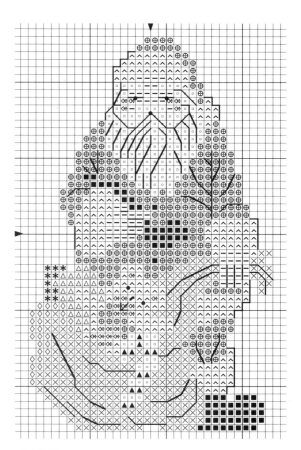

#49

Design size: 26 wide x 52 high

			Anchor	Coats	DMC
□	=	white	2	1001	blanc
∧	=	cream	386	2386	745
⊗	=	lt pink	36	3125	3326
◣	=	med pink	895	3071	3722
●	=	red	19	3500	321
⊕	=	med rose	42	3154	326
		dk rose	44	3073	815
—	=	peach	1012	2331	754
☆	=	yellow	305	2295	743
★	=	gold	890	2876	729
✱	=	orange	329	2327	3340
◇	=	green	226	6227	702
#	=	blue-gray	1034	7051	931
ω	=	med brown	349	5309	3776
×	=	dk brown	352	5471	300
■	=	very dk brown	381	5381	938
		gray	400	8999	414
		black	403	8403	310

• = French Knots: doll's mouth—red; eyes—black

❙ = Backstitch: red (mouth)

❙ = Backstitch: boots—white; robe—dk rose;
cream edges of robe, drum—gold;
brown bag—dk brown; beard—gray; eyes—black

#50

Design size: 32 wide x 52 high

			Anchor	Coats	DMC
□	=	white	2	1001	blanc
∧	=	cream	386	2386	745
⊗	=	lt pink	894	3069	223
⊕	=	med pink	29	3047	309
		dk pink	59	3019	326
▲	=	red	19	3500	321
—	=	peach	881	2331	3774
✱	=	orange	323	2323	3341
◇	=	green	226	6227	702
△	=	blue	1034	7051	931
×	=	lt brown	378	5578	841
◣	=	med brown	936	5936	632
■	=	dk brown	381	5381	938
		gray	235	8513	414
		black	403	8403	310

• = French Knots: mouth—red; bear's eyes—
blue; Santa's eyes—black

❙ = Backstitch: suit—dk pink; fur—lt brown;
bear's mouth, bag—med brown;
beard, hands—gray; eyes—black